P9-BYF-486

February 2020

Dear Sarah,

Good to see you
and with best wishes,

Jimmy

PRAISE FOR FAROOQ KATHWARI'S
TRAILBLAZER

"Farooq Kathwari's journey from the mountains of Kashmir to the highest levels of influence in business and international diplomacy has as many twists and surprises as a fiction thriller. His story demonstrates that when energy, dedication, and values meet American opportunities, remarkable things can happen. No matter your stage in career or life, you'll enjoy and learn from his story."

—JAMES SCHMOTTER, PRESIDENT EMERITUS,
   WESTERN CONNECTICUT STATE UNIVERSITY

"*Trailblazer* takes us through the remarkable journey of a courageous man who came to America with nothing but dreams, avoided deportation, and ultimately rose to lead one of America's iconic corporations. It is a narrative of optimism, hope, and inspiration."

—JOHN HAMRE, PRESIDENT, CENTER FOR STRATEGIC
   AND INTERNATIONAL STUDIES

"A searingly honest and riveting memoir by an iconic corporate leader who became an American statesman. Farooq Kathwari is a role model for top executives who, having achieved success in the boardroom and the marketplace, are destined for even greater contributions and challenges."

—WILLIAM O'SHAUGHNESSY, PRESIDENT & EDITORIAL DIRECTOR,
   WHITNEY GLOBAL MEDIA

"In his engaging autobiography *Trailblazer*, Farooq Kathwari tells the gripping tale of his remarkable life from his volatile youth in Kashmir to his indisputable successes as a leader in global business and international relations. This book is an enormously informative and inspiring account of a life lived to the fullest."

—GEORGE RUPP, FORMER PRESIDENT OF THE INTERNATIONAL
RESCUE COMMITTEE, COLUMBIA UNIVERSITY, AND RICE UNIVERSITY

"*Trailblazer* is the story of a young mountain climber from Kashmir who becomes a captain of industry in America and a passionate global activist for world peace. It's a compelling page-turner full of adventure, passion, and lessons of leadership in life."

—JOHN DOONER, CHAIRMAN EMERITUS OF MCCANN WORLDGROUP

"*Trailblazer* is the unlikely story of one man's unique journey across many worlds, offering lessons in the value of luck, the importance of creative thinking, the power of passion, the centrality of love and family, the pain of tragedy, and the triumph of integrity."

—GARY ACKERMAN, FORMER US HOUSE OF REPRESENTATIVES
REPRESENTATIVE, NEW YORK

"An inspiring life story of leadership, courage, determination, hope, and humanity. Farooq Kathwari perfectly exemplifies the best of the spirit of America."

—STANLEY M. BERGMAN, CHAIRMAN OF THE BOARD AND CEO,
HENRY SCHEIN, INC.

TRAIL
BLAZER

FAROOQ KATHWARI

Chairman, President, and CEO,
Ethan Allen Interiors Inc.

with

KARL WEBER

TRAIL
BLAZER

From the **MOUNTAINS** *of* **KASHMIR**

to the **SUMMIT** *of*

GLOBAL BUSINESS *and* **BEYOND**

GREENLEAF
BOOK GROUP PRESS

In a few cases, the names and identifying characteristics of persons referenced in this book have been changed to protect their privacy.

Published by Greenleaf Book Group Press
Austin, Texas
www.gbgpress.com

Copyright ©2019 Farooq Kathwari

All rights reserved.

Thank you for purchasing an authorized edition of this book and for complying with copyright law. No part of this book may be reproduced, stored in a retrieval system, or transmitted by any means, electronic, mechanical, photocopying, recording, or otherwise, without written permission from the copyright holder.

Distributed by Greenleaf Book Group

For ordering information or special discounts for bulk purchases, please contact Greenleaf Book Group at PO Box 91869, Austin, TX 78709, 512.891.6100.

Design and composition by Greenleaf Book Group and Brian Phillips
Cover design by Greenleaf Book Group and Brian Phillips

Publisher's Cataloging-in-Publication data is available.

Print ISBN: 978-1-62634-645-1

eBook ISBN: 978-1-62634-646-8

Part of the Tree Neutral® program, which offsets the number of trees consumed in the production and printing of this book by taking proactive steps, such as planting trees in direct proportion to the number of trees used: www.treeneutral.com

TreeNeutral®

Printed in the United States of America on acid-free paper

19 20 21 22 23 24   10 9 8 7 6 5 4 3 2 1

First Edition

Dedicated to our children and grandchildren,
so they will know

CONTENTS

TEN LEADERSHIP PRINCIPLES

AS A GROUP, the people of Ethan Allen—the company I've been privileged to serve as chairman and CEO since 1988—embrace ten key leadership principles that define our commitment to excellence. These leadership principles were developed more than twenty-five years ago and have guided us ever since.

Living by these principles is paramount for us. They create the compass that guides us to achieve our full potential, both as individuals within the company and as an organization. I believe these same principles have also enabled me to make my best contributions to the social causes I've embraced. Here they are:

1. **SELF-CONFIDENCE:** "Have the self-confidence to empower others to do their best."

2. **HARD WORK:** "Establish a standard of hard work and practice it consistently."

3. **EXCELLENCE AND INNOVATION:** "Have a passion for being the best you can be."

4. **ACCESSIBILITY**: "Be open and supportive, and recognize the contributions of others."

5. **CUSTOMER FOCUS**: "Encourage everyone around you to make customer service their highest priority."

6. **PRIORITIZATION**: "Clearly differentiate between the big issues and the small ones."

7. **LEADERSHIP**: "Lead by example."

8. **CHANGE**: "Understand that change means opportunity—don't be afraid of it."

9. **SPEED**: "Seize the advantage by reacting quickly to new opportunities."

10. **JUSTICE**: "Make decisions fairly. Justice builds trust, motivation, and teamwork."

As you read the pages that follow, I believe that you will recognize these leadership principles in action in many of the stories I share. I hope you'll find them intriguing and inspiring—perhaps even a source of guidance and insight in the leadership challenges you may face in your own life and work.

A BOYHOOD IN KASHMIR

I GREW UP IN the Himalayan region known as Jammu and Kashmir. It is a beautiful area known for its snowcapped mountains; its lofty lakes and streams filled with rushing, clear, cold water; its lush waterfront gardens; its fragrant fields of rice and saffron; and its dense pine forests.

But it is also a troubled region that for seventy years has been divided by politics, ethnicity, and religion. Those divisions shaped my early life and the life of my entire family.

In 1949, when I was not yet five years old, my father traveled to Pakistan on what we all thought would be a brief business trip. But political conflicts between nations intervened. The two-week journey turned into an enforced separation that would keep my father away from his home for seventeen years. It was just the first of several painful disruptions we would experience over the years to come. I'm sure this helps explain why, in the decades since then, I've devoted much of my time and energy to seeking a solution to the conflict that still brings suffering to the people of the region.

I was born in Srinagar, an ancient city in the heart of the Kashmir Valley that for centuries served as the capital of Kashmir.* The city is famous for the nine bridges that span the Jhelum River and for the lovely lakes to which British tourists traveled to enjoy holidays in grand houseboats. I was the fourth of six children in a prosperous merchant family—in fact, there were well-known merchants on both my father's side and my mother's side.

It was my father's grandfather, Gulam Mohiuddin, who started the business on that side of our family. He passed the business on to his son, my grandfather, Gulam Ahmed, whom I came to know well—although, as I'll explain, our relationship was not always easy.

My grandfather was a merchant who sold various products from central Asia, China, and India, including artifacts ranging from jewelry to rugs to works of traditional craftsmanship made by artisans from Tibet, Tashkent, and elsewhere. He and his father established an arts emporium in Srinagar under the name of Gulam Mohiuddin & Son. The maharajah of Jammu and Kashmir, Hari Singh, used to consult with my grandfather before making any major arts purchases. The family emporium was patronized by well-to-do people from all over the world, especially from England and Scotland. At that time, Kashmir's extraordinary natural beauty, including its snowcapped mountains and its rushing, trout-filled streams, made it a great hub of tourism. Kashmir has also historically been a hub of design and commerce through its links to the famous Silk Road, which connected Europe through Turkey to the Middle East, South Asia, and ultimately China, Korea, and Japan.

The family business took my grandfather and his father to many places in the region. In addition to their arts emporium in Srinagar, they had a shop in Calcutta, India, where they sold Kashmiri crafts, rugs, and art objects mainly to British customers. Their business in

---

* Currently, the most correct term for the entire region is "Jammu and Kashmir," but for the sake of conciseness, I usually refer to it simply as "Kashmir." The Kashmir Valley, where the Kashmiri language is spoken, was independent at various times in its history.

precious stones brought them frequently to the district of Kishtwar, a remote, sparsely populated area that became famous in the 1880s as the source of Kashmiri blue sapphires, some of the most highly prized gemstones in the world. Because Kishtwar is also called Kathwar, my family was sometimes called Kathwaris, although they were also known by the regional family name of Mattoo. I have adopted the name Kathwari, and it has now become the name by which my whole family is known.

My grandfather and great-grandfather were also interested in architecture and design. They commissioned and built a number of beautiful houses in Kashmir. The first one, in downtown Srinagar, was a traditional Kashmiri house with a courtyard in the middle. That's the house where I was born. Then they built three more houses in the suburbs—an English Tudor house, a Victorian-style house, and a Dutch colonial house. These houses reflected the influences on my grandfather during his frequent travels to Europe.

Meanwhile, my grandfather on my mother's side was Abdul Majid Bastel, a well-respected merchant of pashmina wool, with business connections in Tibet and central Asia, where most of this world-famous, high-quality wool came from goats raised at high altitudes. My mother's father was also a well-respected intellectual and a lover of the arts. Like my other grandfather, he built several homes in and around Srinagar, where he often hosted gatherings of writers and poets.

My mother, Maryam, was just a child when she suffered two terrible losses. First, her mother died. Then her father suffered a heart attack and died right before her eyes. An orphan at age twelve, my mother was raised by a couple of uncles. The shock of her two childhood losses had an impact on her that has lasted to this day. (Thankfully, she has been blessed with a long life. As I write, she is a resident of the Hebrew Home for the Aged in Riverdale, New York.)

She married my father, Gulam Mohamed, at the age of sixteen—not unusually young for that time and place.

Before I say more about my family life, I need to turn to the politics of our homeland of Kashmir. To understand the divisions that trouble the region, a little history is necessary.*

. . .

THE CENTRAL PART of the region of Jammu and Kashmir is the Kashmir Valley, where the ethnic Kashmiri-speaking people have lived for centuries. The region has a distinctive linguistic, musical, and cultural heritage, and it enjoyed periods of political independence until October 6, 1586. On that date, the armies of Akbar, the Mughal emperor of India, conquered the valley after having twice been driven back by the defending Kashmiris. Even so, Akbar's armies would not have been able to defeat the Kashmiris if not for the treachery of King Yusuf Shah Chak's brother. Legend has it that this brother aided Akbar in the belief that he himself would be installed on the throne of Kashmir. But after taking control of Kashmir, Akbar instead exiled the traitorous brother into eastern India, saying, "If you betray your brother and your own people, how can I trust you?" The king's brother later died in exile.

Akbar himself made a strategic error that would have fatal consequences for Mughal rule: He granted permission to the British government to set up the East India Company in India. By the late 1700s, the British had largely taken control of the Indian subcontinent, using a policy of divide and conquer to capitalize on conflicts among the local dynasties. In some parts of the region, the British installed their own governors. In others, they ruled indirectly through their influence over local leaders. Under this system, the region from Afghanistan to India was largely divided into provinces called *subas*.

Over time, the power of the Mughal rulers declined. In response,

---

* For a summary and a set of maps showing the evolving geography of this complex corner of the world, see Appendix A, Kashmir and Its Region—A Historical Overview.

the British allowed other groups to take control of portions of the sub-continent. In 1753, with British support, the Afghan general Abdul Khan Isk Aquasi took control of Afghanistan and Kashmir. Kashmir became known as the Kashmir *suba*. The region remained under the control of the Afghan empire until 1819, when armies from a Sikh regime based in Lahore seized Kashmir—again with British support.

In the mid-nineteenth century, much of the region became embroiled in the military, diplomatic, and economic rivalry between Russia and Britain, which battled for control of Afghanistan and neighboring portions of central and southern Asia in what is often referred to as "the Great Game." As one move in this international chess match, the British in 1847 seized control of the Punjab and other areas bordering Afghanistan. Their plan for the region included a treaty with Gulab Singh, Raja of Jammu and a member of the Hindu ethno-linguistic group known as the Dogras.

This Treaty of Amritsar—considered infamous by the people of Kashmir—in effect sold to Gulab Singh, for a price of 7.5 million rupees, all the lands and peoples in a vast region of diverse languages, ethnicities, and religions. This region constituted the state of Jammu and Kashmir, and Gulab Singh was its first maharajah—the first in a series of Hindu rulers over the majority-Muslim region. Giving power over Kashmir to this relative outsider was another aspect of the British Empire's divide-and-conquer strategy, which ensured that no united challenge to British power would arise.

In practice, the British exercised quasi-feudal dominance over Kashmir, pressing the Dogra rulers to adopt policies favorable to them. And while there were limits on what the British could do, they moved in Kashmiri society almost as colonial overlords would. For example, although there were strict laws forbidding any non-Kashmiri from owning land in the state, the British evaded the rules simply by building those lavish houseboats I mentioned earlier—beautiful floating mansions that now serve as hotels.

With help from the British Raj (rule by the British crown), Gulab Singh and his successors extended their control over a number of neighboring regions, including the sparsely populated eastern area; the so-called Northern Areas (once called "tribal areas") lying between Pakistan, Afghanistan, and China; and the Tibetan-influenced area to the east known as Ladakh. By the twentieth century, the state of Jammu and Kashmir was vast, heterogeneous, and hard to govern. In this respect, it resembled some of the countries of today's Middle East and Africa, which also were created with arbitrary borders and stark internal divisions—the result of decisions made by colonial powers more concerned with their own rivalries than with the social, ethnic, and linguistic realities on the ground.

In the first half of the twentieth century, the Kashmiri Muslims suffered greatly under the rule of the Hindu Dogras. The Muslims were largely free to practice their faith, but political activities were forbidden; even small gatherings to discuss political topics were often punished severely. Over time, some Kashmiris of various faiths emigrated to other parts of Asia, mostly to what is now Pakistan and northern India, and many of these emigrant families gained prominence in their new homes. For instance, one of the great poets of South Asia, Sir Muhammad Iqbal, came from a Muslim Kashmiri family that settled in what is now Pakistan. Similarly, Pandit Nehru, the first prime minister of India, was from a Hindu Kashmiri family that settled in northern India.

But in their homeland, Kashmiri Muslims continued to suffer. In the 1930s, my grandfather Gulam Ahmed and a group of associates formed a group called the Kashmir Reading Room, which met in my grandfather's house in downtown Srinagar. Its supposed purpose was to discuss literary issues, but, in reality, it formed the nucleus of what became the Quit Kashmir Movement, with the goal to end the Dogra rule over Kashmir. (Many years later, the Kashmir Reading Room inspired me to establish the Kashmir Study Group, dedicated to finding a peaceful solution to the ongoing political problems of Kashmir and Jammu.)

During the 1930s and the early 1940s, the Quit Kashmir movement worked to build support for Kashmiri self-rule, much as the Quit India movement led by Mohandas K. Gandhi was doing in India. The movement was a nonviolent one, but the government response was not always peaceful. In 1931, a demonstration was held at the Pathar Masjid in Srinagar. This was a mosque built in the seventeenth century by the famous Mughal empress Noor Jehan. The protesters were fired upon by soldiers under orders from the Dogra rulers. Making matters worse, the Dogras refused to allow a decent burial for the bodies of the slain. As a result, the courtyard of Pathar Masjid became known as the Martyrs' Graveyard. It is the site of an annual ceremony, held every July 13, which is known as Martyrs' Day.

This, then, was the political and social situation when I was born—but soon, everything would change dramatically.

■ ■ ■

IN 1947, IN THE AFTERMATH of World War II, and facing ever-growing pressure from the independence movement led by Mohandas K. Gandhi, Muhammad Ali Jinnah, Sardar Vallabhbhai Patel, and other luminaries, Britain decided to relinquish its power over the Indian subcontinent. Unfortunately, it carried out its departure in haste, without adequate planning. Political leaders, especially those from the minority Muslim community, demanded partition of the subcontinent into separate countries—India for the Hindus and Pakistan (in two sections, West Pakistan and East Pakistan) for the Muslims. The partition led to the displacement of millions of people, a vast refugee crisis, and fighting that cost the lives of hundreds of thousands of people.

In Kashmir, the Dogra ruler agreed to hand over power to India temporarily. However, the situation was unstable, with a population deeply divided by religion—their loyalties split between the two emerging nations of India and Pakistan, both of which claimed the right to rule Kashmir and Jammu. The so-called First Kashmir War of 1947–48 was the result. After intervention by the United Nations, a cease-fire was declared, with about 60 percent of the state—including the Kashmir Valley, a highly desirable part of the region—being controlled by India, while the remaining 40 percent was controlled by Pakistan. It was also agreed that a plebiscite (a national referendum) would be held to allow the people of the entire state to decide between joining India or Pakistan. Independence was not proposed as an option.

Flash forward seventy years. No plebiscite has ever been held. The reason is simple: As we now understand, neither India nor Pakistan is likely to want to abide by the result if the vote were to go against them. Instead, the Kashmir and Jammu region remains split into areas—one administered by India, one by Pakistan—along the same dividing line that was established decades ago by the UN cease-fire. This division is now known as the Line of Control. The former state of Jammu and Kashmir still has no clear national identity. Pakistan refers to its people as "natives of the Jammu Kashmir region," while the Indians consider them Indians.

As you can see, the politics of being Kashmiri are very complicated. Although Jammu and Kashmir is sometimes spoken of as a "country," it is not a country but rather a collection of areas inhabited by peoples of different ethnicities, religions, and languages. Rather than enjoying a stable, unified government, it has been ruled for decades by a series of provisional regimes, its peace periodically disturbed by fighting among religious, ethnic, and political groups seeking permanent dominance. Most unique is the Kashmiri-speaking region itself, which enjoyed intermittent periods of independence and more recently has been the center of the ongoing conflict.

Living under these circumstances, it's hard for any thoughtful, concerned person *not* to get involved in politics. Generations of

Kashmiris—and many from outside the region—have found themselves caught up in the search for a fair and peaceful long-term solution to "the Kashmir problem."

My father was no exception. He earned his undergraduate degree in law from Punjab University in Lahore—then in India, now in Pakistan—and his advanced degrees in law from Aligarh Muslim University in the Indian province of Uttar Pradesh. He did not practice law but worked with his father in the family business and also got involved in politics. He participated in the Kashmir Reading Room group founded by my grandfather and his associates, which was focused on ousting the Dogra rulers from Kashmir. This group eventually gave rise to a political organization called the Muslim Conference, which was affiliated with the Muslim League of India. In the 1940s, under the leadership of Sheikh Abdullah, a new organization called the National Conference was established, which included both Hindu and Muslim members.

Since my father was living in the portion of Kashmir that was administered by the Indian government—which also claimed the right to rule all of Kashmir—my father's advocacy of a plebiscite that would allow Kashmiris to decide their own political future made him suspect in the government's eyes. Making matters worse, not only were our family Muslims, but they also had direct political ties to Pakistan. For example, Muhammad Ali Jinnah, the founder of Pakistan and the nation's first governor-general, was friends with my grandfather and used to visit him in Kashmir. As a student, my father was assigned to accompany Jinnah and his sister when they made excursions to visit various parts of Kashmir. These activities were not illegal, but they meant that our family was kept under scrutiny by the Indian authorities in Kashmir.

Perhaps what happened next was almost inevitable. In the fall of 1949, my father traveled to Pakistan on business under a travel permit from the Indian government. His plan was to stay there for a month.

But while he was in Pakistan, my father's travel permit was cancelled. Suddenly he was unable to return to Indian-administered Kashmir—which meant he was separated from his homeland and his family. Although he would be reunited with some members of his immediate family in less than a year, the separation from his homeland would last, more or less, for seventeen years.

The authorities took other steps as well. Soldiers of the Indian army entered our house to search through our father's papers and seized a number of documents, including one of the personal diaries he maintained for many years. Meanwhile, our grandfather was in Calcutta, having just returned from a trip to Europe. Indian police arrested him as he left the ship, also part of the same crackdown.

The man who managed the Calcutta store owned by my grandfather was Gulam Rasul Khan. He was a member of our extended family clan and a stalwart friend of our grandfather's. When the police took our grandfather away, Khan declared, "If you are going to arrest him, you have to arrest me too." The police obliged. The two men were held in prison in Calcutta and in Kashmir for a total of six months, at which point they were released, since they hadn't actually committed any crime.

Gulam Rasul Khan, who bravely supported my grandfather in his time of persecution, would later become my father-in-law.

For several months, my father was frantic, worrying about his father in prison and his wife and five children in Srinagar. The separation was alleviated in March 1950, when my father, with help from the UN, managed to get permission from the Indian authorities to bring my mother and three of us children to join him in Pakistan. (The two eldest children—my older brother and sister, aged ten and nine—remained in Kashmir, as my grandfather did not want them to leave their home.)

I vividly remember the journey, which my uncle Amin arranged. The five of us flew in a small plane from Srinagar to Amritsar in the Indian state of Punjab, near the Pakistani border. There we drove through the international checkpoint in the village of Wagah. On the other side, our father was waiting in a big black car festooned with the green, gold, and white flag of Pakistani-administered Kashmir, also known as "Free Kashmir." We embraced warmly after our months apart. Then we drove together to the city of Muzaffarabad, the capital of the region.

Of course, we were all relieved and happy to be reunited. But we were also longing to return to our home in Srinagar. I remember my mother's unhappiness about being in the hot mountainous city of Muzaffarabad—a far cry from the lush river valley whose pleasant weather she loved. My parents figured that the tensions between India and Pakistan, which were the root cause of our exile, would soon be settled. At the time, everyone still assumed that, one day soon, a plebiscite would be scheduled that would determine once and for all the fate of Kashmir. And so we thought we'd be staying in Pakistan for just six to eight months or so.

Instead, our stay lasted ten years.

■　■　■

IN SEPTEMBER 1948, Jinnah died. In 1949, with my father stranded in Pakistan, Jinnah's successor as the leader of Pakistan, Prime Minister Liaquat Ali Khan, invited him to join the government of Pakistani-administered Kashmir. My father became minister of law and finance and ended up serving in that role for six years before becoming an executive in the Pakistan Industrial Development Corporation, set up by the government to encourage economic growth.

Our prosperous family had been unable to bring any possessions with us to Pakistan. We were designated as refugees, which made us eligible for help from the Pakistani government. In fact, in the wake of the partition of India and the consequent displacement of millions of people, a system had arisen whereby refugees were sometimes given property seized from others who'd fled in the opposite direction. My mother's family properties had been taken by authorities in the Indian-administered region of Kashmir. So she was given a house in Murree, which would be our home for most of the next several years. (When my mother returned to the Indian-administered side of Kashmir in 1960, she returned the Murree house to the government—an unusual step that reflected the strong ethical standards she always upheld.)

Murree is located high in the Pir Panjal Range of the Himalayan Mountains. When I lived in Murree in the 1950s, it was a poor area and very cold in the winter. Our house, called Katrina, had been built by an Englishman and was located on top of a mountain, more than 8,000 feet above sea level. It had no running water; instead, a supply of drinking water was delivered daily from a local spring, and we collected rainwater from the tin roofs for bathing.

As a small child back in Srinagar, I'd attended a Protestant missionary school with both Kashmiri and non-Kashmiri teachers. Now, in Murree, I was sent to Presentation Convent boarding school as a day student. Many of the students—including most of the boarders—came from the tribal areas bordering Afghanistan. These students were physically tough, instinctively aggressive, and quick to recognize any sign of weakness—and to take advantage of it. Kids seven years old carried knives, which they used in battles that often pitted the day students against the boarders.

My first test came early. Although Punjabi and Urdu were the main languages spoken in Murree, I knew only Kashmiri. One of the older boys started taunting me with the nickname *gur*, which means "horse" in Kashmiri. (He'd heard me using the word in reference to the horses that I saw all around in Murree.) The other boys picked up the insult. I was incensed, and I came up with an idea. My father had a bodyguard who slept in our house—and I knew he kept his gun in a holster, hanging from a hook in his room. I got ahold of the pistol, marched straight up to the boy who'd taunted me, and demanded that he stop. When the boy refused, I pointed the gun right at him and pulled the trigger. Fortunately, the pistol was equipped with a safety lock, so nothing happened.

Of course, my father was very upset with me. But the boy never called me *gur* again. And as word about my action spread through the school, the other kids began to treat me with respect—even fear.

I soon learned Urdu—the language that most of my classmates spoke—and at age ten I became the leader of one of the school's toughest cliques. One day, angry about the latest beating I'd suffered at the hands of the nuns, I assembled ten or so of my followers and declared, "We'll teach them a lesson—let's burn the school down!" One of us got a can of kerosene from somewhere, another got a box of matches, and we tried to carry out the plot. But the stone walls of the school proved fire resistant. One of our friends betrayed the rest of us by telling somebody's parents, and we all got yet another good thrashing.

During the winters, our family would move to warmer places, such as Muzaffarabad (where my brother Tariq was born in 1951) and Rawalpindi—with the exception of one winter, when we stayed in Murree and had to cope with snow accumulations more than six feet deep. During one of our winters in Rawalpindi, a near-tragedy struck. My sister Mahmuda took our brothers Rafiq and Tariq to bathe in the bathroom, and they were almost killed by carbon monoxide poisoning.

After sixth grade, at age twelve, I was sent to St. Mary's School in Rawalpindi, where my father rented a townhouse about thirty-five miles down the mountain from Murree—a two-hour trip by bus. What's odd is that most weeks, I lived in the townhouse by myself. My parents usually stayed behind in Murree, although my father would travel to stay with me periodically. I would travel on Friday afternoon to be with them in Murree, then return to Rawalpindi on Sunday evening. So at the age of twelve, I became a commuter.

Concerned about how isolated I was during the week, my father arranged for me to have dinners with neighbors—military men and their families (Rawalpindi is the headquarters of the Pakistani army).

Looking back on this years later, I realized that he must have paid them for this favor.

Since I'd been toughened up by being a gang leader at the convent school, living alone in Rawalpindi didn't bother me. That's not to say I wasn't a little anxious. Exploring the townhouse, I discovered that my father had a gun locked up in a safe, and I learned the combination by watching closely when he opened it. I took out the gun and kept it under my pillow while I slept. I never had a reason to use it.

I rode the four miles to and from school every day on a grown-up bike that I found in the townhouse. It was too big for me, so I couldn't use the seat; instead, I straddled the top tube of the bike frame and cranked away on the pedals.

The culture at St. Mary's School turned out to be just as tough as at Presentation Convent. On the second day of school, one of the other kids—his nickname was *Ganda*, which means "rhino" in Urdu—came up to me out of the blue and demanded, "Do you want to fight?"

I had nothing against Ganda; I didn't even know him. "No," I responded.

"In that case, I'll call you *Darpok*," he announced. That means "scared"—like giving someone the nickname "Chicken."

I didn't care for that. So the next morning when I saw Ganda sitting around before class, I picked up a wooden chair and with all my strength hit him over the head.

"That's what you get for calling me Darpok!" I told him.

Naturally, this caused quite a commotion. A teacher and a priest rushed over, saw Ganda's bloody head, and asked, "What happened?"

After a moment, Ganda told them, "I slipped and fell." Ganda might have been a bully, but he had an ethical code, and ratting on a fellow student wasn't permitted. He and I ended up becoming good friends.

An experience in Rawalpindi foreshadowed my future. Our townhouse fronted on the main street of the town—the address was 31 The Mall—and, on the first floor, it had a store called the Kashmir Arts

Emporium. It was a consignment shop that my father had organized with the government, run by a hired manager. Its purpose was to provide a market for goods made by Kashmiri artisans who were refugees in Pakistan. At the age of thirteen, I started working there after school, keeping the stock neatly displayed and helping customers choose craft items—lamps, bowls made of wood or papier-mâché, embroidered fabrics, and so on. It was both the first time I'd participated in my family's merchant tradition, and the first time I sold home furnishings—a suitable apprenticeship for a future CEO of Ethan Allen.

As you can see from the stories I've told, I must have been quite a handful for my parents. Unfortunately, dealing with a headstrong young son wasn't the most difficult thing in my mother's life. I've mentioned how she tragically became an orphan by the age of twelve, even seeing her father die in front of her. Perhaps partly as a result of this trauma, she developed psychological issues that included schizophrenia and obsessive-compulsive disorder. During our time in Pakistan, our family consulted physicians about her condition, and they prescribed electroconvulsive therapy—a common treatment throughout the world in the 1940s and 1950s. The electric shocks were administered in our home, and I had to hold down my mother's legs while the jolts of electricity surged through her head and body—a frightening and disturbing thing for me. The shock treatments, including my involvement, continued later when we returned to Srinagar in Kashmir.

Having a mother who was suffering both from severe mental health problems and the debilitating effects of shock treatments increased my sense of isolation. In some children, such experiences might have led to antisocial behavior—perhaps even a tendency toward crime, violence, or alcohol abuse. But not for me. I outgrew the aggressiveness I'd used to survive in school and instead became self-reliant and independent at a young age.

I must add that there is another side to my mother that is much happier to speak about. She has always been an exceptionally smart woman with strong intellectual and social interests. She speaks knowledgeably about politics, geography, and history, and has periodically gotten engaged in social issues. For example, back in the 1950s she wrote a thoughtful letter to President Eisenhower about resolving the Kashmir issue to help the people of the region and to enable her to reunite with her two children. I'm happy to have been blessed with her presence throughout her long and eventful life.

• • •

IN 1960, AFTER A DECADE in Pakistan, most of our family—with the exception of our father—were given permission to leave the country. I was fifteen at the time. My mother, my three siblings, and I were all given Pakistani traveling documents with a five-year term. We were also given three-month visas that would allow us to enter India and visit Amritsar and Delhi. As we had done in 1950, we again traveled to the international crossing point at Wagah. My grandfather's car was waiting for us on the other side of the border. We were received by Gulam Rasul Khan, my grandfather's business partner who had insisted on joining him in prison.

Despite the fact that we were not technically allowed to travel to Kashmir, we drove straight home to Srinagar, a trip of twelve hours or more. There was a checkpoint at the crossing from India, but because we had a car with Kashmiri license plates—and we all looked like Kashmiris—we were not asked to show any papers. And once we were in Srinagar, everyone who heard about what we'd done—up to and including Bakshi Ghulam Mohammad, then the prime minister of Jammu and Kashmir—simply shrugged: "Forget it! You're home now. You don't have to worry about papers anymore."

Before long, however, my less-than-perfect travel documents would cause me some significant problems.

Meanwhile, my family devoted its attention to settling back into life in Srinagar, the place we all still thought of as home. Close relatives and members of our larger extended clan came from near and far to welcome us, some by automobile, some in the horse carriages called *tongas* that were widely used at the time as a sort of taxi. Many stayed for a while in our large house, extending the welcome party over a number of days.

We were now reunited with many family members, including our great-grandmother (known as Apa), our grandmother (called Boba), and our grandfather (called Tathoo, meaning "loved one"). I was also now reunited with my older sister Aisha and my older brother Aslum.

During this period when our house was bustling with friends and relations, one day I bumped into an attractive girl in a hallway.

"Excuse me," I said. And then, "Who are you?"

"My name is Farida," she said, and we stared into one another's eyes. It was the first time I'd ever seen my future wife. I was fifteen and Farida was fourteen. Within a few seconds, it was clear that something important had happened to both of us.

Returning to Srinagar turned out to be quite an adjustment for me. I had changed during my years in Murree and Rawalpindi. My grandmother and great-grandmother captured the difference in their new nickname for me: "Mountain Boy." I had become tough, self-confident, bold, and outspoken. By contrast, the city boys I got to know were quiet, respectful, and careful about the things they said. It took awhile for me to overcome the cultural shock and to adjust my own behavior to fit in a little better to my new surroundings.

I joined a Catholic missionary school called Burn Hall and quickly became involved in several sports teams. Within a few months, I was captain of the cricket team, and in my last year of high school—which was tenth grade in Kashmir—I won most of the medals for sprinting and long-distance running.

After graduation, I enrolled in Kashmir University. I became a student in Sri Pratap College—universally known as SP College—which is named after one of the Dogra rulers of Kashmir. Many of the students there were aspiring physicians or engineers (or at least those were the hopes of their parents). But my most serious interest was sports. I would walk to the college early in the morning—it was not far from our family home—and stay there until well into the evening, taking classes, doing things with friends, and above all taking part in sports practices and matches.

By now, I had little in common with my brothers and sisters; my father was still in Pakistan; my poor mother was not well; and the head of the household, my paternal grandfather, was a distant and imposing figure with whom I found it hard to communicate. So there wasn't much to engage my interest at home. It was mostly just the place where I slept every night, in between sporting events.

I liked all sports, but I developed an especially strong love for cricket—a love that at one point almost permanently derailed my college education.

It was near the end of my first year at the university. Final exams were approaching, and my scores would help determine my future. But I had a couple of problems. The first problem was that I'd skipped so many classes in my science courses that I didn't have the skills required to pass the final lab exam.

Luckily for me, a peculiarity in the university's examination system worked in my favor. At that time, a single university served students in the two major cities of Jammu and Kashmir—Srinagar in Kashmir, and Jammu itself. Classes were held on campuses in both cities. And in an effort to avoid favoritism, the university had developed a system whereby professors from Jammu would come to the Srinagar campus to administer the final exams, and vice versa—thus ensuring that every student would be tested by a teacher who did not know him.

This created an opening for me. I approached a very smart student and asked him to take the lab exam in my place. He agreed to do it, mainly because of my popularity as one of the leaders on the college sports teams—everyone liked me and would have been happy to do a favor for me. This was an unusual and inappropriate way of handling the situation. However, when I was in a fix, I'd developed the habit of simply improvising—and that's what I was doing in this case.

I still had a second problem to deal with. University regulations required students to attend a specified percentage of classes to be eligible to sit for their written exams—and my attendance record fell short. I wasn't what we might today call a slacker; I'd been missing classes not simply to loaf or hang out with my friends, but rather to participate in sports—in particular, to play and practice cricket and to help organize our college cricket team. Nonetheless, rules were rules. And if I couldn't take my exams, my future at the university might be in jeopardy, along with my hopes for a successful life and career.

To appeal my case, I visited Amin Chisti in his office. He was the registrar of Kashmir University (equivalent to a vice chancellor in the US academic system) and known as a stern, no-nonsense administrator—a man who'd recently had the audacity to stand up to the prime minister himself during a dispute about changes in university policies.

I decided to be forthright about what I'd done. "Sir, it is true that I was not present for some of my classes," I said, "but I believe it would be fair to mark me as present. I was on the cricket field, and I consider cricket an education in itself!"

Mr. Chisti laughed. "This is the first time I've heard such an excuse!" he declared. "Tell me, what have you learned from this education in cricket?"

"The main thing I've learned is that being able to live and work successfully with people is the most important skill in life," I replied. "This is why I've spent so much time with my teammates, getting to know them and talking about how we can make our team better." I elaborated on my discovery, and the registrar's expression gradually changed from one of skepticism to one of thoughtful understanding.

Before our conversation ended, he agreed to grant me permission to take my year-end exams—in effect, marking me as present in class during my practice sessions on the cricket field. I took the tests and passed them, which made me eligible to continue my education the following semester.

Not long ago, in April 2017, I had the bittersweet experience of attending a memorial service for Mr. Chisti in New York City. Had he not been willing to give me a second chance at a college education, I might never have come to America and enjoyed the career and life I've experienced.

• • •

I DID PAY A PRICE for my careless attitude toward exams during that first year. Indirectly, it started a downward spiral in my relationship with the most important male figure in my life at that time—my paternal grandfather.

Having floundered academically during my first year in college, and lacking interest in either medicine or engineering, I decided to change my major field of study from science to the arts and humanities. Accordingly, in my second and third years of college, I signed up mostly for classes like political science and English literature, which I enjoyed and did well in. At the same time, I continued to dedicate most of my energies to sports. The problem was that I made these potentially important decisions without consulting anyone.

Finally, in my third year, my grandfather discovered what I was doing all day at school—and he was furious. "I thought you were studying to be an engineer!" he thundered. "What will you do with your life? Do you expect to be a forest ranger or a police officer?" (These were jobs that someone with a "useless" humanities degree might take.)

Nothing I said seemed to placate him, and this troubled me. I wasn't concerned about money. College education was free to all students, and I relied on my grandfather for practically nothing financially. But I felt bad about making him feel disrespected. I decided I'd better do something to make him happy.

Trying to resuscitate an engineering major was out of the question. I had no gift for the subject and very little desire to study it. The only academic subject I found interesting that I thought my grandfather might approve of was business; after all, he was a successful merchant and businessman. The problem was that SP College offered no business program. So I came up with a plan.

There was another college in Kashmir, called Islamia College, which offered a program in economics and commerce. I went to the head of that college and said, "I would like to transfer from SP College to your school." He was delighted—not because of my academic brilliance, but because I was known as a good athlete who would be an asset to the school's teams. With his acceptance in my pocket, I went back to Mr. Saif Uddin, the principal of SP College, and announced my imminent departure.

"Not so fast," he replied. "Let's see what we can do."

He called Professor Abdullah Punoo, the head of the economics department, and asked, "How can we keep Farooq here? Our sports teams need him!" Professor Punoo suggested a solution: "Let's create an economics honors program with a focus on business. All we need is a minimum of three students to make it eligible for certification."

Mr. Saif Uddin liked that idea. They put out the word and soon found two other students who were willing to sign on to the new program. I was now able to proudly announce to my grandfather that I had become a major in economics and business. That patched things up between us, at least for a time.

But soon more friction grew between us. Perhaps that was inevitable, given how independent minded and willful I was. Our quarrels were often about small things. For example, one time I needed a new set of spiked shoes for cricket. These were a little more expensive than

I could afford on my own. (I was making some pocket money by working as an umpire for cricket matches in my spare time, but it was not enough for cricket spikes.) So I visited my grandfather in his office to ask for the money.

Busy at his desk, he merely glanced at me and said, "Why don't you go to my assistant and write an application?"

For some reason, this callous reply made me furious. "That does it," I said. "I don't want anything from you, and I will have nothing to do with you or your property ever again." I stalked out of the room.

Those were big words. But now I had to follow up on them. After all, I was living in his house at the time! Where would I sleep that night?

As always when faced with a dilemma, I was resourceful. I went to the cowshed in the back of my grandfather's estate, some distance from the main house, almost touching one of the outside walls of the property. It was a small mud hut with two floors; the cow lived in the first floor, and upstairs were two tiny rooms with no water, no electricity, cracked walls, and windows with no panes of glass. Those upstairs rooms, I decided, would be my new home. I got handfuls of wet clay, which I used to plaster the walls and the floor to keep the wind out. Then I got some sheets of clear plastic to cover the windows. Finally, I realized that there was a pole for electric wires just on the other side of the cowshed wall. So I climbed the pole with a couple of tools and a length of wire in my hand, and I spliced a connection to the power line. Yes, it was very dangerous—as well as illegal. But it worked. My first construction job was a success!

My grandfather and everyone else in the family watched all this with amazement and amusement. They thought I was crazy and would come slinking back to my comfortable room in the main house within a day or two. But they didn't know me. I lived in that cowshed for two years. I called it my *gam lari*, or "village hut." I carried a bed and some blankets up there, and during the winter months, I wore a knitted ski cap and a pair of gloves while sleeping. All the while, the cow lived down below. I went into the main house only to eat and to use the bathroom—which meant I was still somewhat dependent on my grandfather, but little enough so that I considered myself the winner in this battle. It was all about independence and my determination to control my own destiny.

During my college years, I developed my lifelong love of mountaineering. Our home in Srinagar was already at an elevation of 5,200 feet, but I wanted to go higher. So I got into the habit of leaving my house every morning around five o'clock to climb a nearby mountain before my college classes began. This mountain has two names. The Muslims call it the Throne of Suleiman, while the Hindus call it Shankaracharya in honor of Adi Shankara, an Indian philosopher of the eighth century who used to visit the ancient temple on its peak.

Weather permitting, I would start my day by climbing up Shankaracharya. Occasionally I was joined by a friend of mine, also named Farooq. One time I hiked up Shankaracharya with Farida, the girl I'd met in the hallway of my home soon after returning to Kashmir. My sister and Farida's sister also came along, but of course my attention was focused entirely on Farida. I remember taking her hand to help her with a difficult part of the hike, then holding on to her hand for a while—not exactly improper for a Muslim boy and girl in that time and place, but not typical either.

Farida and I were beginning to develop a special bond with one another. On a different occasion, we went to a movie together—again with our sisters in tow—and held hands briefly while enjoying the show. These are moments that have remained vivid for me after all these years.

Maybe most memorable were the times when Farida would visit my sisters to listen to music from the radio in my *gam lari*. The story of the radio requires its own explanation.

Being a cricket player brought me many benefits during my boyhood in Kashmir—extending far beyond the opportunity to talk my way back into my first year of college exams. One benefit was the chance to travel widely. The various colleges of Kashmir University, based in both Srinagar and Jammu, all had cricket teams that would play matches against one another; so as a member of the SP College team I got to travel within the Kashmir region.

Later, as a member of the Kashmir-wide cricket team that included the best players from the whole region, I got to travel far more extensively. We played cricket matches in various cities in northern India, including Delhi and Agra (home to the magnificent Taj Mahal). I enjoyed travel and seized opportunities to visit other places in India, such as Calcutta and Bombay, generally traveling via the Indian railroads, which at the time lacked most modern amenities but nonetheless constituted one of the world's busiest and most extensive rail networks. (This is still true today.)

In 1963, when I was eighteen years old, I went with the Kashmir cricket team to play in Allahabad, an important city in northern India. I decided to visit Calcutta, where, as I've mentioned, my grandfather had a shop that Farida's father helped run. This was not a short trip. Today a superfast train can go from Allahabad to Calcutta in about ten hours, but in those days it took much longer. I was young and hardy, however, and I thought nothing of it.

In Calcutta, I visited the townhouse where Farida's father lived, and while curiously poking around in the attic, I came across an old RCA radio almost the size of a trunk. I asked Farida's father if it worked.

"I doubt it," he replied, "We haven't touched it in years, maybe decades."

"Can I take it?" I asked.

"Take it where?"

"To Kashmir."

"You know, it's more than 2,000 miles from here. How will you take it?"

I told him I was traveling by train and bus.

Farida's father shrugged. "Well, if you want to take it, take it."

And so I did. This would be a journey that would make the Allahabad-to-Calcutta trip seem like a little jaunt. I had to ride the train for some fifty hours to get from Calcutta to Pathankot, the city nearest to Srinagar where the Indian train lines finally ended. (Even today there is no direct railroad line to Srinagar, because the mountains are too high.) The final leg of the journey to my home would be another twelve or fourteen hours by bus. The idea of doing all this while lugging a giant old radio in a huge wooden cabinet must have seemed crazy. But off I went.

I got on the train in Calcutta and put the radio on the floor next to my seat, attracting quite a few stares from my fellow passengers. The trip was uneventful until the train arrived at the border between one Indian state and the next. The train stopped, and a pair of uniformed government officials came up and down the aisles to collect the mandated tax on "goods movement"—something I'd never heard about before. I had very little money in my pocket, and I had no interest in sparing any of it to pay tax.

When the officials spotted me, one of them pointed to the huge object by my side and asked, "What is this?"

"It's a radio."

"Well, you have to pay tax on it."

"Tax! I don't think it even works."

"You still have to pay tax."

"I won't pay it," I said firmly. "If you want, you can take the radio. But I won't pay tax."

The officials looked at one another. There was no way they were going to take the radio—and be saddled with figuring out what to do with it.

"Forget it," they said and moved on to the next passenger.

Over the next fifty hours, the same thing happened at additional border crossings.

Finally the railroad journey to Pathankot ended, and the bus ride to Srinagar began. The first challenge was getting the radio onto the bus.

Like most Indian buses, this one had a luggage rack on the roof, and the bus driver and the conductor manfully wrestled the radio all the way up there.

"I need to check on it," I said and began climbing up the side of the bus. The driver protested, but I insisted. So I scrambled up, saw where the radio was nestled among all kinds of other belongings—bedding, tin trunks, wooden boxes, and other luggage—and made sure it was properly covered with a tarpaulin in case of rain or snow.

Ten hours later, the odyssey of the radio finally ended. I hauled it to my cottage and took it to the local radio repair shop, where they had it in working order within a few days. I lugged it up to my room in the cowshed, plugged it into my jerry-rigged wiring, and stretched the yards of fabric antenna around the ceiling, tacking it in place with nails. Soon my cottage was filled with the sound of music. It was a minor miracle.

Radios were unusual in Kashmir at that time—televisions were completely unknown—and so my cottage became a local curiosity and an attraction. My sisters, Farida, and her sister would come to listen to broadcasts with me. Thinking it might not be proper for them to come into the cottage, they stood outside in the nearby garden, listening to music or news through the windows. Sometimes I turned the volume up loud enough so that my grandfather could hear it from his room in the main house—another salvo in my ongoing "cold war" against him. Like my cottage dwelling itself, my radio was a symbol of my willingness to do almost anything, no matter how crazy, in pursuit of independence.

■ ■ ■

DURING MY THIRD YEAR at university, I was made captain of the cricket team—the first Muslim to be so honored. Cricket was played mostly by Kashmiri Pandits and by the Dogras of Jammu. Kashmiri Muslims generally played soccer, while the Sikhs favored field hockey.

I was not a deeply religious person. My family and I rarely went to mosque, and we seldom discussed our faith. But we understood, of course, that in Kashmir, the Dogras and the Pandits represented the ruling elite. This caused resentment that helped fuel social conflict. It also meant that Muslims tended to band together, offering mutual support against the perceived discrimination they faced from the Hindus. So I imagine that when I gradually emerged as a student leader, my fellow Muslims, consciously or unconsciously, desired to support me: "He's one of us—we should help him."

The existence of prejudice and a history of discrimination were not things I thought about much at the time. I had many friends among the Pandits and Punjabi-speaking Hindus who made up the majority of our cricket team. I'm still in touch with many of them today, and some still like to call me "Captain."

Eventually, my status as a student leader led to my receiving some unique privileges. One day the principal said, "You know, you're so much involved with sports and activities, I'm going to give you the title of sports secretary, and you should have an office here." He gave me a small office at the college, and equally important, a stove for making tea. I used the office for sports-related meetings, and sometimes one of my economics or English classes, with just a handful of students, would be held there. The only other student who had previously enjoyed the right to an office alongside those of the faculty members and administrators had been the crown prince of Kashmir.

In addition, a special document was created that I could use to grant any member of a college sports team an exemption from a class meeting, provided he was needed for an important game or practice session. I used the form very selectively, of course, not to make life easy for my teammates. And I'm sure this is what the university expected me to do—otherwise they would never have granted a student such power in the first place.

In a curious way, cricket became, for me, much more than just a game or a pastime. In a sense, I grew up on the cricket field, not just physically but intellectually and morally as well. And to this day, I believe that the game of cricket, as I learned to play it during my boyhood in Kashmir, exemplifies many of the principles of teamwork and leadership that have helped make me successful in my later life.

For many people in America, cricket is an unfamiliar sport. They associate it with England, they know it vaguely resembles baseball, and they may even know that cricket matches sometimes last for many hours or even days; beyond that, cricket is largely a mystery. So let me explain a bit about the game and the kind of leadership it demands.

Cricket is played by two teams of eleven players, and it shares some features with baseball. As in baseball, the objective is for the batting team to score runs while the opposition tries to field the ball. But one major way cricket differs from baseball is in team leadership. Unlike the manager in baseball, the cricket captain is also a player. He doesn't sit on a bench in the dugout, orchestrating strategy from afar; instead, he is on the field, taking part in almost every play and contributing directly to the success or failure of the team. On most cricket teams, the captain is also one of the best players, if not the very best. He must be able to lead by example.

Because the cricket captain is both player and leader, he must be accessible, accountable, and personally connected to his teammates. He motivates the other players not through exhortations, rule setting, or punishment, but by showing his own enthusiasm and commitment. The cricket captain thinks continually about the game, his team, and what he can do to make the team better; he views his leadership role not just as a hobby or an avocation but a life mission. This level of dedication is transmitted naturally to his teammates, who in turn become exceptionally engaged and devoted.

This helps to explain the motto that our college team lived by: "If you're not playing, you're practicing!" During my captaincy, we worked out almost every evening and weekend, more than any other team I knew—which played a huge role in our competitive success.

At the same time the cricket captain is performing on the field, he has special responsibility for team strategy. He sets the team's batting order before the game starts, makes changes in the order during the game, and selects the bowler (roughly the equivalent of the pitcher in baseball). The captain also positions his teammates around the field depending on the particular characteristics of the batsman and the bowler, the kinds of deliveries the bowler intends to pitch (fast bowls, spinners, swing bowls, and so on), weather conditions, the varying skills of the fielders, and other considerations. So the captain must have an intimate understanding of the game and of the strengths and weaknesses of each of his teammates, as well as those of the opposing players.

As you can see from this brief description, leadership in cricket is not just about technical knowledge—although technical knowledge is quite important. It is very much a "people" skill. The captain who chooses the bowler based on favoritism or friendship rather than on merit and strategic fit for the situation may doom his team to defeat. The captain who is aloof or arrogant and so fails to engage and motivate his teammates is unlikely to enjoy lasting success. By contrast, the captain who is sensitive to the moods of his teammates, understands the nuances of each player's strengths and weaknesses, and knows which one is more likely to be energized by a word of praise and which by a gentle rebuke or a stern challenge—such a captain will win the loyalty and support of the whole team and will enable them to perform at their very best.

All of this interpersonal drama plays out against a backdrop of crucial cricket matches that may last as long as five days—a challenge to the athletes' physical and emotional stamina that underscores the importance of team cohesion and camaraderie.

During my years as captain of the Kashmir University team, I had the opportunity to learn and practice the varied leadership skills that cricket demands. Some of the biggest challenges arose off the field, such as the time when our team bus was stranded in several feet of snow in a Himalayan mountain pass as we traveled from Jammu to Srinagar. As captain, I had to make the tough decision about what we should do. After gathering input from my teammates, I concluded that our best chance of getting food and rest lay in abandoning the bus and walking to our destination. Ill equipped and poorly dressed for the trek, we nonetheless managed to cross the mountain gap—an unplanned but powerful bonding experience that none of us would ever forget.

Our team achieved some exhilarating successes on the playing field. In 1963, we competed for the national championship against the powerful team from Jammu, located in Jammu's largest city, which was the winter seat of government for the Kashmiri state. When we defeated Jammu on their home field, the local fans were outraged that our upstart team had beaten the "royals," and some even pelted our team bus with stones. We proved that our victory was no fluke the following year when we won the championship again, this time defeating the team from Jammu on our home field in Srinagar.

In later years, after I came to America, I played on the cricket team at New York University. My teammates were from various far-flung parts of the former British Empire in the Caribbean, Australia, Canada, and South Asia. And once again, I ended up being asked to serve as team captain.

In various ways, then, cricket served as a connecting thread in my life as well as a proving ground where I developed my character and leadership skills. But as my college career neared its end, I was still not clear about my direction in life. The following year proved to be a pivotal one that would shape my future profoundly.

2

UPRISING IN THE KASHMIR VALLEY

WHEN YOU GROW UP in a region that is politically divided and torn by social and sectarian strife, it's almost impossible to be unengaged or uninvolved—that is, to have what most people would consider a "normal" childhood. I imagine this is true today for children growing up in war-torn areas, and it was certainly true for me growing up in Kashmir in the 1950s and 1960s.

As I've explained, the conflict over Kashmir had many elements, including ethnicity, language, and religion. Prior to 1947, many members of the Muslim majority in Kashmir resented being ruled by a Hindu-dominated government, and communal solidarity was one of the driving forces behind the rivalry between India and Pakistan over control of the region.

However, for my family, dedication to Islam and a desire to take control away from Hindu politicians was not at the core of our political views. I grew up hearing the familiar call to prayer from the local mosques several times a day, whether in Pakistan or in Kashmir, but my family and I attended services only a few times a year. This is not to say that we were agnostics or atheists. Over time, I came to learn that my parents' worldview included a touch of mysticism; they were definitely believers in a higher power that shapes and guides human destiny, as am I. My brothers and sisters and I were taught that Islam meant "submission"—that God's main attribute was goodness, and that submission to Him should be the core of our religion. And our parents certainly encouraged their children always to think and behave in accordance with what we believed was right. However, although we were tutored to read the Koran in Arabic, studying scripture was not part of our daily experience. It was only later in life, after tragedy touched my family, that I turned to the Koran for solace and wisdom . . . which I found there in abundance.

All in all, religious feeling was not a strong motivating factor in my family's political engagement. However, when I was growing up, it was always clear to me that my father—like my grandfather before him—believed that Kashmir's position of dependency on the larger countries along its borders was fundamentally unfair. Rather than being a football over which the great powers of India and Pakistan would wrestle with little real concern for the well-being of its people, Kashmir should have the same power to shape its own destiny that most regions of the world take for granted. It was natural for me to share this perspective, and I think that, to this day, most Kashmiris share the same desire for self-governance.

Of course, it's relatively simple and obvious to declare that Kashmiris should have control over their own destiny. It's more difficult to define precisely what form that destiny should take. Like many Kashmiris, my father had political views that shifted over time. When he was young, he believed that Kashmir should become part of Pakistan. I think this is the attitude he took when he joined the government of Pakistan-administered Kashmir. But after a while, his views evolved. He started believing in self-governance or independence for

Kashmir—especially for the Kashmiri-speaking region, which has its own unique culture, sometimes referred to as *Kashmiryat*. This region also has a history that includes long periods of political independence.

My father's belief in independence was one he shared with many of our fellow Kashmiris—although they were not very clear as to what independence meant. What parts of the region should be included in an independent Kashmir? What connections would it have with neighboring powers? What form of government would it have? In what ways would the rights and freedoms of people from varying ethnic, religious, and linguistic groups be protected? How would governmental power be distributed among these groups?

The complexity of these issues is one reason behind my founding of the Kashmir Study Group many years later. That organization brought together an array of experts from many perspectives to help clarify—for the peoples of Kashmir and for the world—some of the many challenges involved in settling the "Kashmir problem." The study group has also worked to propose practical steps toward resolving these challenges in ways that are peaceful, honorable, and feasible—that is, acceptable to all the relevant parties. As I'll explain later in this book, developing realistic solutions to these complicated issues is a tricky balancing act. The best direction—the one most likely to lead to a lasting peace in the region—will probably involve creating several self-governing units.

It was against this complicated backdrop that my family's engagement in the politics of Kashmir—including my own—evolved.

By the early 1960s, my father had been exiled from Kashmir for more than a decade. Following his departure in 1949, he had not seen his mother, his two children, other family members, or the city and home in which he had grown up. But he had remained connected with us and deeply concerned about the future of his children. And in 1964, a number of events occurred that would have a profound impact on my life—including a journey by my father to the country that would soon become my own new home.

Nowadays only old people are likely to remember the New York World's Fair of 1964–65. World's fairs themselves have become rare events, largely superseded by theme parks like Disney's Epcot. But for several decades in the twentieth century, these fairs were grand spectacles that attracted millions of people to experience the wonders of the world, including futuristic technologies and the cultures of many nations.

My father was given the job of organizing and managing a pavilion representing the nation of Pakistan at the New York World's Fair, which would be held in what is now Flushing Meadows Park in the borough of Queens. He moved to the city in 1964 and soon began developing friendships with some of the people he met there. Among others, he encountered a woman who was working in the Indian pavilion whose family was friendly with our family—an example of the many personal connections that exist between the peoples of Pakistan and India. She was a Muslim married to a Hindu man, an officer in the Indian army. This Indian woman, in turn, had developed a friendship with a family from the borough of Brooklyn named the Levys, and she introduced them to my father. They all got along very well, and soon the group were sharing meals and learning about one another's cultures—an interesting case of Muslim-Hindu-Jewish fellowship in one of the most diverse and tolerant cities in the world.

As my father explored New York City and spoke with his new friends, he began to formulate an idea about my future. I was then getting ready to begin my fourth year in college back in Srinagar, and I was still uncertain as to what I should do next. So my father made a long-distance telephone call to me with a suggestion: Why not apply to attend graduate school in New York City?

I liked the idea. But I really had no clear idea what I should study. I'd been focusing on economics, literature, and political science in my undergraduate studies, but these didn't necessarily spell out a career for me. I'd been toying with the idea of some kind of sports career. So my father made the decision for me. "I think you should apply to graduate business school," he said. He collected application forms from the three leading business schools in New York City—Columbia University, the City University of New York, and New York University—and sent them off to me.

I didn't know exactly how to handle these forms, so I took them to Saif Uddin, the principal of SP College. He called in the professors to help—the head of the English department, a Kashmiri Hindu named Professor J. N. Kaul, and the head of the economics department, a Kashmiri Muslim named Professor A. Punoo—and he instructed them, "Help Farooq fill out these applications." Of course, the professors were as unfamiliar with the forms as I was, but at least they understood the American academic system and were able to translate the terms for me. For example, my average class grade in Kashmir had been 60, which was quite high—not at all the equivalent of a 60 in the United States. So the professors decided I was what Americans would call an "A student," and they created a specially tailored transcript for me to use. And each professor, along with Principal Saif Uddin, wrote a letter of recommendation for me.

I sent the completed forms to my father in New York and waited to find out what the universities would say. I didn't even think about what sort of travel documents I would need if the time came when I would actually have to move to the United States.

This was a complicated problem in itself. As I've mentioned, when my family returned to Kashmir from Pakistan in 1960, we were each given three-month visas that allowed us to enter India. I didn't think very much about the legal restrictions these entailed.

For example, in 1963, I was one of two young people from Kashmir selected for a six-week course in advanced military training with the Indian army. This was at a time of heightened tensions with China, when all college students were being asked to participate in compulsory military training, and a few were selected for advanced training with what was called the National Cadet Corps. My most memorable experience in the corps was when my fellow Kashmiri and I were approached by a colonel who said, "You Kashmiris are great meat eaters. Can you cook a delicious meal for us?" Though we had no cooking experience, we improvised a recipe for spicy lamb, potatoes, and rice that we cooked in two or three giant pots over open wood fires, then served to a hundred of our fellow trainees. It came out pretty well!

For this stint of military training, I'd been sent to an army camp near the city of Pune in western India—and I made the trip to and from the army camp without incident, despite the fact that my Indian visa had long since expired. I later realized that I should have applied for an Indian passport then. The only other travel document I had was Pakistani, good through March 1965. But I hadn't thought much about it, because I hadn't been planning any travel; in any case, I had no plans to return to Pakistan. As I'll recount shortly, the lack of travel papers would end up complicating my life rather dramatically.

Meanwhile, my father was living in New York as a representative of Pakistan and working at the World's Fair. Of course, he still wanted very badly to be able to return to Kashmir to see his wife, his children, his parents, and the rest of his family. So he was working any connection he could find to obtain permission to make the trip. These efforts finally bore fruit in 1964. My father managed to meet with Braj Kumar Nehru, the Indian ambassador to the United States, who happened to be a friend of my grandfather's. My father also appealed to an old school friend of his, Durga Prasad Dhar, who was an associate of Lal Bahadur Shastri, the Indian prime minister. Somehow their combined interventions made the difference, and my father was given permission to make a return visit to Kashmir for ten days in January 1965.

The trip was an arduous one. The winter weather was bad, closing many of the roads into Kashmir. After an all-night journey, cold and exhausted, my father finally arrived at my grandfather's house, where he enjoyed a long-awaited reunion with my mother, his children, and his own mother and grandmother. (My grandfather himself was spending the winter in India—in Bombay or Calcutta, as he usually did.)

Soon after his arrival, my father noticed that there was no sign of me anywhere in the main house. He asked, "Where's Farooq?" When the answer came back, "He's in *gam lari*" (the village hut), he replied, "What's he doing there?"

Of course, he quickly came to visit me in my little room above the cowshed, and he was shocked and moved to see me there—partly, I'm sure, because I'd grown up so much during the five years since we'd been together. He began to cry, and the two of us greeted one another warmly.

"Why have they made you sleep out here?" my father asked. I guess he thought I was being punished.

"I love it here!" I said. "Look at my radio!" And I told him the story about how I'd organized the room for myself and brought the radio from Calcutta.

We enjoyed ten days of family reunion together.

Among other things, I shared with my father the story of how I'd gotten involved in the Kashmir protests of 1964. The immediate cause of the protests, amazingly enough, was a missing strand of hair. But the full story had its roots much further back in the history of the region.

One of the most important leaders in the history of Kashmir was Sheikh Mohammad Abdullah, sometimes known as "The Lion of Kashmir." He was a friend of my grandfather's, a schoolteacher, and a member of the Quit Kashmir movement. Supporters of that movement during the period of rule by the Dogras promoted him as a potential national leader. He had friends among both Muslims and Hindus, as well as among Indians and Pakistanis. For example, one of his political allies was Jawaharlal Nehru, who later became the prime minister of India. The political organization that Sheikh Abdullah helped found, the Kashmir Muslim Conference, firmly stated that its purpose was to struggle on behalf of the rights of all oppressed members of society, not just Muslims. Reflecting this breadth of purpose, the party later changed its name to the National Conference.

Because of his work as an activist and agitator on behalf of rights for the Kashmiri people, Sheikh Abdullah spent some time in prison. Then in October 1947, after the independence and partition of India, a major portion of Jammu and Kashmir came under Indian control, and Sheikh Abdullah became head of an emergency administration. He became prime minister of Kashmir in March 1948, and served in that role for five years. (At the same time, Dr. Karan Singh, son of a former ruler of Jammu and Kashmir, was named *Sadr-i-Riyasat,* or "head of the state.") Sheikh Abdullah's administration was troubled, in part because he continued to make veiled statements demanding independence, which alienated the Indian sponsors who had helped him achieve power. At the same time, many Muslims in Jammu and Kashmir were dissatisfied with him because he rejected the notion of making the region part of Pakistan.

Sheikh Abdullah lost his insecure grasp on power in August 1953. He was dismissed as prime minister on the charge that he had lost the confidence of his cabinet, though he was never given an opportunity to contest this claim. He was then immediately arrested on trumped-up conspiracy charges, along with many other notable Kashmiri leaders, including a member of our extended family. A dissident cabinet member, Bakshi Ghulam Mohammad, who had collaborated with the Indians, was then named prime minister. In 1960 when my family returned home, Bakshi was still in power—and Sheikh Abdullah was still in prison.

Bakshi is said to have been an able administrator; many say he played a role in bringing Kashmir into the modern era. But he also earned the enmity of many in Kashmir through his heavy-handed tactics, which included reliance on secret police to control dissent and even the use of torture. Over time, his reputation among the Kashmiri people gradually worsened.

By 1963, the Indian leadership in Delhi had had enough. They decided to replace Bakshi with Ghulam Mohammed Sadiq, whom they named chief minister. As a kind of fig leaf, they described Bakshi's dismissal as a "promotion" to the job of special advisor to Indian Prime Minister Nehru.

But Bakshi was not happy about relinquishing his hold on power. In response, he orchestrated a strange historical episode, one that he hoped might show his former sponsors in the Indian government that he was still needed at the helm of the state—at least, this is the version of the story I was told as a young Kashmiri.

In Srinagar, there is a major Muslim site known as the Hazratbal Shrine, which contains what is thought to be a strand of hair from the beard of the Prophet Mohammad. Among most orthodox Muslims, it's considered sacrilegious to revere something like a strand of hair simply because it came from the body of the Prophet. But millions of ordinary Muslims feel differently. So when it was announced on December 27, 1963, that the relic had disappeared from the Hazratbal Shrine, the news created havoc in Kashmir.

Despite the frigid winter weather, around two million Muslims took to the roads in outrage and anger, heading toward the shrine from all corners of Kashmir. Many blamed Bakshi, the former prime minister, for the disappearance of the relic, believing he had arranged for it to be stolen. His motive, they said, was the hope of provoking demonstrations that would prove to the Indians that only Bakshi was capable of maintaining order in Kashmir. Some began setting fire to properties known to be owned by Bakshi. Others began converting the demonstrations from anti-Bakshi protests into anti-India protests. "First you stole our liberty," they said, "but now you have stolen something even more precious to us, our relic of the Prophet."

It's impossible to say whether Bakshi was really the mastermind behind the disappearance of the strand of hair. If he was, the response quickly overwhelmed whatever he'd intended. Rather than showing the firm control Bakshi had over the Kashmiri people, the demonstrations revealed the opposite. The residents of the Kashmir Valley were on the verge of rising up, not just against Bakshi but against Indian rule.

In late December 1963, I was in Delhi playing cricket with the university team when we received the alarming news about the protests back home. Most of my teammates decided to remain in Delhi. It was the safest choice, after all. But I felt driven to return home. I needed to be with my people at this time of crisis. And as a Kashmiri who had long shared my family's dream that our country should be free, I felt excited by the thought that this might be the spark that would lead to a democratic revolution to free Kashmir. I caught the next flight for Srinagar.

Sitting next to me on the plane was an American—not a very common sight on a flight to Kashmir. "Why are you traveling to Kashmir?" I asked.

"I want to see what's happening there," he replied. "My name is Richard Critchfield, and I'm a journalist with the *Washington Evening Star*."

"Well, you're not going to see anything," I told him. "I hear that there's no way to get around—no buses, no taxis, nothing. Millions of people have filled the streets and the roads."

"Yes, that's a problem," he admitted.

"So who is going to take you around?" I asked.

"I don't know. I thought I would start by checking in with the government people."

"The government people are not going to let you see what is really happening," I said. "Why not let me take you around?"

In retrospect, it was foolish of me to make such an offer. I was well aware that I would be risking retribution by the security forces, who had no desire to let the outside world understand the depths of unhappiness felt by the majority of Kashmiri people. But I was a headstrong, independent young man, and I'd seen the examples of my grandfather and father, both of whom had had the courage to stand up for their beliefs in the face of government opposition. I wanted the truth to get out, and if I could do anything to help that happen, I would.

Critchfield accepted my offer. When we arrived in Srinagar, I got a car to drive me from the airport to our home on the outskirts of the city, dropping the journalist off at his hotel along the way. The next morning, without telling my family what I was doing, I met him in the city and began walking the streets with him, mingling with the crowds of protesters, witnessing one major demonstration after another, and explaining the political and social situation in Kashmir as best I understood it. From what we both could see, Critchfield was the only foreign journalist on the scene.

At various times when people had gathered in a city square, the leaders of the demonstrations would climb up on a couple of city buses that had been pushed together to form an impromptu speaker's platform, from which they would address the crowds. When they saw Critchfield and me in the throngs below, they would call out, "Come up!" and the two of us would clamber up the sides of the buses to join the leaders.

Of course, this meant that the security police, who were photographing everything, were well aware of our involvement with the demonstrations. But fortunately no crackdown was attempted—perhaps because the crowds were so vast, perhaps because the protests remained peaceful. So neither Critchfield nor I were ever stopped.

I had the opportunity to introduce Critchfield to a few local leaders I knew. They included Mirwaiz Farooq, a respected Muslim teacher, and Farooq Abdullah, a physician and one of the sons of Sheikh Abdullah. Both were leading the demonstrations. Mirwaiz Farooq would later be one of the so-called secessionist leaders in the 1990 Kashmiri uprising and was killed by unknown gunmen that same year. His son, Mirwaiz

Omar Farooq, took his place and today continues to lead the organization his father co-founded, which is called Hurriyet (freedom).

Critchfield and I were also invited to the homes of various respected families for meals during this period of uprising, including Farida's home in downtown Srinagar. This was a great opportunity for him to deepen his understanding of what was happening in Kashmir and to collect a variety of perspectives. Naturally, many people knew who I was, and it was clear that, by befriending this foreign journalist and introducing him to leaders of the movement, I was taking a personal stand on its behalf.

The uprising ended almost as suddenly as it began. On January 4, word spread that the relic had been found and returned to the shrine, and that the thieves—whoever they were—had been arrested. (Some claimed the recovered relic was a fake, but of course it was impossible to know this for certain.) The crowds dispersed, and life returned more or less to normal—except for that, for the first time in many years, virtually the whole population of the Kashmir Valley had taken a united stand against Indian rule. Everyone sensed that this fact—the knowledge that such united action was even possible—had enormous potential significance.

Richard Critchfield thanked me for my help and told me that he would be returning to his usual journalistic post in Delhi. "Is there any way you can let me know if things heat up again in Kashmir?" he asked.

I didn't want to run the risk of attracting the attention of the security services. "If things get bad," I told him, "I'll send you a telegram with the message 'All is well.'" We shook hands, and Critchfield flew off to Delhi.

Critchfield's journalistic instincts were sound. Within a month, things did heat up. With the vast crowds back in their homes, the authorities quietly began rounding up the demonstration leaders and throwing them in jail. I went to the telegraph office and sent this message to Delhi: "All is well."

But the security agents monitoring the wires weren't naive. They registered the fact that this student from Srinagar was in touch with the American reporter in Delhi, and they cracked down by alerting one of the few people they figured would have power over me: my grandfather.

When my grandfather returned home from his business office in Calcutta, he confronted me. "I've heard from the government about what you've been up to. You've been talking to journalists, meeting with protest leaders. You're lucky you haven't been arrested! This has to stop. No more talking to reporters. No more talking to Americans of any kind. Otherwise, you're going to be in big trouble—and I won't be able to protect you."

Of course, I promised my grandfather that I would be good. But that didn't stop me when the next opportunity arose. In fact, he and I were sitting in the same room at home one day when the telephone rang. It was about two months after Critchfield's visit to Kashmir. Grandfather answered it and handed the receiver to me. "It's for you," he said.

"My name is Howard Schaffer," said the voice on the phone. "Your name has been given to me by Richard Critchfield. I'm a diplomat in the American embassy at Delhi, and Critchfield says you're the best person for me to meet in Kashmir."

I glanced at my grandfather, sitting just a few feet away. "Yes," I said into the phone, "I'd be happy to get together to talk about cricket. Where are you staying?"

Schaffer quickly picked up on my little deception. We arranged to meet that evening at Nedou's Hotel, a nineteenth-century hotel once favored by British businessmen and travelers, which is still in operation today. I agreed to help Schaffer meet some of the local students and dissident leaders, much as I had done for Richard Critchfield.

Of course, by now it was clear that the intelligence service had me in its sights. They did not choose to arrest me. Instead, they decided to keep close tabs on me, perhaps figuring they would learn more this way. They assigned a Kashmiri officer to follow me—which he did, quite openly. So much so that, after a few days, my grandmother asked me, "Who is this person sitting outside our gate all the time?" When I explained, she said, "Tell him to go and sit in the kitchen. He can warm up." I did.

Eventually, it got so that in the evenings the agent, sitting in the kitchen, would simply ask me, "Mr. Farooq, are you going anywhere?" I would say, "No, you can go home," and he would.

Eager to help Ambassador Schaffer meet with some of the local student leaders, I spoke frankly with him about the difficulties. "Nobody's going to want to talk with you now. There are too many intelligence agents and police officers around, and too many of the movement leaders are in jail. But I think I can come up with a plan. Tomorrow morning, come to my college, SP College, around nine or ten o'clock. Meet me there, and I'll figure out how you can meet some students."

The next morning, I went straight to Principal Saif Uddin's office. "Please don't get upset with me," I said, "but last night, I met an American diplomat who wants to learn how the people in Kashmir are feeling. I've invited him to come here and see you. I think we should ask Professor Duloo to take him around and meet some of the students. But we'll call Ambassador Schaffer an educator, not a diplomat. And that way, nothing's going to happen."

Principal Saif Uddin was quite upset with me. "You're really going to get me into trouble!" he said. "How dare you do these things!" But the arrangements had all been made. I understood I was taking a risk. But I thought it just had to be done.

In a short time, Ambassador Schaffer arrived. He met Principal Saif Uddin, and we called in Professor Duloo, to whom we introduced Schaffer as an American educator. Professor Duloo agreed to escort Schaffer around the campus. Meanwhile, to take advantage of Schaffer's presence, I'd already organized a student protest against Indian rule. Just as quickly, a smaller counter-demonstration by Kashmiri Pandits in favor of Indian rule sprang up—so Ambassador Schaffer suddenly found himself in the middle of a heated debate, much like those that were occurring everywhere in Kashmir.

It was just the first of a number of meetings that Ambassador Schaffer participated in, including some others that were arranged with my help. These encounters greatly enriched his understanding of the widespread unhappiness felt by the people of the Kashmir Valley. As Schaffer wrote at the time in a missive to the State Department summarizing his findings, "The most fundamental cause for this acute dissatisfaction is the Kashmiri Muslims' feeling of separateness. They do not consider themselves Indians." This insight would be crucial in any attempt to formulate a meaningful solution to the Kashmir dilemma.

As 1964 wore on, protests against Indian rule throughout the Kashmir Valley continued, and my own involvement deepened. I participated in a number of demonstrations, including some in which the police attacked students and beat them up.

The most frightening moment occurred one time when the Kashmiri police knocked on the door of our home in the middle of the night, looking for me. "You have to come with us," they demanded.

"Why?" I asked. "Do you have a warrant?"

"Please don't ask that," the police responded. "Just bring your bedding roll and come with us." Something in their manner told me that I'd better obey their orders, so I went with them.

It became clear that this was one of the routine sweeps made by the police to gather up political dissidents, including students. They'd gotten my name from a fellow cricket player, who'd "ratted on me" for no reason other than his desire to have a friend by his side in prison. Soon I found myself stuck in a dark jail cell with a couple of cellmates, including my friend from the cricket team and a man from the village who'd assaulted someone with an axe.

In the morning, when I had a chance to speak to one of the Indian police officers from the Central Reserve Police, I seized the moment to ask for a cup of tea. After all, I'd had nothing to eat or drink for hours.

"How dare you!" he shouted, then pointed a gun at my head. "Shut up or I'll shoot."

"Go ahead!" I said. I didn't want to die—but I also didn't want to kowtow to a bully with a weapon.

Luckily for me, a Kashmiri police officer intervened. "Never mind," he said to his hotheaded colleague. "Just put that thing down. I'll get him some tea." And he did.

Years later, after I'd begun my business career in America, when disputes in the office or around the boardroom table became especially heated, people would sometimes express surprise that I could remain so calm while others were losing their heads. Perhaps the fact that I remembered staring down a police officer with a gun pointed at my head while I was just a teenager helps to explain why I've always been able to put other, less directly threatening, confrontations into perspective.

Fortunately for me, I didn't end up spending any real time in prison. A lucky acquaintance with a neighbor of our family was the reason. His name was Mr. Agha, and he was head of the Home Department in the Kashmiri government—which meant that all the Kashmir police reported to him. I'd become close with Mr. Agha after helping him with his son, a married student who was undisciplined in his habits. At his father's request, I'd taken this fellow—also named Farooq—under my wing. I made him go mountain climbing with me in the mornings near our home as a way of getting him to work off some of his extra fat, and I pushed him to become more serious about completing his studies. Mr. Agha was very grateful to me for my help with his son. So now, when Mr. Agha heard I'd been caught up in one of the police sweeps, he quickly intervened to get me freed.

■ ■ ■

BY APRIL 1964, Indian Prime Minister Nehru decided that he simply could no longer allow the situation in Kashmir to fester. The step he took was a surprising one. He decided to drop the false conspiracy charges against Sheikh Abdullah and all the members of his cabinet, who'd been held in prison in Jammu province for more than ten years.

I vividly remember the day when the newly freed Sheikh Abdullah came home to Srinagar. Nearly a million jubilant people lined the road to welcome the bus convoy in which he was traveling along with his associates, who'd also been freed. A decade in prison had transformed Sheikh Abdullah from a controversial politician into a national hero, respected by Kashmiris. Within months, he would be on his way to Pakistan to meet with that country's new president, Ayub Khan, seeking a solution to the Kashmir dilemma.

Unfortunately, a real solution was still as far away as ever. In May 1964, while Sheikh Abdullah was in Pakistan meeting with President Ayub Khan, Nehru died. He was succeeded by a new prime minister, Lal Bahadur Shastri. Under pressure to assert his authority, both in Kashmir and closer to home, Shastri returned Sheikh Abdullah to prison.

Meanwhile, the leaders of Pakistan decided to take advantage of the disaffection with Indian rule to deliberately foment unrest in Kashmir. They started developing plans to send outside fighters into the Kashmir region to fight India. Thus, they transformed what had been a homegrown uprising into a regional conflict driven by the India-Pakistan rivalry—a disastrous change.

In January 1965, when my father was home for those ten days to be with the family in Kashmir, we were able to talk about my experiences during the protests of the previous year and much more. I was now well into my final year of college and beginning to think seriously about the next step in my life.

One day during my father's visit, he asked to see my travel document, which, as I've said, was a Pakistani form set to expire in March. I'd basically ignored the problem, but my father wisely recognized its significance. He realized that I might not get an Indian passport in time for me to leave for New York, and he wanted me to have another travel option. "Let me take your paper to Delhi and see if they can extend it," he said. After leaving Kashmir, while stopping in Delhi on his way to New York, he was able to get the Pakistan embassy there to extend my travel document to September 1965, and then mailed it back to me.

In February, I traveled from Kashmir to Jammu. I'd been invited there by Mr. Agha, the official who'd secured my release from prison. Every winter, he and his family along with other members of the government moved to Jammu to take advantage of the warmer climate. "Please come with us," Mr. Agha had said to me. "You can make sure that my son keeps up with his studies."

I liked his offer. So I went to Jammu for six weeks during the winter of 1965. And while I was there, I received a letter from New York University. It said that if I could earn a passing score on the entrance exam, they would grant me admission to their graduate business school.

This would prove to be a major turning point in my life.

3

JOURNEY TO AMERICA

IN 1965, MY FATHER was in his second year as a resident of New York, helping run the Pakistan pavilion at the historic 1964–65 World's Fair in Queens. In February, I'd received my conditional acceptance to New York University's School of Business, and I was excited about the idea of joining him there. But making my way from Indian-administered Kashmir to the United States would not be easy. In fact, it turned into a months-long ordeal that could easily have ended in failure, if not for a series of happy accidents, coincidences, and acts of generosity that I experienced along the way.

The first hurdle was the standardized exam that NYU required me to take. The Admission Test for Graduate Study in Business was to be held in March in Bombay—the closest location to my home in Kashmir. I'd never taken such an exam, so this would be a challenge—though the biggest challenge would turn out to be the trip to Bombay itself.

In those days, Indian Airlines used to fly a small plane called a DC-3 from Srinagar to Delhi, a short hop of a little over 500 miles. Then there would be a separate flight of another 700 miles from Delhi to

Bombay. So a couple of days before my test, I went to Srinagar Airport, where I encountered the first obstacle in my way.

The flight from Srinagar to Delhi had to cross the Banihal Pass through the Pir Panjal Range, at an elevation of some 15,000 feet. Bad weather and low visibility sometimes made this journey treacherous, so the pilots were given the leeway to decide whether the trip was safe or not. Furthermore, their decisions were not always completely unbiased. The climate in Kashmir was so much more pleasant than in the plains that pilots were known to delay making the trip back from Kashmir for a few days, claiming safety as the reason.

That's what happened this time. After having lunch at the Srinagar Airport, we passengers waited to learn when the flight would depart, only to hear the pilot announce, "Sorry, the pass is closed. Go home and come back tomorrow."

I went home and returned for another lunch the next day, knowing that now I *had* to make the journey to Delhi. If I didn't, I would miss the exam and lose my shot at attending graduate school in New York. So you can imagine how I felt when the pilot came on the loudspeaker and again announced, "Sorry, but the Banihal Pass is closed because of cloud cover. We'll try again tomorrow."

The other passengers were disappointed and began to gather their things to leave the airport, but I went in search of the pilot. When I found him, I told him, "Sir, you *have* to go!"

"What do you mean, I *have* to go?" he responded.

"I have to appear for an exam tomorrow," I said. "If I don't, I will not be able to go to America."

He shook his head. "But the weather is bad. We can't make the flight."

I was persistent. "Can't you do me a favor?" I asked. "Just make an announcement. Tell the passengers not to leave, but to wait for a few minutes. Then you and I can talk about what you should do. Please, do that for me."

Somewhat to my surprise, he agreed.

Now I set about persuading him. "Why don't you just try making the trip? My future depends on this flight. Check into the conditions further. Maybe the clouds are beginning to clear. Maybe they're not so bad. You're an experienced pilot. I believe you can make the journey safely."

"I see you are very determined," he said.

I continued to plead with him. "Please, do me this favor. Of course, I understand that you won't go if it's truly dangerous. But if there's a chance to make the trip, don't you think you ought to try?"

I could see the pilot beginning to bend—whether because my arguments were so powerful or because he was getting tired of listening to me. He walked back and forth into the room where the weather reports were being received, shook his head, and conferred with a couple of his colleagues. Finally, he returned to the public address system: "The pilot has determined that the pass is safe for travel. Please prepare to board."

It was one of the most successful—and most important—sales jobs of my career.

I made it to Bombay and took the first multiple-choice test of my life. I must have done all right, because a month later, NYU sent me a letter confirming my admission to the university.

Now I faced another challenge. How was I going to get to America? The school semester was scheduled to begin in late August, which left me about four months to figure out how to make the necessary arrangements.

The most important problem was that I lacked the legal documents required for international travel. I'd come to Indian-administered Kashmir from Pakistan on a Pakistani travel document, which fortunately—at the request of my father—had been extended by the Pakistani embassy in Delhi to September 1965. But my visa for travel to India had expired five years earlier, so technically I was living in Kashmir illegally. For me to get an Indian passport, my status in India first had to be "regularized." And any attempt to regularize my status in India would be particularly difficult because of the political situation at the time—the demonstrations in Kashmir by protesters opposed to Indian rule. In the aftermath of those protests, fighting was still going on in Kashmir by insurgents against the Indian army. This led to major tensions between India and Pakistan, because India accused Pakistan of fomenting the unrest in Kashmir.

Still, I needed to do something if I was going to travel to America. So I asked everyone I knew for suggestions. A number of people recommended that I try to meet with some high Indian government officials. My friend Mr. Agha offered a very specific proposal. He said, "You should see my associate, Peer Ghulam Hassan Shah. He is a Kashmiri and the head of the intelligence office that is in charge of affairs in Kashmir. Maybe he will be able to help you."

So I arranged to meet with Mr. Shah at his office in Srinagar, taking my Pakistani travel document with its expired Indian visa. I told him that I needed somehow to get official travel documents that would allow me to make my way to America. Could he do anything to help?

He looked at me and said, "You know, we know you. Are you not the person who took the American journalist around Srinagar during the demonstrations after the relic was lost?"

I said, "Yes, sir, I did."

He said, "Are you not the one who later sent him a coded telegram saying, 'All is well'?"

I said, "Yes, I did." I knew there was no use denying it.

Then he said, "You're also the one who took that American diplomat around, telling people that he was an educator." They knew everything.

I said, "I did."

Then he looked at me and said, "But you are also the captain of a cricket team, aren't you? Haven't I read about you in the newspaper? It seems you are a star at several sports."

I humbly said, "I am."

He sat and thought for a moment, then said, "I have no authority to do this. But give me your papers. I'm going to authorize you to stay in India for the time being." And he stamped my visa, officially extending it through September 1965—matching the date on my Pakistani travel document. "I don't know whether you can travel with this document," he said, "but I hope it will help you."

Why did Mr. Shah try to help me? It could have been my exploits on the cricket field. I also think he felt that I was trustworthy. Those things that I did in showing the diplomat and the journalist around were not serious acts of rebellion or insurrection. I had never been charged with a crime.

Perhaps most important was the fact that Mr. Shah, like me, was a Kashmiri Muslim. Deep inside, despite the fact that he was the head of the intelligence office, he was pleased to have the opportunity to do something to help a promising young person who shared his background.

Neither of us knew it then, but this was the start of a long-term relationship. Mr. Shah got into the habit of calling me at the holiday season of Eid, to check in on how I was doing and to wish me well. He is now retired and living in Kashmir, but until very recently he had called me faithfully every year. Once I asked him, "Why do you call me every year, Mr. Shah?"

He said, "I want to thank you."

"To thank me? Why? You were the one who did me a favor."

"I want to thank you because, by helping you get to New York, I helped make your whole career possible. So I am grateful to you because you gave me an opportunity to show the world what a young Kashmiri can do."

I went home with my newly stamped visa and travel document, and I made my preparations for a journey to New York. But I still had no US visa, my travel documents were not endorsed for travel to the US, and it was still uncertain whether I'd be allowed to get an Indian passport. Given the hostile relations between India and Pakistan and the confusing status of Kashmir, that possibility seemed very dubious. So when August came, and classes at NYU were almost due to begin, some of my family members came up with a plan. They arranged for me to meet a family friend in Delhi who was an official at Kashmir House, which served almost like an informal embassy for Kashmiri people in India. "Go and meet the commissioner at Kashmir House," they said. "Perhaps he will help you."

So I flew from Srinagar, arriving at Delhi Airport around 11:00 a.m. As I was walking through the terminal, I noticed a sign: "Indian Airlines flight to Lahore, Pakistan, leaving at 4:00 p.m." I went outside, carrying my suitcase, and caught a taxi to Kashmir House.

Unfortunately, the commissioner whose name I'd been given was not in the office. "Come back later," they said. I felt discouraged. I had no idea whether this commissioner could really help me. I began to feel as though I would be wasting my time to hang around in Delhi, hoping for a miracle.

Somehow the sign I'd seen in the airport flashed back into my mind. "Forget about Kashmir House," I said. "I'm going to see if I can get to Lahore. Then I'll work on flying to America from Pakistan."

So I went to the Indian Airlines office. I had just enough money to buy a ticket for Lahore. But when I asked for one, the man behind the counter asked me, "Do you have the income tax clearance certificate? Do you have the P-form? You need these to leave India legally."

"I don't," I admitted.

Suddenly, hearing my voice, a man came out from a back office. "Hello, Farooq. How are you?" he said. I recognized him immediately. I'd met him a year earlier when he was a member of a cricket team made up of Indian Airlines employees, which had visited Kashmir and played against my team. I greeted him happily, and we exclaimed over the remarkable coincidence that had brought us together.

"What seems to be the problem?" he asked. I explained that I wanted to fly to Lahore in hopes to traveling to America from there—but that I was missing some of the necessary papers.

"Let me see what I can do," he said. He vanished into the back office, where I could hear him questioning another administrator. In a moment, he reappeared.

"You don't need a P-form," he said, "but you've got to go to the tax office to show that you don't owe any taxes. You're a student, so that shouldn't be a problem." He gave me the address of the tax office and said, "Go there right now. Leave your bag with me."

I ended up making two trips to the tax office—the first time I went, I discovered I'd left my student identification paper in my suitcase at the airline office, so I had to rush back to pick it up. But in the end, the tax people gave me a clean bill of health, and I rushed back to the Indian Airlines office.

By now, it was getting late—just a few minutes before the scheduled 4:00 p.m. departure time for the flight to Lahore. "We've called the airport," my friend at the airline office told me. "They're holding the plane for you. Show us all your papers." Feeling a bit nervous, I handed him the Pakistani travel document, in which Mr. Shah had extended the Indian visa without any real power to do so. But the airline officials found my papers acceptable, and I jumped in a taxi for the airport.

At the gate, an immigration official was waiting impatiently. "Are you Farooq? Hurry up, we're late." He gave my papers a quick glance, immediately stamped them, and waved me on board.

The first leg of my journey to America had begun. But I was far from relaxed. I sensed I had many more hurdles to leap before I'd reach my destination.

When I disembarked from the hour-long flight to Lahore, immigration agents were waiting to check every passenger's passport right at the gate. The tight security was understandable: Pakistan and India were reported to be on the verge of war, and anyone traveling between the two countries was automatically treated with suspicion.

The agent who scanned my travel document held up his hand to stop me. "What is this?" he asked.

"I've just come from Kashmir," I explained. "I'm in Lahore to catch a plane to America."

"What do you mean, you've come from Kashmir?" At that time, such a journey was considered impossible. I was quickly surrounded by immigration officers and security police, who drew me into an inner office and began plying me with questions: "How is this possible? You're telling us you stayed in Kashmir for five years, and now you're coming back to Pakistan? How did you get on this flight? And who extended the date on this travel document?"

"It was extended in Delhi," I replied, hoping they would consider that a reasonable answer. The look on their faces told me it hadn't worked. I could tell they were wondering who I was and what I was trying to do. Perhaps I was here to spy on behalf of India.

"You'll need to come with us to headquarters," the chief official decided. My imagination quickly conjured up the possibility of days in detention—or something worse. I began to search my brain, trying to think of something I could say or do to wriggle out of the trap I was in.

Suddenly I remembered something. "Isn't there a police official here named Mr. Rizvi?" This was a friend of my father's whom I'd met while in Pakistan. I'd even stayed in his home in Lahore for a week or so, some eight years earlier. "I know Mr. Rizvi," I declared, "and before you take me anywhere, I want to speak with him."

The name sparked a real reaction. "He's the head of our police," the official said. "We're not going to bother him at six in the evening."

"Please, I insist," I replied. "I need to speak with Mr. Rizvi. He would want me to call."

Somehow I talked them into placing the call to Mr. Rizvi's home—and luckily for me, he answered the phone.

"*Salaams, Rizvi Sahib,*" I said. "This is Farooq, son of *Khawaja* Gulam Mohamed." (In Kashmir, *Khawaja* is an honorific, more or less the equivalent of "Mister.") "I've just come from Kashmir. I'm here in Lahore, and I've got to go to New York to where my father is. But the police here at the airport are holding me for questions."

As you can imagine, Mr. Rizvi was very surprised—and a little suspicious. "Yes," he said, "I know that Khawaja Sahib is in the US. But how do I know you are really his son?" And he started quizzing me, asking questions only I would be likely to know—my mother's name, the names of my brothers and sisters, even the names of Mr. Rizvi's own children whom I'd met a number of times. I couldn't blame him—after all, he hadn't laid eyes on me for at least five years. But I answered all his questions correctly.

"I'm glad you called me, Farooq," he finally said. "Let me speak to the officer in charge."

On Mr. Rizvi's order, the immigration and security officers allowed me to proceed to the city of Lahore. They asked me for a contact there, and I gave them the name and address of a relative of my father's, Mr. Habib Kakru. Mr. Rizvi also called the head of the Pakistan intelligence office in charge of Kashmiri affairs to inform him of my whereabouts. Then the officers stamped my papers and let me go.

I left the airport and got into a taxi—with no Pakistan money and very little cash of any kind. But at least I remembered where my father's relative was. He owned a business that sold appliances—washers, refrigerators, stoves—in a building on the main street in Lahore. "Take me to the Alfala Building," I told the driver.

Fortunately for me, Mr. Kakru was at the store. He was surprised to see me, especially since I was now all grown up. "Are you sure you are Farooq?" he asked me.

"Of course I'm sure."

Once he was convinced, he embraced me. He was very happy to see a long-lost relative, especially one from Kashmir—a rare thing at that time. I then said, "Habib Sahib, the first thing to do is to please pay the taxi driver." Which he kindly did.

Then he took me home, where his wife and his children were amazed and delighted to greet me.

That evening, I got a call from Mr. Malik Habib-Ullah, the head of the Pakistan intelligence office in charge of Kashmir. "Mr. Rizvi called to tell us about you," he said. "We'd like you to come to Rawalpindi. We're eager to talk with you, because we want to know your perspectives regarding the situation in Kashmir. We'll arrange for you to fly here the day after tomorrow."

I had to agree. Two days later, a police car drove me to the airport for the 200-mile flight to Rawalpindi, where Pakistani intelligence is headquartered, along with the Pakistani army. Of course, it's also the city where my father had a house and an arts emporium, and where I had stayed while going to school—back when I was a twelve-year-old commuter to the tough St. Mary's School. So I knew the city and still had friends there.

Upon my arrival, another police car picked me up and drove me to the intelligence headquarters, where I was met by Mr. Malik and several other officers. All had been closely monitoring the unrest in Kashmir. Right away they began plying me with questions about what was happening in Kashmir.

I answered their questions as best I could, but I soon became exasperated. In my usual forthright way, I began to push back. "Mr. Malik," I said, "you're asking me all these questions, but I don't know the answers any more than you, even though I live in Kashmir. What do *you* think is happening? You're from the government. Aren't you supposed to have a plan?"

"What do you mean, a plan?"

"You know what I mean. Doesn't Pakistan have a plan for resolving the Kashmir issue?"

He sensed the sarcasm in my voice. "I hope you're not one of those Kashmiris who want to have an *independent* Kashmir," he said.

By this time, I was exhausted. "Malik Sahib," I said, "please don't tell me what to think. My family has suffered greatly because of this conflict. I'm here because I need to get the papers that will let me travel to America to go to school. If you don't want to give them to me, just send me back to the other side." And I looked him straight in the eye.

I could have ruined all my hopes with those words. As the head of Pakistani intelligence for Kashmir, Malik Habib-Ullah had it in his power to tear up my documents and make sure I never received another set. I wondered whether I'd gone too far.

But after a moment, Mr. Malik smiled and said, "Don't worry, son. Everything is okay." Turning to his assistant, he said, "Tomorrow, take Farooq to the head of immigration and see he gets the right papers." And he let me go.

By now, I had been in Pakistan for three days—all completely unplanned, since my original intention had been simply to travel to Delhi to meet with the commissioner at Kashmir House. My family back home had no idea of my whereabouts, and at that time it was impossible to make a telephone call or send a telegram from Pakistan to Kashmir. They were very worried, and in fact began calling everyone they knew in Delhi, convinced that I'd been arrested.

Luckily, I figured out a way to assuage their fears. I sent a telegram from Lahore to a friend in Bombay, saying, "Please send a telegram to my family. Tell them I'm well and in Pakistan, making arrangements to travel to America."

I spent the night in my father's house in Rawalpindi and even met with some of my old school friends who were still in town. Then I went to the immigration office, where I was assured that a new travel document that would allow me to leave the country would be presented to me. But I still had a couple of other hurdles to get over. I needed guarantees from two responsible individuals who would promise that, if I had to return from America, they would take care of my transportation personally. (At the time, this was required by the Pakistani government, which didn't want to bear responsibility for citizens who might be unable to fend for themselves while abroad.) I would also need a visa from the US government.

So I began to ponder who might provide me with a guarantee that the government would consider acceptable. Finally, I thought of someone: a good friend of my father's, a man named Habib-ur-Rehman from the Pakistani-administered region of Kashmir, who had an interesting background. A military officer, he had fought against the British with Subhas Chandra Bose, the Indian nationalist leader. In 1945, he was traveling with Bose on the flight that crashed in Taiwan, supposedly costing Bose his life (though many rumors and legends reject that story). Habib-ur-Rehman survived the crash, though he suffered serious burns. Later he became a brigadier general in the army of Pakistan-administered Kashmir. At the time I met him, he was serving as secretary of the Ministry of Kashmiri Affairs in Rawalpindi.

I called Mr. Habib, and he promptly invited me to visit with him. I found him sitting with the director general of Foreign Affairs of Pakistan, who had immigrated to Pakistan from the Kargil region of Jammu and Kashmir. He had come to visit Brigadier Habib-ur-Rehman. Both men knew and respected my father, and both had known me as a youngster. His presence there was a great coincidence.

When I explained what I needed, they both offered to provide me the guarantees required, and in fact they signed the papers then and there. They also offered to contact my father in New York to tell him what I was doing. I delivered the guarantee forms to the passport officer, where I was told, "Come tomorrow, and we'll give you a traveling document to America." Sure enough, the next day, I picked up my new passport, which referred to me, under the "Citizenship" heading, as a "native of the former state of Jammu and Kashmir." This wording reflected the fact that Pakistan considered my homeland a disputed region.

The matter of the US visa, however, remained unsettled.

I had another day to spend in Rawalpindi. I recalled the name of a woman my father had mentioned to me. Like my father, she worked for a Pakistani industrial development corporation, and her job was to manage the corporation's gift store in Rawalpindi. I decided to pay Mrs. Anees a visit at the store.

She greeted me in friendly fashion and introduced me to a lady sitting nearby—a Mrs. Nusrat Bhutto. "Young Farooq is the son of a friend of mine," she said, "He comes from Kashmir."

Mrs. Bhutto was amazed—as I've said, at that time it was very rare to meet someone who had come from Kashmir. So of course she asked me many questions about myself, my background, and my purpose in coming to Rawalpindi. I told her the whole story about my quest for a way to travel to America, and I concluded by saying, "Now I just have to figure out how to get an American visa."

Mrs. Bhutto smiled. "My husband is the foreign minister of Pakistan, and I know the American ambassador. Let me call him right now."

The very next day, I visited the American embassy and filled out the application for a student visa. My letter of acceptance from NYU made it possible for me to qualify. I also informed the embassy officials about having met Ambassador Howard Schaffer in Kashmir. I later learned that they contacted him, and he gave them a strong recommendation in my favor.

I also owed a debt of gratitude to my new friend, Mrs. Bhutto, and to her husband, the foreign minister, who streamlined the path for me. And of course, as you may have guessed, in meeting them, I brushed up against a bit of world history. Her husband would go on to serve as prime minister and president of Pakistan. And some twenty-three years later, their daughter Benazir Bhutto would herself become prime minister, the first woman to head an elected government in a Muslim-majority nation. I had the opportunity of interacting with her in 1994 as my involvement in the Kashmir issue got started.

Once I'd applied for my visa, it seemed as if my long battle for the right to travel to America might be at an end—but, yet again, it turned out that there was "just one more" requirement. "You need to pass a medical exam," the embassy officer told me. "Here's the name of a doctor who can help you."

I made my way to the doctor's office and submitted to a thorough physical exam. As he listened to my heart and tested my reflexes, he seemed impressed by my fitness. "What do you do, young man?"

"I'm an athlete, a cricket player," I told him, and he nodded as if to say, "That explains it."

But when he took what should have been a routine X-ray of my chest, he became concerned. "See these spots on your lungs?" he asked, pointing to white blotches on the black background of the image. "Those are signs of TB—tuberculosis. When was the last time you had a checkup?"

"I've never had one before," I replied. "In fact, I don't recall ever visiting a doctor or a dentist. There was no need to."

The doctor raised his eyebrows at that one. Then, after a moment of thought, he asked, "Tell me, have you been drinking milk?"

"Yes," I replied, "every morning, straight from the cow."

He nodded. "Now I understand the problem. You should only drink pasteurized milk, young man," he told me. "That explains the TB spots. But if you stop drinking unpasteurized milk, they'll go away."

Now I was worried. "What does this mean for my trip to America?" I asked.

"I'm not supposed to do this," the doctor replied, "but I'm going to disregard the spots. Just promise me you'll give up drinking milk fresh from the cow." And he signed off on a clean health report for me.

The next day, I had a beautiful new US visa pasted into my passport. Now, nothing could stop me from getting to America. Or so I believed.

My father had learned that I was in Rawalpindi, working on organizing my papers for the journey to the US. Having lived there for years, he still had an account at the local bank, so he arranged for some money to be deposited there for me. I used it to buy a plane ticket from Karachi—at the time, the only city in Pakistan from which international flights departed—to New York. By now, it was September 1, and I was already late for the start of classes at NYU. But my father had been in touch with the administrators at the school, and they understood the reasons for my delay. I was scheduled to depart in a few days.

I decided I had time to take care of one more responsibility before leaving for America. I'd go back to Lahore to thank Mr. Rizvi, the police chief who'd been instrumental in getting me admitted to Pakistan. So I spent the equivalent of a US dollar to buy a ticket for the seven-hour trip by minibus from Rawalpindi to Lahore. I planned to start early the next morning.

In warm weather, it's common for people in Rawalpindi to sleep on the rooftops of their homes, under netting that protects them from mosquitos. That's where I was in the wee hours of the morning when I was awakened by what seemed like fireworks exploding overhead. Sitting bolt upright, I asked myself, "What's happening?"

I soon found out. India and Pakistan had gone to war, and the Indian Air Force had launched an attack on Rawalpindi.

I wondered what I should do. I still wanted to see Mr. Rizvi, and I was unwilling to waste the money I'd spent on my bus ticket. I decided to stick to my plan. The minibus journey to Lahore took twelve hours rather than the usual seven, because the roads were crowded both with Pakistani troops on the march and with ordinary civilians fleeing the fighting. We arrived in Lahore late that evening.

I went first to the home of my father's relative, Mr. Habib, in the Gulberg area of Lahore. There was a guard outside their empty house. "They've left Lahore because of the war," he told me. "If you need a place to sleep, try the little hotel around the corner."

I slept in a room at the hotel that night. It was the first time in my life that I ever saw a television or experienced air conditioning.

In the morning, I took a taxi to Mr. Rizvi's house. He and his family were not expecting me. "Why are you here at such a troubled time?" he asked.

"I came to thank you for helping me enter Pakistan," I explained.

I noticed that he and his family members were cleaning their guns. "The Indian army is just eight miles away," Mr. Rizvi said. "There's going to be house-to-house fighting, and we're getting ready to do our part."

That night, Mr. Rizvi put me on a train back to Rawalpindi. Along the way, the train passed border towns where fighting was going on. Before the journey's end, the train was filled with wounded soldiers.

Meanwhile, my travel plans—along with those of many other people—were put on hold. Ayub Khan, the president of Pakistan, decreed that no one could leave the country until the war ended. So I was stuck in Rawalpindi as long as the fighting lasted.

Thankfully, the war was a brief one. Twenty-one days later, I boarded a Pakistan International Airlines plane in Karachi, bound for Beirut. After a second overnight stop in London, I took a British Overseas Airways flight to New York's John F. Kennedy Airport.

My father was waiting for me—looking very pleased but also very haggard. He had lost weight worrying about me during my month of misadventures, near-disasters, amazing coincidences, and acts of extraordinary kindness and generosity.

He gave me a hug and welcomed me to America. A new phase of my life was about to begin.

4

NEW LAND, NEW LIFE

MY FATHER TOOK ME HOME from the airport to his apartment in Queens, in a middle-class neighborhood known as Elmhurst. The next morning, he took me to NYU's Graduate School of Business in downtown Manhattan, in the canyons of Wall Street. The fall semester of classes had already been under way for over a month. The streets were teeming not just with businesspeople scurrying to and from their offices but also with countless New Yorkers of all kinds, including students.

The first person I met at NYU was a foreign student advisor who had been assigned to help me. I later learned that he was himself a graduate student, a Jewish New Yorker pursuing a career in investment banking. I'd had very few occasions to know Jewish people before coming to America (Ambassador Schaffer was Jewish, though I didn't know it at the time we met). Many of the close friends I would make in America happened to be Jewish.

My advisor—I'll call him Harry—asked me a few questions about my background and my plans. The first step in assigning me to classes would be an English proficiency test. Because I'd been using English practically all my life back in Kashmir, I passed the test easily.

"Well, your English is better than that of most students," Harry said. "Now the question is, What do you want to major in?"

My answer was simple: "I have no idea."

"Well, how about accounting?" Apparently accounting had always been a popular field of study among business students.

"If you say so," I responded.

Harry signed me up for an introductory accounting class. But after an hour trying to make sense of jargon I'd never heard before and that the professor didn't bother to explain—probably because I'd already missed the first several weeks of class—I headed back to Harry's office.

"Accounting is not for me," I told him. "I don't like all that stuff about debits and credits."

"Hmm," Harry said. "Okay, you're not an accounting major. How about economics?"

"Okay," I said. At least I had some inkling of what economics was about—I'd studied it in college back in Kashmir.

I went off for my first economics class at NYU. It was a class in microeconomics, and most of the discussion seemed to center on graphs, charts, and tables. I heard more numbers in that classroom than words, which for me, as a lover of literature and history, was rather disconcerting.

I sought out Harry one more time. "Sorry, I don't like economics, either."

Harry was a very patient man. "What about marketing?" he suggested.

I'd never heard the word before. "What is it?" I asked.

"It's about buying and selling," Harry said.

"That's sounds okay," I told him.

Fortunately, when I attended my first marketing class, the teacher used words I understood rather than numbers, equations, and formulas. So I liked it. That's how I ended up majoring in international marketing.

My first couple of months at NYU included some surprises. My graduate business classes were filled with students who worked in the nearby financial industry. (The NYU Graduate School of Business was then located on Church Street, just steps from Wall Street.) I had never before seen a student who was thirty or forty years old, so I was rather shocked to discover that some of my classmates were older than the professors. I was also surprised to observe many of them smoking in class. Some would prop their feet up on the desks, and occasionally they even argued with the teachers. This kind of behavior would have been considered tremendously disrespectful back in Kashmir.

I realized I was in a new world.

Then as now, case studies were an important part of learning in business school. The first case study I was given had to do with an American company working in Mexico. The professor gave us a lot of background materials to read and also told us that we should type our papers. The deadline was short, and I didn't have time to read all the materials. What's more, I didn't own a typewriter. (Of course, there were no such things as personal computers in those days.) So I read the case study and developed my own answers for the issues it presented. The whole paper was about three handwritten pages.

After a week, the professor called me to his office. He seemed a little puzzled by the work I'd handed in.

"Which of the background materials did you read?" he asked me.

My first instinct was to bend the truth. But then I decided it was better to be honest. "I didn't have time to read them," I admitted.

"I see," the professor said. "And why did you hand in your paper without typing it?"

"I'm sorry," I said, "but I don't have a typewriter, and I didn't have time to go to the library." I was beginning to think that I was doomed to failure in this class.

The professor sighed. "Well, it would have been better if you'd read the materials. Please do that next time. But I'm giving you an A on this paper because your answers are exactly right."

I realized that common sense was an important part of learning.

Many years later, the case study about operating in Mexico became real to me when Ethan Allen established a major manufacturing hub in the Mexican state of Guanajuato, employing over 1,100 people.

One of the reasons I'd felt too busy to read the background materials was because I was working by day and attending classes at night. That had been my plan all along—in fact, I'd chosen NYU in part because it was easy to attend night classes there.

My first job in America was working near my father at the World's Fair. There was a gift shop at the Pakistan pavilion, and I took a job behind the counter, putting out goods for display and helping customers select souvenirs to purchase. It was a little like the work I'd done back home at the crafts emporium in Rawalpindi.

I took advantage of the opportunity to tour the rest of the World's Fair. It was a blend of national pavilions and exhibits hosted by giant corporations, promoting their products and showing off the latest technological advances. I still remember some of the highlights of the fair, including the giant Unisphere, which remains a centerpiece of Flushing Meadows Park; GE's colorful Carousel of Progress (still on display, in an updated version, at Disney World in Orlando, Florida); and the General Motors pavilion, which featured a ride through a giant diorama displaying the world of the future—a world coincidentally filled with countless GM cars. During that summer and fall of 1965, the World's Fair was my main source of recreation, and I was sorry when it closed for good in October.

During these first months in New York, I was living with my father in his Queens apartment. Some of the first people I got to know were the Levys, the Jewish family from Flatbush that my father had met at the fair. They'd become good friends, and I quickly became a member of their circle. My father and I used to visit with them almost every weekend. Gerald Levy, always called Jerry, was a cardiologist, and his wife, Mildred, known as Mimi, was a homemaker. They had three small children, sons Joseph and Nathan, and a daughter named Lanis-Ruth. I remember them sitting on my lap in those days; now, of course, they are all grown up, and we still remain friends. In later years, Mimi even visited Kashmir with me and my family.

A few months after the fair closed, my father went back to Pakistan. That meant I had to find a place of my own to live. Somehow I found another overseas student, a fellow named Sultan from Karachi, Pakistan, who was also looking for a place to stay. He was in New York on a student visa, taking classes in practical skills like dry cleaning. Sultan and I agreed to share a place, and we moved into a studio apartment in Queens.

One day, Sultan came to me and said, "I'd love to be able to drive around New York and even outside of the city. But I'm scared to drive. If I buy a car, would you drive it?"

I'd learned to drive back in Kashmir, although I was basically self-taught. You may recall "the other Farooq," the student whose father had asked me to help him become more disciplined about his studies. Farooq had owned a British Vauxhall, and he let me drive it around. I remember the brakes didn't work, so I had to use the handbrake to stop the car. Still, I learned how to get around. Later, in Queens, I passed the test for my driver's license in the station wagon that my father owned, and he let me use it until his departure from the US. Mimi Levy also occasionally lent me her car, one of those big Oldsmobiles with giant tailfins that were stylish in the early 1960s. So I figured I was a good enough driver. "Sure," I said to Sultan. "If you buy a car, I'll drive it."

Sultan went shopping and ended up buying a used Corvair. This was a compact Chevrolet model that eventually got a reputation as one of the historic lemons of all time. In fact, consumer advocate Ralph Nader became famous for his scathing criticisms of the Corvair in his 1965 book, *Unsafe at Any Speed*.

Of course, Sultan and I didn't know any of this. So whenever we wanted to take a ride somewhere, we got in his Corvair. The results turned out to be quite adventurous. One time we were on the Van Wyck Expressway in Queens when the engine literally fell out of the car. (It was held in place with just a small handful of screws.) Luckily I was able to safely maneuver the vehicle over to the side of the road. Poor Sultan had to pay a tow-truck operator to have the car taken to a service station, where they patched it back together.

Later, we took the Corvair on a trip to Glens Falls in upstate New York to visit an engineer friend of mine who had moved there from Kashmir. Once again, the engine fell out. "I'm not taking this thing to be fixed anymore," Sultan declared, and this time he junked it.

Meanwhile, even after my father's departure, my friendship with the Levy family continued to blossom. Most weekends I would take the long subway trip from Queens to Brooklyn, via Manhattan, to have dinner with them. Mimi Levy was a marvelous cook, and in addition to typical American foods, she would prepare for me some Kashmiri dishes that my father had taught her—concoctions with lamb, chicken, vegetables, and rice. Mimi's dinners were a wonderful change from the unimpressive meals I cooked in my own apartment.

After a few months, Sultan was called back home after his young brother died in an accident in Karachi. At that point, the Levys suggested, "Why don't you move to a place near us? Your school is in downtown Manhattan, and your daily commute will be quicker and easier from here than from Queens."

I liked the idea. So I looked around in the Flatbush area, and I found a nice little studio apartment at 805 Ditmas Avenue near Ocean Parkway, close to the subway and just a ten-minute walk from the Levys. It was on the second floor of an eight- or ten-story apartment building, and it cost me about $75 a month. Nat Levy helped me move, using a company van I had borrowed from one of his relatives who owned a home heating oil business.

Around this time I also bought my first television, a small wooden cabinet model that I purchased for $25 from a Manhattan hotel that was selling all their old stuff. This gave me something to do in the evenings during the relatively rare times when I wasn't working or studying.

. . .

THE CLOSING OF THE World's Fair meant that I needed to find a new job. In those days, classified newspaper ads were the main way one looked for an opening. Scanning the paper one day, I spotted an ad for a job as assistant to a supervisor in a small factory in Queens. I showed up for an interview and was given the job, although I have to admit I had no idea what my responsibilities were or even what kinds of products they made in the factory.

Obviously my confusion affected my job performance, because after a couple of weeks my boss called me into his office on Friday afternoon.

"Don't bother coming in on Monday," he told me.

"Okay," I said. "I'll see you on Tuesday."

"No, don't come on Tuesday, either."

"Oh. What about Wednesday, then?"

"No, you don't need to come in on Wednesday."

Eventually it dawned on me that I was being fired.

I was very upset. I went home and wrote an angry letter to the company management, asking, "How can you treat people this way?" Somehow I'd imagined that this position was the first rung on a promising career ladder—despite the fact that I had no idea what I was doing.

My next job started out in a way that was just as unpromising. But the results ended up being very different.

Looking for a new position, I spotted a newspaper ad that said: "Bookkeeper needed."

I asked a couple of my classmates at NYU, "What's a bookkeeper?"

They offered me some advice that was actually pretty sound: "If you don't know, don't apply."

I decided to apply anyway. I found the office in a loft building on

446 Broadway near Canal Street in Lower Manhattan. I walked in. The company was called Imperial Envelope Company, and it was run by two partners, Jesse Isaacson and Richard King, who were sitting on partners' desks facing each other. Right next to them was their assistant—then known as a "Gal Friday"—a woman named Sally. Working in the back was Abe, who printed the envelopes on a big, greasy black machine.

I walked in and asked to apply for the vacant bookkeeper's job. Richard King took me over to a nearby desk, opened up a ledger, and pointed to a giant mechanical calculator operated with a hand crank. "Go ahead and foot the ledger," he said.

I looked up at him and said, "What's that in English?"

He said, "What do you mean? Where did you learn bookkeeping?"

Thinking fast, I replied, "England." In reality, the only thing I'd ever done in England was change from one plane to another.

Luckily for me, it was around noon. King said, "Jesse and I are going out for lunch. Why don't you come back later, and we'll talk about the job. Or you can wait if you like."

"I'll wait," I replied. The two partners left.

Sally had observed the whole thing. "Do you know anything about bookkeeping?" she asked.

"Not a thing," I confessed, "but I need this job. Can you help me? What are these books about? How do you operate this machine?"

Sally took her lunch hour to give me a forty-five-minute tutorial on bookkeeping—cash receipts, cash disbursement, balancing accounts. She explained to me that "footing" is simply adding the figures in a column and entering the sum at the bottom (the "foot") of the page. By the time King and Isaacson returned from lunch, I had at least a rudimentary understanding of how bookkeeping worked.

King asked me, "So, do you think you can do the job?"

"Well, I've taken a look at your ledger," I responded, "and it looks okay, but I think your bookkeeping methods need improvement."

King was startled. "What?" Sally was watching and barely repressing her giggles. I'd promised her that, if I got the job, I'd take her out to lunch on my first day.

I got the job. It paid $1.75 an hour.

I was still not interested in numbers, which is why I'd rejected accounting as a major on my first day at NYU. But bookkeeping, as explained by Sally, seemed pretty straightforward and down-to-earth. And, of course, I needed a job.

I'm sure I made some mistakes during my first few weeks at work. Sally kept giving me pointers. I don't know what I would have done without her. Even so, it's pretty amazing that Richard and Jesse kept me on.

I soon struck up a friendship with Abe, the printer. Whenever I had a few minutes free from my office job, I would visit him in the back room and help him out with his work. I learned how his printing machinery worked, and he appreciated my assistance.

I also discovered some new ways to make myself useful around the office.

It turned out that the partners, Richard and Jesse, had very different personalities. As a result, they were constantly squabbling, mostly over insignificant things. It made for an unpleasant atmosphere, especially since the group of us was all confined to the same tiny office together.

I had just turned twenty-one years old, and Richard and Jesse were old, experienced businessmen. But as captain of the cricket team back in Kashmir, I'd developed a feel for how to resolve disputes. So one day I decided to intervene.

"Mr. King and Mr. Isaacson, I see you're always arguing. Can you tell me what the problem is? Maybe I can help you."

At first, they were incredulous. But when I insisted, they decided to try me.

"Today," Richard told me, "we're arguing about how much money each of us should be allowed to take out of petty cash."

"That's an easy one," I said. "I'm your bookkeeper, and I know exactly how the company cash flow stands. My recommendation is that each of you should get $100 a month from petty cash, and I should get $10."

The two men stared at me. "Why should *you* get $10?" Jesse demanded.

I said, "I'm the one giving you the advice."

They laughed and said, "Okay." The argument for the day was settled—and I walked away with $10 a month in the bargain.

I learned a couple of important lessons from that experience. I learned that most of the problems in life are pretty simple—and that they are fundamentally the same, whether on the cricket pitch in Kashmir or in an office building in downtown Manhattan. If you have the intelligence and the instincts to solve problems in one setting, you can probably solve them in another setting.

I also learned that it never hurts to ask for a share for yourself!

In three months' time, I'd learned enough about bookkeeping to be handling all the financial matters for the company, which entitled me to a nice raise in salary. After three more months, my salary was doubled.

Eventually, I became good friends with Richard King and Jesse Isaacson. Here's a story that illustrates just how close our friendship grew.

During my year at the Imperial Envelope Company, the issue of the future of Kashmir was a major topic of discussion in international circles and a subject of heated debates at the United Nations. I followed the news coverage closely. Eager to play a role in shaping the future of my homeland, I decided to establish a committee for the future of Kashmir, renting a post office box on Wall Street to serve as its address. When I wrote a manifesto making the case for a free Kashmir, Richard King offered to help by printing it for me.

But Richard's help to me extended much further than this. Three years later, when I was no longer working for Richard and Jesse, Sheikh Abdullah, the former prime minister of Kashmir, was released from prison after ten years of confinement. He organized an international conference in Kashmir, which I would have liked to attend. But because I lacked proper travel papers, I could not travel to the conference—so Richard and his wife decided to go in my place. They presented the manifesto I'd drafted, representing the people of Kashmir in the United States—meaning, in effect, me, Farida, and two other Kashmiri families then living in New York. I later heard that the conference attendees were surprised and impressed to see two lifelong Americans speaking in support of the rights of Kashmiris.

Meanwhile, my life in New York had become extremely busy and rewarding. I was working all day and attending classes at night. I had also renewed my love of sports. One of the first things I'd asked when I arrived in New York was whether NYU had a cricket team. I learned that they did, and that any student at the university could play if he was good enough. I joined a team made up mostly of students from Caribbean countries like Guyana and Jamaica. In those days, students from South Asia were very rare in New York. So on the weekends, I took the long subway ride from Brooklyn to the Bronx to play cricket in Van Cortlandt Park. Three months later, my teammates elected me captain of the NYU team, and that fall we traveled to Toronto to play a Canadian team.

After a year or so, Richard King and Jesse Isaacson realized that I wasn't going to remain their bookkeeper forever. They realized it—I didn't. I was happy working for them. But, to their credit, the partners recognized I had more talent than they could use in their little business. So around the end of 1966, they came to me with a suggestion: "Farooq, why don't you look for a job on Wall Street? It's close to your school, and there's a lot of room for advancement for a smart young man like you."

I had no financial background at that time, other than what I'd learned as their bookkeeper. So I was a bit baffled at the suggestion. "What will I do on Wall Street?" I asked.

"Tell them you're a financial analyst," Richard said.

I decided to give it a try. I went to One Wall Street, an Art Deco skyscraper then known as the Irving Trust Company Building, and rode up in the elevator to visit the companies on each floor—something anyone could do in those days when the kind of tight security we're now accustomed to was unknown.

When I arrived at Bear Stearns and mentioned I was interested in a Wall Street job, I was ushered into the office of one of the personnel directors, a man named Jacobs. He gave me an application form to fill out. In the space that asked about "extracurricular activities," I listed "sports, cricket, badminton, aquatics, mountain climbing." The last item caught Jacobs's eye: "Mountain climbing, really?"

"Yes, I lived in Kashmir."

"Oh, I love the mountains," Jacobs said. "Let me see what I can do to get you a job here."

He made a few calls and discovered that there was an opening for a junior financial analyst in the payroll department. By this time, I had learned about bookkeeping, and I was studying marketing at NYU. So I got the job.

■ ■ ■

YOU MIGHT ASSUME THAT the transition from Kashmir to the biggest city in the United States would involve a drastic culture shock—but I didn't find that to be the case.

Perhaps one reason is that I didn't come to America with any fixed preconceptions. I'd never lived in a big city, so life in a great metropolis was all new to me—and because I was very flexible and open to new experiences, I found it all interesting and absorbing.

Of course, there were things I had to get used to. For instance, one of the first things I did in New York was ride the subway with my father. The very idea made me quite nervous. When I heard we were going to go underground, my first reaction was, "How will we breathe?" The first couple of times I went down into the tunnel, I actually felt I had some trouble breathing. But I realize now that was purely psychological. I quickly got used to the experience, and soon I was traveling all over the city by subway just like millions of other New Yorkers.

Another hurdle I had to overcome was figuring out what to order in restaurants. Near NYU was a Horn & Hardart Automat, a self-service restaurant that let you buy food by inserting coins into a slot. I went in, asked for a cup of tea, and was baffled to be given a cup of hot water and a curious-looking white bag. I started to tear the tea bag open to release the tea leaves inside when a man sitting nearby stopped me. "No," he said, "don't open the tea bag—just drop it in the hot water, and you'll soon have a cup of tea."

I thanked him and followed his advice. But then I spotted a little paper packet of sugar on the table. Ah, I know what to do! I thought, and I dropped the whole packet into the teacup.

"No, no!" my new friend explained, "You tear open the pack and pour out the sugar!" I was thoroughly confused.

On the whole, however, my transition to American life was an easy one. I was fortunate in that I had no fixed ideas about Americans that I needed to discard. I'd seen a few cowboy movies and glamorous pictures set in Hollywood, but it took just a few minutes for me to realize that those images had nothing to do with typical Americans. Walking the streets of the city, riding the subway, or sitting in my classes at NYU, I saw that Americans were ordinary people much like the ones I'd known at home. They're no different from me, I thought, and I immediately decided I would have no trouble living and working with them.

I happen to be a very sociable person, which means that I like to talk to people, even if we haven't met before. I couldn't help noticing that people riding on the subway didn't talk to one another, which I found a little strange. But I followed my usual practice and started conversations with the people nearby: "How are you, and where are you from?"

I got a few looks of shock or suspicion. But three quarters of the people I approached were happy to talk with me—and I find that still to be the case when I am in a strange place to this day.

Perhaps the most striking and delightful thing I discovered about America was the sense of freedom it gave me. I had come from an area of conflict, where people had to be very careful about what they said and did. I was amazed to realize that people in America are free. No one asks to see your papers. There's no "lights out" curfew at night. You don't have to worry that the authorities will come to your home to arrest you because of your political opinions or activities. This is a wonderful fact of life in America that we too often take for granted.

I never took it for granted. And though I was technically a "stateless" person, I quickly came to feel very much at home in America.

This is partly a reflection of my personality. Many people who settle in a new country go on referring to their original country as "home," even after many years have passed. I was never that kind of person. To this day, I am the kind of person who feels at home anywhere I go. I've spent a lot of time traveling the world. I've been to Mexico, Honduras, Italy, China, Korea, the Middle East, and many other places, and no matter where I am, I never feel any different. And perhaps in part as a reaction to me, the people I meet have almost always treated me with friendship and respect.

Still, the governments of the world have a way of erecting boundaries that make it hard for human beings to interact with one another in a free and friendly fashion.

During my first year in New York, I was technically not supposed to work. Under the rules at that time, foreign students were permitted to work only during the summer. I ignored the rule for a time, but finally decided that it would be safer to apply for a permit. So I got all the forms, sent them in along with my traveling documents, and applied to the US immigration service for a work permit.

In the spring of 1966, near the end of my first year at NYU, I was called in to the local office of the immigration service. It turned out that applying for the work permit had been a big mistake. My irregular travel documents were a problem, the answers I gave to the questions they asked me were a problem, and the fact that I'd submitted my own application without advice or help from a lawyer was a problem. I could see from the faces of the people who examined me that they weren't happy with me.

A week later, I got a deportation letter. In effect, it said, "You cannot stay in America as a student because you are stateless. You must leave the country in two weeks."

Once again, the Levys were there to help. Mimi Levy's sister, Shirley Cherin, was a lawyer, and her partner at the firm, a Mr. Galef, specialized in immigration law. They agreed to take my case.

But even as they set to work to get my deportation order revoked, I realized that my situation was very precarious. Not wanting to take a chance, I decided to look for a backup plan. I wrote a letter to the Canadian minister of immigration, explaining my entire history. In just a month, I got a reply from a high Canadian official saying, in effect, "If America asks you to leave, you're welcome in Canada. Show this letter at any Canadian border, and we'll welcome you to our country as a permanent resident, eligible for citizenship." To confirm the arrangement, I traveled to Montreal for a few days and so became a Canadian resident, equivalent to the green card coveted by residents of the US. When I returned to New York, I felt more secure, knowing that if I was expelled from the US, I had a second home right next door.

In the end, the US immigration service decided not to follow through on its threat to deport me. I understand that the State Department itself intervened in the case. The reason is not that I was especially favored but because the US was confronted with an unusual situation—a technically stateless person from a disputed territory, living in the US at a time when the status of his homeland was being hotly debated at the UN. The immigration authorities did not officially give me an approved status. They just said, "We're going to take no action in this case."

In other words, I could stay in the US and go on working, and the government would turn a blind eye to my status.

I still have the letter I received all those years ago from the government of Canada, offering me their country's welcome. I don't suppose I'll ever need to take them up on their generous offer, but it's nice to know that I have the option.

By the way, in later years, the son of Shirley Cherin's law partner, named Steve Galef, became a good friend and advisor of mine. Also an attorney, he served on the board of Ethan Allen until his untimely death in 1998, when he was just fifty-eight years old.

. . .

LOOKING BACK, IT IS STRIKING to think about the number and variety of individuals who played crucial roles in my early journey. These "human angels" include Principal Saif Uddin of SP College in Srinagar, who recognized my leadership potential and helped me apply to NYU, and the Indian Airlines pilot who decided to fly to Delhi from Srinagar after initially canceling the flight due to bad weather—and so made it possible for me to take the graduate admissions test in Bombay the next day.

They include Peer Ghulam Hassan Shah, the chief of intelligence of Kashmir, who exceeded his authority by signing the documents that enabled me to leave India, and the Indian Airlines official at Delhi who helped process my airline tickets and allowed me to leave the country that same day.

They include Ambassador Schaffer, the American diplomat who helped me get a visa for travel to the US; Mr. Rizvi, the Pakistani head of police who decided to authorize the traveling document I needed for travel to the US; and my father's friend, Brigadier

Habib-ur-Rehman, who gave his personal guarantee that enabled me to make my journey.

They include the Levy family of Brooklyn, who adopted me when I was a stranger in their land and made me feel welcome in New York City; Richard King, Jesse Isaacson, Sally, and Abe of the Imperial Envelope company, who gave me a job I wasn't qualified for and then helped me learn about business and life; and Mr. Jacobs, who helped me get a job at Bear Stearns because he shared my love of mountain climbing.

I can't think of these people, and the many others who helped me, without reflecting on how fortunate I've been. They gave me the opportunity; I was lucky enough to recognize it, and to know how to use it.

And I must also reflect on the fact that those of us who succeed with the help of generous friends also have an obligation to try to make the same kinds of opportunities available to as many others as possible, so all can thrive to the best of their abilities. That's what I've been trying to do my whole life.

5

THE MAKING OF A MERCHANT

WHEN WE REFLECT ON the past, we see how events that seemed small at the time sometimes end up having a major influence on our lives. One such event occurred while I was working at the Imperial Envelope Company.

My father suggested an idea to my grandfather and his colleague, Farida's father. "Why don't you send Farooq some arts and crafts from Kashmir? Maybe he can sell those items in America. He'll pay you what they cost, and the profits can help support him."

When my grandfather approached me with this idea, I said okay, thinking it was worth a try. It didn't occur to me that I was quietly being initiated into my family's business as merchants—or that this casual decision would help shape my life and career for decades to come.

In a few weeks, twelve wicker baskets arrived in New York, filled with colorful art objects made of papier-mâché, home decor accessories, and similar things. I'd had no idea how big and bulky they were going to be. I wondered what I was going to do with all this stuff.

Fortunately, the Levys had a neighbor who owned several buildings in the Williamsburg section of Brooklyn. "I can help you out," he said.

"I have this warehouse building with some space you can use. I warn you, it's got no security, and there are some rats living there. The neighborhood's pretty tough, and I can't promise your stuff will be safe. But I can let you have it cheap."

I checked out the space, and it was just as he described. "Let's make a deal," I said. "Let me use the space for my merchandise, and I'll pay you 5 percent of my revenues." We shook hands on it.

Now I had to figure out how to turn my twelve baskets full of products into a real business. The first thing I did was get a post office box near Wall Street, where I worked and studied. Then I had envelopes printed bearing the name Kashmir Products Limited. I hadn't formally registered the business—but as far as I was concerned, I was now officially an entrepreneur.

But where was I going to find customers? A chance encounter gave me an opportunity. My first-year marketing class at NYU featured a guest lecture by a well-known retailer—Marvin Traub, the CEO of Bloomingdale's department store. Impressed by his presentation, I called his office and told his assistant, "I'm a student who heard Mr. Traub speak, and I have something I'd like to discuss with him."

"Mr. Traub is a very busy man," I was told.

"Okay, I'll call back later," I responded. "Please let him know that I called." And I called every day for the next week, leaving a message with my name and phone number each time.

Eventually, my persistence paid off. "Come into the office, and Mr. Traub will give you a few minutes," the assistant told me.

At the appointed time, I showed up carrying a few samples of my Kashmiri merchandise, and in a little while I was ushered into Marvin Traub's office.

Here a bit of good luck worked in my favor. Marvin Traub was interested in the culture of South Asia. His stores carried products from the region, and Traub had visited India as well as Kashmir. So when I introduced myself and explained my mission, he was intrigued. He picked up his phone and asked one of his buyers to join us. And when she examined my sample products, she liked their quality and said she thought they might be saleable in New York.

So Bloomingdale's became my first significant customer, placing an order for several thousand dollars' worth of Kashmiri goods—a pretty big purchase at that time.

I soon added another customer—the gift shop for tourists and dignitaries visiting the United Nations headquarters in New York. I used to drop in at the UN rather frequently in the 1960s to listen to the Security Council debates about the Kashmir issue. After launching my crafts business, I got to know the manager of the gift shop, and he agreed to add Kashmiri items to the store's inventory.

Around this time, my grandfather made one of his regular trips to the United States—partly on business and partly to see his American friends. And of course he spent some time with me as well, staying in a hotel in Manhattan and visiting with me in Brooklyn. Now that I was an adult living on my own, our relationship had changed from the prickly one we'd had when I was a teenager. He understood that I was determined never to accept anything material from him, and he accepted that. He also developed a new respect for me and for my accomplishments—attending business school, beginning a business career, and even launching my little company. Over the next decade, between his visits to America and my own visits back home to Kashmir, we developed a new, mutually respectful friendship.

. . .

AS I MENTIONED in chapter four, I soon outgrew my job at Imperial Envelope and went to work at Bear Stearns on Wall Street. I was assigned to work in the controller's office with two much older associates—an orthodox Jewish man and a gregarious Irish gentleman. They took me under their wings and taught me so much about finance that, within less than a year, I was involved in meaningful business projects on behalf of some of the company's senior partners.

Soon thereafter, I received a call from a newly established Wall Street firm by the name of New Court Securities. Was I interested in considering a job opportunity? I was always open to new possibilities, so I went for an interview with an assistant vice president, a man named Larry Harris.

I learned from Harris that New Court Securities had been organized by Peter Fleck, a Dutch man associated with the Rothschild family, the world-renowned European bankers. Fleck had helped the Rothschilds bring substantial assets from Europe to America in advance of the Nazi occupation. They'd used some of these funds to establish a $100 million fund headquartered in Curaçao, a Caribbean island affiliated with the Netherlands. It was called the Five Arrows Fund, referring to the five branches of the Rothschild family, each of which had invested in the fund. New Court Securities was the name of the company that now ran the fund. Peter Fleck was the fund's chairman, while the CEO of New Court was a younger, very aggressive and capable person whose name was John Birkelund.

Larry Harris took a liking to me—perhaps in part because I was attending NYU, his own alma mater. He was also fascinated by my cricket playing and my involvement with the cause of democratic freedom for Kashmir. "If you come to work with New Court, the job will be harder than what you're doing at Bear Stearns. But I'd like to see you join us. Your next interview will be with our chief financial officer, Stanley Gluck, and he's pretty tough. He's a CPA, an accountant through and through, with an MBA from NYU. Let me walk you through the questions he's going to ask you and suggest the kinds of answers you should give."

Thanks in part to Harris's coaching, I got the job. I was named assistant to Ken Merrill, the portfolio manager of the Five Arrows Fund. I was the youngest of the twenty or so professionals working at the firm, most of them highly experienced and with impressive credentials from Ivy League universities—Harvard, Princeton, Yale. Fortunately for me, I was a quick learner, and with advice and guidance from my colleagues I soon began to feel comfortable with the work. A number of members of the New Court team became lifelong friends of mine, including Ken Merrill, Roger Widmann, Richard Sandberg, Richard Smith, Charlie Flood, and Kristin Gamble.

After a few months on the job, I was invited to an investment meeting attended by all the professionals, presided over by the company's CEO, John Birkelund. For some reason, Birkelund was in a terrible temper that day. I was shocked to hear him spend a number of minutes angrily castigating each of his senior associates in turn. No one dared to respond to him. As you can imagine, the mood in the room was very uncomfortable.

Eventually, Birkelund's focus turned to me. As he'd done with the others, he began berating me in a loud voice.

The moment he paused for breath, I spoke up. "Mr. Birkelund," I said in a quiet voice, "I don't like being shouted at."

There was a moment of utter silence, and then Birkelund said, "What did you say?"

"I said, please don't shout at me," I responded.

Birkelund stared at me in shock and then said, "Come with me to my office." I followed him down the hall, thinking to myself, *this is probably my last day working at New Court Securities.*

Birkelund closed the door behind us, and I took a seat. Pacing up and down, Birkelund demanded, "Why did you say what you did?"

"Because I think it is better not to shout at people. I don't understand why you feel the need to do this."

"Don't psychoanalyze me, young man!" Birkelund answered. And then, after a moment of silence, he simply said, "Let's go back to the meeting."

We did, and I think my colleagues were a bit surprised to see that

I'd been allowed to remain. They were also surprised at my audacity in standing up to John Birkelund. None of them knew the full story of my life—the ways I'd been called upon to live independently from an early age, my involvement in political conflicts in Kashmir, and the way I'd had a police officer threaten me with a gun. After facing down challenges like these, a raised voice in a Wall Street conference room didn't hold much terror for me.

In the months that followed, John Birkelund and I never talked about that incident, though others did. In fact, I've found that many of those who worked with us remember it to this day.

More important, Birkelund never again raised his voice at me. In fact, he took me under his wing and helped me learn an enormous amount about finance and business. I came to consider him one of my most important business mentors.

Another was Peter Fleck. A member of the Council on Foreign Relations, he was intrigued by my interest in the Kashmir question and often engaged me in long conversations about it. (Sometimes during the business day, a colleague looking for me would be told, "Farooq is in the chairman's office discussing foreign affairs.") He and John Birkelund invited me to one of the regular meetings they convened for financial professionals at the prestigious University Club on Fifth Avenue, and years later Birkelund sponsored my membership in the club. Birkelund, Sandberg, Gamble, and Smith would all later serve on the Ethan Allen board of directors.

In less than three years, I became a vice president and the chief financial officer of New Court Securities. I'd learned a lot about finance by then, of course. But I think my rapid ascent was due mainly to the fact that my nature is to be a problem solver. Unlike many people in business, I would never simply bring a problem to my boss and ask, "What should I do?" Instead, I would analyze the issues and say to my boss, "Here is a problem that has arisen—and here is what I think we should do."

The usual response I got was, "Okay, go and do it." And I think the people I worked for appreciated the fact that I would fix things rather than merely complaining about them.

. . .

MEANWHILE, I WAS CONTINUING to become accustomed to life in America. One of my rites of passage was buying my first car—a brand-new 1968 Ford Mustang, burgundy red, that cost me around $2,000. I was able to afford it with the help of my friend, Dr. Levy. One of his patients was a Ford dealer in Brooklyn, and Jerry Levy insisted that he give me a good deal on the car.

I also had help from Muriel Hyland, the manager of the First National City Bank branch on Madison Avenue at 65th Street, where my father had set up a bank account for me. I had just a hundred dollars to spare, so Muriel arranged a car loan for the rest of the cost. It was a pretty basic car—standard shift, no air conditioning, an AM radio only—but it took me where I wanted to go. Today, it would be considered a classic.

Another rite of passage that most New Yorkers have experienced is looking for a better but still affordable place to live. I found myself feeling a bit claustrophobic after a year in my tiny studio apartment in Flatbush, and my eye was caught by a newspaper ad for a cottage in Manhattan Beach. "Imagine that," I said, "a beach in Manhattan." But when I inquired, I discovered that the neighborhood of Manhattan Beach is actually located at the southern tip of Brooklyn. I took the long ride to the end of the D train line, crossed over the wooden Sheepshead Bay Bridge, and ultimately found my way to 1608 Shore Boulevard, just about a block from the beach.

The cottage consisted of a small living room, a bedroom just large enough for a bed, a small kitchen, and a little garden, all tucked away behind the main house in which the Bedfords, a conservative Jewish family, lived. Mrs. Bedford's mom had lived in the cottage until she'd passed away, and now the family was ready to rent it out.

The Bedfords were curious about this young man who was interested in occupying their extra house. "What kind of furniture do you have?" they asked me.

"Enough," I said. "A bed, a table, a chair."

Mrs. Bedford was pleased. "That's perfect!" she exclaimed. And she explained that the cottage was filled with all her mother's furniture, pots and pans, dishes, silverware, and other things—and that if I could use them, it would save her the trouble of having to donate them. The rent would be $90 per month, utilities included. I happily accepted the offer and moved in as soon as I could. I developed the habit of going swimming at the nearby beach almost every day during that summer of 1967. The other cottages in the neighborhood were occupied mostly by retired people, and I became friendly with many of them.

I also began participating in one of the typical activities of young American students—namely, going out with girls. I developed a particular attachment to Sara Johnson, who was studying music at NYU. We kept in touch for a year or so, mostly going out to dinner together, taking in movies, and going to an occasional concert.

I even met Sara's parents, who lived in the New Jersey suburbs, which reflects a certain amount of seriousness on Sara's part. But I never really got close to her. Instead, my thoughts were increasingly drawn in a different direction—toward Farida, the girl I'd met in my grandfather's house back in Srinagar.

Since my move to America, Farida and I had exchanged just a few friendly letters. She'd finished college with an education degree and was teaching school. I'd always been attracted to her, and I suspected that she felt something similar about me. But there was no understanding between us or our families. As time passed, I realized that, unless I made a move, Farida would probably marry someone else.

I decided that I'd better take action. But this was easier said than done, given the vast distance between us.

I got in touch with my father, who'd moved back home to Kashmir in 1967 after eighteen years away, and I asked him whether he would discuss with her parents the possibility of my marrying Farida. (As I've mentioned, her father was a business associate of my grandfather, so our families knew each other well.) This would be in accordance with Kashmiri tradition, in which families are often involved in a couple's courtship. To my pleasure, Farida's parents approved the plan, and—more important—so did Farida. We were officially engaged.

Looking back, I suppose that my life would have been rather different if I'd decided to marry an American girl rather than a Kashmiri. At age twenty-three, I was still deeply immersed in the culture of my homeland, as well as its complicated political situation, and I cared deeply about it. Although I was building a new life and a business career halfway around the world, I really wanted to maintain my connection to Kashmir—and one important way to do that was to marry the young woman I loved who shared that same heritage with me. In the years since then, my ties to Kashmir have remained strong, and my marriage to Farida is one reason why.

But now that the choice was made, the question was, how would we get married? I was unable to travel to Kashmir, because I still lacked proper travel documents. If I were to leave the US, there would be no guarantee I could return. And Farida and her family would not have wanted to send her to America before her marriage. So what could we do?

A little research revealed the existence of an Indian law that permitted people to get married from different locations—even different countries—using the telephone. As far as I can tell, no Kashmiris before Farida and me had ever taken advantage of this option. But we decided to do it. We obtained a special proxy form signed by the counsel general of India in the United States, and I signed a number of documents that were needed to make the ceremony legal. We also arranged for two legal witnesses in each location, and we planned a long-distance telephone call for September 1, 1968, scheduling it for the evening in Srinagar, which was early morning for me over in New York.

Then, as now, I was very concerned about the social implications of my choices and my family's choices. As the wedding date approached, I told my father, "Please don't spend any money on arranging an extravagant wedding. I think it's a waste, and anyway, the groom is not even going to be physically present! Give the money to the poor instead. And tell Farida's family that I feel this way."

Both fathers responded to me in the same way. "We understand and respect your point of view," they said, "but a family wedding is a very important event. We are going to celebrate it in the way we think is appropriate." And so they organized a traditional four-day-long celebration that included hundreds of guests.

When the big day arrived, Farida and the wedding party assembled in the large hall of her home. Farida wore the traditional wedding garment of a Kashmiri bride, and she looked very beautiful—as revealed by the photos I saw much later. In addition to family members, a number of prominent community leaders were in attendance, including Sheikh Abdullah, the former prime minister of Kashmir. The celebrant was Mirwaiz Farooq, a prominent religious leader who was also a friend of mine, a political activist, and a fellow cricketer. In accordance with the custom in that part of the world, the whole group was seated on cushions on the carpet.

Back in Brooklyn, my telephone rang with the pre-arranged call at 6:00 a.m. The *mirwaiz* led me through a series of prescribed questions and statements. In accordance with Muslim custom, Farida's answers were provided on her behalf by two uncles, who had been given the power to represent her. In this way, we affirmed our desire to be married in accordance with the law and with our faith. The whole conversation took just three or four minutes. When it ended, Farida and I were husband and wife.

I was very excited, as you can imagine. But once I hung up the phone, there was nothing more for me to do. So I went outside with a bucket and a sponge and gave my Mustang a wash, thinking happily about the life I would enjoy with my new bride. That evening, Mimi Levy prepared a beautiful dinner in my honor, and we celebrated my wedding with her family and a few friends at the Levys' home.

Later, our unusual wedding ceremony would be the subject of newspaper stories back in Kashmir: "Bride in Kashmir, bridegroom in New York are married by telephone." We still have those yellowing clippings in an album.

Now that she was officially the wife of a student in America, Farida applied to the US embassy in Delhi for a visa that would let her travel to New York. She arrived in December, bearing two large suitcases filled with traditional Kashmiri clothing and feeling a bit dazed from her long journey. Along with the Levys and a couple of my friends from New York, I met her at the airport. It was a wonderfully joyous reunion for us.

The next day, the Levys welcomed Farida with a second wedding dinner. Our life in America was under way.

One day that first week, Farida and I sat down in our cottage for an important conversation.

"Farida," I said, "now that you are here in America, there are three things I think you ought to do."

"What are they?" she asked.

"First, I think you should keep your Kashmiri clothes put away in the suitcases." Farida had brought outfits that we call *shalwar kameez*, including a tunic and loose-fitting trousers that are narrow at the ankle. "The clothes are beautiful, but they are not what American women wear. We'll go shopping together and buy you some new clothes that will help you fit in to your new home country."

"All right," Farida agreed.

"Second, you need to improve your English. The better you speak, the more comfortable you will feel. Just two blocks from here is Kingsborough Community College. We'll go there and sign you up for English classes." Again, Farida agreed.

"Finally, you'll need to get a job. You will meet people and get to know about life here. And we can use the money."

Farida willingly accepted all three of my suggestions. We went shopping together in Manhattan and bought her a new wardrobe, including several of the miniskirts that young women in America were wearing. She looked very nice and quickly got used to this new style. She enrolled in English classes and soon was speaking almost like a native. And after a few months, she got a job selling small appliances at the (now-defunct) Korvettes department store on 34th Street in Manhattan. Before long, she was promoted to a supervisor's position.

Like millions of others before her, Farida had transformed herself from an immigrant into an American.

Little by little, we created a comfortable and happy life for ourselves in New York. Before Farida's arrival, I'd bought a Castro convertible sofa for us to sleep on in our Manhattan Beach cottage. But after a few months, Mrs. Bedford noticed that we didn't have a "real" bed to share, and she kindly gave us her old four-poster. Today that bed is in our farmhouse in Livingston, New York.

We found a place where Farida could buy the ingredients and spices needed to prepare traditional Kashmiri dishes—an Armenian store at Lexington Avenue and 28th Street called Kalustyan's, patronized by most New Yorkers with South Asian backgrounds. (Farida has since become an expert at preparing all kinds of food, including American food, of course.)

We adopted a stray dog and named him Nar, which is the Kashmiri word for "fire"—he had reddish fur and a lot of energy. Unfortunately, he turned out to be aggressive and attacked a couple of cats, so we donated him to the ASPCA. I hope they found him an appropriate home. In his place, we took in a stray cat that we called Jay.

We also welcomed some family members to New York. My uncle Amin came to visit us in the summer of 1969. I arranged for him to use a spare bedroom in a nearby cottage in exchange for my trimming the hedges for its owner, a disabled war veteran. Amin still visits us in America practically every year.

In September 1970, my younger brother Tariq came to New York. At the time, he was a high school student without much interest in studying, and my father thought he might benefit from a visit with me. I signed him up to study television repair at a school run by RCA. Our idea was that Tariq could stay in the attic of our cottage—I even got a rope ladder he could use to climb up there—until we realized the attic was unbearably hot.

We needed to find a new, larger home in New York. We found a suitable place—the second floor of a house at 181 Falmouth Street in Manhattan Beach. However, we couldn't move in until the end of August, and the lease on our cottage ended in June. Farida and I rented a furnished room on Long Beach island for the summer, only to discover that the house was right in the path of planes landing at JFK airport. Somehow, we got used to the earthquake-like roar of their engines overhead, and I enjoyed swimming in the ocean off beautiful Long Beach. We even made space for Farida's father when he visited New York, pushing two twin beds together to create a larger bed that the three of us shared, sleeping sideways.

At the end of August, we moved to 181 Falmouth Street, where we had two bedrooms and a basement that provided a storage place for the arts and crafts products I was continuing to sell. Tariq came and stayed with us.

A year later, my younger brother Rafiq joined us. He had gotten into trouble for signing a paper threatening a revolt against Indian authorities in Kashmir. When he was released from prison after about six months, my father decided his best option might be to come to America and live with us. He arrived on a tourist visa in 1971.

Tariq and Rafiq both enrolled in colleges, and in their spare time I put them to work as salesmen for Kashmir Products Ltd. They stayed with us, enjoying Farida's cooking. In time, Rafiq earned two master's degrees—one in political science from the New School, the other in creative writing from Columbia University. Today he is a poet and divides his time among three places—New York, Kashmir, and Ireland, where he has a little cottage.

Sadly, our brother Tariq is no longer with us, having drowned while swimming in Goa in 2015.

• • •

WHILE WORKING FULL TIME for New Court Securities, I was continuing to build my business in Kashmiri products. In addition to selling traditional goods like those my grandfather had sent me, I was imagining new products, sharing the concepts with craftspeople back home, and offering the samples they created to my retail clients.

Even at that time, I was thinking in terms of branding—part of my mental DNA, which could be traced back to my family's history as merchants as well as to the marketing classes I'd taken at NYU. For example, I began to sell two kinds of traditional rugs made in Kashmir—one called a *numda,* made of wool felt with decorative embroidery, and one referred to as a chain-stitch rug with embroidery on cotton. I decided to give these two types of rugs my own distinctive brand names. I called the numda rugs Nagin, named after a lake in Kashmir, and the chain-stitch rugs Chinar, after the famous Kashmiri maple tree, known for its very large leaves and centuries-long lifespan.

I also began working on innovative design ideas. For example, while visiting a design center in Manhattan, I noticed a big photograph of the Grand Canyon. Finding it very striking, I got a similar photo and sent it back to Farida's father in Kashmir. "Is it possible for a craftsperson to turn this image into the chain-stitched design on a rug?" I asked.

"They can try," he responded. To that point, all the rugs we'd sold had traditional patterns, floral or geometric in style. Now the crafts-people responded to my request with a new type of rug, one with an abstract design that resembled the Grand Canyon photo I'd provided. I now had a new option to offer designers looking for something fresh and unique to bring to their clients.

In 1970, a new client relationship fell into my lap—one that would change my life forever.

It started with a remark from Roger Widmann, my friend and col-league from New Court Securities. "You know, our family is friendly with Nat Ancell, one of the founders of Ethan Allen. Would you like me to introduce you to him?"

I had no idea what Ethan Allen was, but I was always ready to meet a prospective customer. I went with Roger to see Nat Ancell at the Ethan Allen offices at 215 Lexington Avenue, near 33rd Street.

Nat greeted me and, after hearing about my background, called in one of his merchants. "This young man is from Kashmir," he told her. "Do we buy any products from there?"

"Yes," she replied. "We purchase crewel fabric from there. It's used in upholstering chairs and sofas, and also for other purposes like drap-eries. It's very good stuff. But we have a real problem with the supply. It never comes on time. I wish we could find a better source."

Nat turned to me and asked, "Can you help?"

"Absolutely," I replied, although I had no idea exactly how that would happen. I asked for more details about the problem.

The merchant explained that Ethan Allen was buying crewel fabric in four patterns from a New York supplier who imported goods from Kashmir, including a famous historic pattern called the Tree of Life. (This pattern, which originated in the Middle East over two thousand years ago, has been popular in Western cultures since the seventeenth century.) They gave me small samples, a yard or so in size, for each of these patterns.

"Okay," I said, "I'll send these to Kashmir and let you know what we can do."

I sent the samples to Farida's father, who had some of the local craftspeople produce copies that were returned to me. I visited Nat and his merchant again, and they looked them over.

"These look very good," the merchant said. "But the person whose quality approval you need is Hazel Hilton. If they pass muster with her, she'll start placing orders with you."

"Very good," I said, "I'll see her in the morning."

Nat and his merchant gave me a funny look. "In the morning?" they repeated. "You know, she's based in Maiden, North Carolina."

I'd never been there before. But how hard could it be to get there? "That's fine," I said. "I'll visit her tomorrow." And I made plans to take a sick day from New Court Securities.

The next day, I took a crack-of-dawn flight to Charlotte, rented a car, and drove to Maiden—a two-hour trip, since there was no highway to Maiden at that time.

Hazel Hilton turned out to be a feisty, no-nonsense lady with deep knowledge of the furniture business—especially the details of upholstery. She studied the fabric samples I showed her, turning them around in her hands to judge their quality, durability, and detailing.

"This is good work, young man," she finally declared. "And we've been having a lot of trouble with our usual supplier. So I'm ready to place an order with you. But I warn you—if the quality doesn't stand up, we're going to send it right back."

"Miss Hilton," I replied, "Do you mind if I ask a favor of you?"

"What's that?" she asked.

"May I have your photograph?"

She was startled. Was I trying to flirt with her, or even worse, make fun of her? "What do you want that for?" she demanded.

"I want to send your photograph to my craftspeople in Kashmir," I said. "I'm going to tell them that you are the person who's got to approve their work and that you are a very tough person. I want them to see your photograph and think about pleasing you as they do their work."

Hazel laughed. She gave me an order for four crewel fabric designs, 1,000 yards each—worth about $40,000, the equivalent of $250,000 in today's money. I sent the orders to Kashmir, for delivery in six months or so.

And in a few days I received Hazel's photo in the mail, which I also passed along to Kashmir.

When the fabric was ready, it was shipped to Ethan Allen's plant in Maiden for Hazel's approval. A few days later, she called me. "The fabric is good quality," she said, "but what's the bird doing in there?"

I was confused. At first I thought that perhaps a dead bird had somehow gotten into one of the packages. But Hazel went on to explain that the Tree of Life pattern used by Ethan Allen was a variant that did *not* include the image of a bird perched on a tree branch. The pattern my suppliers had followed was a slightly different version that included the bird. "This is not our design," Hazel said, "so we'll have to reject this batch of fabric." I realized that I should have sent my suppliers the full pattern, which would have shown them that no bird was featured.

"I understand," I said, and Hazel and I agreed that my craftspeople would produce a new supply of Tree of Life fabric with the pattern preferred by Ethan Allen.

"Meanwhile," I then said, "can you please send me one full cutting of the fabric, with a full repeat, showing the bird on it?" And she did.

I asked around and learned the names of some of the big interior design companies in New York—companies with names like Schumacher and Scalamandre, which dealt extensively in high-end fabrics. I arranged to visit one of the buyers at Schumacher, bringing with me samples of our products, including, for example, the embroidered Grand Canyon design.

"I like these fabrics," the buyer said, "and my favorite is this Tree of Life design." I'd shown him the pattern with the bird, which Ethan Allen was going to return.

"You know, you're very lucky," I told him. "This is one of our best patterns. And if you move fast, I might be able to set aside a thousand yards for you." So not only did I salvage a potentially costly mistake, but I also attracted a valuable new customer. I did the same with a number of other companies. In this way, I began developing relationships with many of the leading figures in the furniture and design industries.

A year later, in 1971, I got a call from Nat Ancell. He said, "Farooq, my vice president of merchandising says we're having big trouble getting a steady supply of rugs from India and Romania. Do you think you can help?"

Once again, I said, "Absolutely." Then I set about trying to figure out how to make it happen. At the time, I had no knowledge of rugs or their sourcing. I didn't even know where Romania was.

Ethan Allen was supplied by a leading rug importer, Couristan, which was owned by David Murad, a member of an Armenian family with decades of experience in rugs. I called him up. "Mr. Murad," I said, "I understand from your customer, Nat Ancell of Ethan Allen, that you are having trouble organizing the delivery of rugs. I'd like to help." And I invited him to have tea with me at our apartment.

Mr. Murad said he'd be happy to receive help. So we discussed the challenges of rug sourcing. He later showed me several small rugs, four by six feet in size, that were samples of the rugs they were having trouble buying. I asked him to cut the rugs in half to make them easier to carry and made plans to take my yearly week's vacation from New Court Securities.

Our family had a friend who was in the rug business in Agra. So I flew to India on a US travel document, carrying the sample rugs as my baggage, and I went with Farida's father to meet this man. He looked over the rugs and said, "This type of rug is not made here. They're made in the villages near Benares." Benares—now known as Varanasi—is a city in the northern Indian state of Uttar Pradesh. "In fact," he went on, "I know a man in the rug business in a village called Aurai, about forty miles south of the Benares airport. His name is Mr. Hai."

Farida's father and I traveled by overnight train to Benares and then took a taxi to Aurai, arriving there around six in the morning. Not knowing where the rug merchants might be, I simply started asking people on the street, "Where is Mr. Hai?" They wondered whether there was some kind of trouble afoot. But eventually, Mr. Hai appeared and asked us, in Urdu, "What's the problem?"

"No problem," I replied. "In fact, I've come from America to see you. I understand you are a fine supplier of rugs. Can you take a look at these rugs and tell me whether you can supply rugs to me on a regular basis?"

It quickly became clear that we had come to the right place. Mr. Hai had a large group of local rug makers who worked for him—men, women, and children, working in their homes, buying and dyeing the wool and then turning it into finished rugs through painstaking handwork, using skills passed down through the generations. (Today, children are no longer permitted to work in such businesses.) What's more, Mr. Hai had recently lost one of his best customers—an Australian company that had gone out of business—and so he was looking for someone to sell rugs to. Our timing was perfect.

"Do you sell any rugs in America?" I asked.

"No," Mr. Hai said.

"Then I will be your agent there," I told him. "In addition to buying rugs for Ethan Allen, I will line up other customers for you, and you'll give me 5 percent of the money they pay you. Give me a piece of paper, and we will draw up an agreement." We signed the document then and there.

The first sample rugs provided by Mr. Hai and his craftspeople were of high quality, so the executives at Couristan were very pleased—as was

Nat Ancell. So I became the supplier of Indian rugs to Couristan, who in turn sold them to Ethan Allen. And because Couristan was a well-known and highly regarded rug merchant, I was able to visit several other leading importers and say, "We have a significant rug manufacturing operation in India," using our deal with Couristan as my calling card. Soon I was channeling a lot of additional work to Mr. Hai and his craftspeople.

In this way, I was building my business as an importer of products not just from Kashmir but from other areas too. Of course, I was also beginning to develop a strong relationship of trust with one particular customer—Ethan Allen. I didn't know it at the time, but that would prove to be the most important relationship of all.

■ ■ ■

AT THE SAME TIME I was building the successful Kashmir Products Ltd., I was working full time for the Rothschilds at New Court Securities. However, after I completed my MBA studies at NYU in 1968, I decided to apply for some other jobs. I liked the people at New Court, and my career there had been successful, but I'd never really felt committed to working in finance. Marketing remained my greatest interest. So I sent out my resume to a range of companies.

The greatest interest I received came from Toronto Dominion Bank. After a positive interview in New York, they were almost ready to make me an offer, but the final hurdle was an interview at the home office in Canada.

One Friday evening, having had a successful interview in Toronto, I was about to fly home to New York when the American immigration officials took me off the plane. "What kind of papers are these?" they asked me. "You aren't supposed to be allowed to remain in the US with papers like these."

"That may be so," I said, "but I've been living peaceably in the US for years with these papers."

"Well, we're sorry, but there's no way we can let you reenter the US with these documents."

I called Farida, explained the problem, and she phoned our friends the Levys, who'd already helped me on so many previous occasions. Shirley Cherin got in touch with her partner, Mr. Galef, who promised to intervene on my behalf. But he warned me that nothing could be done over the weekend. So I took a room in a small motel near the Toronto airport and waited until Monday.

On Monday morning, I was surprised to get a call from the US immigration officer stationed at the Toronto Airport. He asked me to visit his office. When I did, he shook my hand and said, "You know, I've been doing this work for a long time, and this is the first time I've gotten a call from the head of immigration in New York saying about a detainee, 'Don't ask any questions. Just let him in.'" Within a couple of hours, I was on my way back to JFK.

Once again, my unusual immigration status, and the desire of the US not to create an international incident in regard to a region of the world where tensions ran high, had worked in my favor.

But I didn't want to have to deal with the uncertainty any longer. I went to John Birkelund, who by this time had become a friend and a mentor, and told him, "John, I've been thinking about taking another job. But I've decided that I want to stay here." He was pleased to hear this.

I also explained the problems with my immigration status and the anxiety it had caused me. "New Court Securities can help," John said. "We will sponsor your application for legal immigrant status."

I submitted the proper paperwork, and in less than six months, I got the green card that millions of people covet, which would allow me to remain and work in the United States permanently.

The green card was followed almost immediately by a notice to register for the draft. I went down to my local draft board and gave them all my information. Fortunately for me, the Vietnam War was finally beginning to wind down at that time, which reduced the demand for soldiers. I was never called to serve, which left me free to focus on my career and my family.

I continued to work hard at New Court and was rewarded with a series of promotions: to assistant vice president, to vice president, and finally, in 1972, to chief financial officer. I was deeply engaged in the company's financial dealings, helping administer the Five Arrows Fund, working on computerizing the company's records, and arranging to have the firm registered on the stock exchanges of Chicago and Luxembourg.

Even the chairman of the holding company that owned New Court, Baron Guy de Rothschild, came to know me. On one of his visits from Paris, he asked John Birkelund (in my presence), "I see this young man has the authority to make decisions involving millions of dollars on behalf of the company. Why have you given him so much power?"

Before John could respond, I chimed in. "Let me explain, Baron Guy," I said. "I was born in Kashmir, which the people from the region call Kasheer. And a person from Kasheer is called Koshur." Koshur is pronounced the same as the English word kosher. "So it's only right that I should be given authority in a firm owned by the Rothschilds, because I am more kosher than anyone here!"

As I was offering this explanation, John Birkelund was smiling. I've used this line many times since then, and it always seems to get a positive response. Baron Guy certainly found it amusing.

Of course, there's a more serious reason why I'd been given so much authority at such a young age, and that is my instinctive readiness to take the lead when confronted with a problem—to study an issue, develop a plan of action, and execute it. Every human being has a distinctive set of strengths, weaknesses, and gifts, and success comes from making the most of the traits you've been given. I've been lucky enough to understand this from an early age.

. . .

FOR FARIDA AND ME, THE 1970s brought many changes. Our first child, our son Irfan, was born at Maimonides Hospital in Brooklyn on November 22, 1971. He was followed by a sister, Farah, on October 23, 1974, and a brother, Omar, on August 12, 1977, both born in New Rochelle Hospital. All three children were healthy and strong, but in the process of childbirth Farida discovered that she suffered from a heart problem that the doctors called mitral valve prolapse. It may have been the result of an untreated case of strep throat when she was a child. It caused her no problems at the time, but it would have consequences later.

Our family also made two moves—first to Manhattan, then to New Rochelle.

I'd commuted for years from Brooklyn to Manhattan on the D train, where I got to know a fellow straphanger named Mr. Mitzkin. One day, Mr. Mitzkin asked, "Farooq, why don't you live in Manhattan? You won't need to take this long subway ride every day." When he found my reasons unconvincing, he said, "Come with me, I'll show you something." And he took me to see a building he owned—1049 Park Avenue, near 86th Street, famous as the apartment building in which Felix Unger and Oscar Madison live in the movie *The Odd Couple*. Mr. Mitzkin offered me a six-room apartment at a very reasonable rent of $600, so Farida and I decided to make the move.

At the time, Rafiq and Tariq were living with us. We rented a truck to move our things, including all the crewel fabric and rugs we had in our basement. When the doorman saw the three of us unloading the truck, he turned up his nose and announced, "Delivery men use the back entrance." We followed his instructions. Of course, the next day he saw us coming out the front door in our suits and ties, and he realized we were residents, not delivery men at all.

A year later, we were on the move again. Farida and I were invited for lunch at the home of Dick Sandberg, a colleague from New Court who lived in New Rochelle. We fell in love with the diverse community and decided it would be a beautiful place to raise our children. When we discovered an empty house built in the 1920s just around the corner from Dick, we quickly bought it. It had an old, unused, and overgrown clay tennis court that we cleared and refurbished, and I became an avid tennis player. I discovered that Nat Ancell also lived in New Rochelle, and he became not just a customer but a family friend. Our children learned to call him Bumpa, an Eastern European nickname for Grandpa. My grandchildren now use the same name for me.

All in all, New Rochelle proved to be the perfect home for our growing family.

In 1973, I was finally able to get a visa from the Indian government that would allow me to travel back home to Kashmir. Farida and I made the journey with our young son Irfan.

My grandfather arranged a get-together in his home where we had the opportunity to meet with many notable people from Srinagar. Two of those in attendance were Sheikh Abdullah, the great Kashmiri leader I've mentioned before, and Mirwaiz Farooq, the chief religious leader of Kashmir, who had performed our telephone wedding.

We all sat cross-legged on the carpet in the great hall, exchanging stories and talking about our lives. At a certain point in the conversation, Sheikh Abdullah turned to me and asked, "What are your plans?" I think he was wondering whether I would remain in America or return home to Kashmir—perhaps to become involved in government, as my father had done.

"Sheikh Sahib," I replied, "I did not leave Kashmir completely willingly. But when I was invited to study in America, it was logical for me to go. As for the future, tell me—what do you think someone like me should do?"

"You should come and join me," he replied.

This was no light statement from a very highly respected leader. So I chose the words of my response carefully. "Well, sir," I said, "with all due respect, I'd have a tough time joining you, because I really don't know what you stand for."

My grandfather was sitting next to me. I felt his hand touch my leg, as if to caution me, *Watch what you are saying.*

"You don't know what I stand for?" Sheikh Abdullah replied.

"No, sir," I said.

He responded with a long story about his own life—about how he and his father had felt humiliated by the Dogras, the Jammu-based rulers of Kashmir, and about how this experience had led him to make a vow to fight them.

I did not completely understand how his story would forward the work of bringing dignity to the people of Kashmir. When he looked at me for a response, I said, "Sir, you have said it all, and I understand and appreciate it. But what I want to know is, Do you stand for independence for Kashmir, or not?"

Sheikh Abdullah paused, then said, "How can we be independent? We have to deal with India. We have no choice."

"I see, sir," I replied. "If that is your answer, then I am not going to join you."

This was a daring statement to make—the kind of language very few people had ever used when speaking to Sheikh Abdullah, I'm sure. It was even more surprising because the setting was quasi-public, since a number of well-connected journalists were among those in attendance.

In fact, the exchange between us made news, because it was the first time that Sheikh Abdullah had explicitly renounced the idea of independence from India. And it soon became known that, at that very time, Sheikh Abdullah had been engaging in talks with Indian prime minister Indira Gandhi that would lead to his being named prime minister of Kashmir again just a year later.

After a couple of weeks in Kashmir, Farida, Irfan, and I returned home. This was the first of a series of such trips that we would make in the years to come, allowing us to nurture our ties with our homeland and also to let our children learn about their heritage.

Three years later, in 1976—the year of the American bicentennial celebration—I passed the test to become a US citizen. I took the oath of allegiance in downtown Manhattan. A few years later, Farida followed suit.

We will always love and cherish our ancestral ties to Kashmir. But we and our children are happy and proud to call America our home.

6

SPREADING MY ENTREPRENEURIAL WINGS

IN 1973, NAT ANCELL made me a proposition. "Farooq, you're a merchant at heart," he told me. "Why don't you leave New Court Securities and join Ethan Allen?"

I'd thought about the idea before, and I was ready with an answer. "I'm flattered by your offer, Nat," I said. "But why don't we set up a joint venture instead?"

By then, I'd been supplying Ethan Allen with merchandise through Kashmir Products Ltd. for about three years. I'd gotten to know Ethan Allen well. Founded in 1932 by Nat Ancell and Ted Baumritter, it had grown into the world's leading maker of American colonial-style furniture, with some thirty manufacturing plants, mostly in the Northeast and Southeast regions of the US. In the 1930s and 1940s, Ethan Allen had also pioneered the gallery concept in furniture retailing, persuading department stores to set up Ethan Allen showrooms within their furniture departments. Later, in the 1960s, the company worked with families and individual entrepreneurs to open up freestanding Ethan

Allen galleries. By the 1970s, there were some 250 independent stores operating under the Ethan Allen gallery umbrella, selling furniture as well as additional items—lighting fixtures, rugs, accessories—from a variety of sources, including, of course, Kashmir Products Ltd.

As for Nat Ancell, the company CEO, he was a complicated person. His family had its roots in Eastern Europe and had been impacted by the Holocaust. Nat himself had been trained as a lawyer. He was bright, very opinionated, and in his own way a visionary, having largely developed the Ethan Allen gallery concept.

His brother-in-law and co-founder, Ted Baumritter, was more of a salesman—the man who used his powers of persuasion to convince the dealers to support Nat's ideas. Ted had long played a lesser role in managing Ethan Allen. Ted's daughter was married to Howard Jacobs, who owned and ran several Ethan Allen stores in Orange County, California. Nat and Ted had taken Ethan Allen public in the mid-1960s.

I respected Ethan Allen and enjoyed having the company as my customer. I wasn't sure I wanted to become an employee of Ethan Allen.

"A joint venture, eh?" Nat replied. "It's an interesting idea. Why don't you draw up a detailed proposal?"

So I did. I suggested we create a company called KEA International, which would, in effect, absorb the old Kashmir Products Ltd. The goal of the business would be to serve as a supplier of all kinds of non-furniture products to Ethan Allen dealers and to other customers—things like lighting fixtures, rugs, decorative items, accessories, and so on. I would own 60 percent of the business, while Ethan Allen would own 40 percent. We'd need $100,000 in capital to start with, of which I would provide $10,000. (I only had about half that amount in the bank at that time, so I got the rest through a cash advance against a credit card.) The rest would be loaned to the new business by Ethan Allen.

Nat invited me to discuss the proposal over lunch with him and two of his top lieutenants. Clint Walker was president of Ethan Allen. A New Englander and an engineer by training, he'd joined the company before the war, taken time out to serve in the military, then rejoined the firm, focusing on manufacturing. Tom Swanston was senior vice president of marketing, a very bright man with an MBA from Harvard. The three of us met in Nat's office, and all agreed that my proposal was fair and that the prospects for the business seemed strong. So the notion of a joint venture—a first for Ethan Allen—was accepted.

Now I had to break the news to John Birkelund, the CEO of New Court Securities, who had done so much to support and help me in my career.

After hearing about my business plan, Birkelund's response was characteristically thoughtful. "Are you sure you want to give up everything you've achieved at New Court for an unproven venture? Any new business is risky. You have a good job here and a great future. We'd hate to see you go. In time, we could see our way to giving you a share in our firm's equity."

"I appreciate what you're saying, John," I replied, "but I've realized I'm an entrepreneur by nature. I feel as though I've got to give this new business a try."

"Okay," Birkelund said. "But do me a favor—and do yourself one at the same time. Take a couple of months to work out the details of your business, make your plans, and so on. Meanwhile, don't say a word to anyone here. After two months, if you're still convinced it's the right move, then go ahead, with our blessing."

This was wise advice. I did as Birkelund suggested, and after two months I went to him and said, "John, I'm going to go out on my own. The more I think about it, the more I realize that there's only one reason for me *not* to do it—because I'm scared, and being scared is not a good reason."

And so I became president of KEA International.

. . .

The first thing I needed was an office. It happened that Ethan Allen had just built its new headquarters in Danbury, Connecticut. So Nat Ancell said to me, "How about taking over my old office in Manhattan? It's on the top floor of a good building with great views and plenty of space."

At first, the idea seemed silly. At the moment, KEA International would consist of one employee (me) with perhaps a part-time assistant to answer the telephone. I had no use for 3,000 square feet of office space, and I'd figured that my budget for rent was all of $400 per month. "What would I do with all that space?" I asked Nat.

"Well, I'm sure I'll be visiting the city from time to time. You can set aside an office for me to use."

"All right," I said. "If you rent me the whole place for $400, I'll keep an eye on things for you and make sure an office is ready for your visits."

"Okay, kiddo," Nat said with a smile. "But you've also got to buy all our old office furniture. That includes the boardroom table with the fifty captain's chairs." We talked it over and agreed on a relatively modest price that my cash flow would bear. So now I had a huge, well-furnished office suite that I hoped my new business would some-day grow to fit.

I also needed a warehouse for my fabrics. First, I rented one in a loft on East 28th Street in Manhattan. But because I had only a short-term lease there, I kept my eyes open for an alternative. I spotted one near the train station in suburban Larchmont, where I used to catch the commuter line from my home into the city. It was a vacant building that formerly housed a bowling alley. The entire place was 22,000 square feet, but I only needed a fraction of that; so I struck a deal with the owner, Mr. Friedman, to rent 1,000 square feet for around $150 a month.

A few months later, Mr. Friedman stopped by and noticed that KEA International was using almost the entire building. "What's going on?" he demanded.

"The building is empty, so I'm keeping an eye on it for you," I explained.

"Sorry, that won't fly," Mr. Friedman responded. "If you're going to use the whole place, either rent it all or buy it from me."

I agreed to buy the building if Mr. Friedman would give me a mortgage, which he did. So the former Larchmont Lanes became the new headquarters of KEA International.

Now that I had official use of the entire space, I realized the building needed quite a bit of work. I asked Mr. Friedman about a reliable contractor, and he introduced me to Lou Grasso, based in New Rochelle. I hired Lou to renovate the building for me, and that began forty years (so far) of an enjoyable relationship between us, with Lou managing countless construction jobs, big and small, both for Ethan Allen and for me and my family.

The launch of KEA as a joint venture also meant that I would now be working much more closely with the whole Ethan Allen team. Up to that time, I had dealt mainly with Nat Ancell and with a few of his key buyers, such as Hazel Hilton and the rug specialist. Now I began to meet many of the company's long-serving executives. In addition to Clint Walker and Tom Swanston, there was Pat Norton, a decorated war hero who was the vice president of sales, a man with a very strong personality. There was Larry Thompson, a native of Vermont, who was the senior vice president of distribution and logistics. And there was Philip Caroselli, an industry veteran who had recently been hired from Macy's to serve as the vice president of merchandising.

Other company leaders I got to know included Bob Ficks, vice president of advertising; Stanley Harris, vice president of store development; Lenny Silverman, vice president of finance; Skip Curcio, vice president of human resources; Walter Biadasz, vice president of upholstery manufacturing; and Hank Walker (Clint Walker's brother), vice president of wood manufacturing. Other vice presidents were in charge of manufacturing operations in various regions of the country—the Northeast, the South, and the Midwest.

All in all, the company employed close to five thousand people, including over 550 at the Danbury headquarters. It was by far the largest organization I'd ever been associated with. I realized quickly that I had to invest time and energy in getting to know people, and in letting them know me.

Like most furniture makers, Ethan Allen exhibited its products at the semiannual High Point Market in North Carolina. Nat Ancell and I got into the habit of traveling to this show together, flying down to Greensboro and then renting a car, which I would drive. This sent a signal to the industry that I had taken on a significant role in the leadership of our company. It also gave me an opportunity to meet many Ethan Allen dealers, themselves important figures in the business. Some owned multiple galleries in various locations, which meant that their opinions of the new styles and products we introduced could play a big role in determining how successful these would be. I befriended many of these dealers and paid a lot of attention to the ideas they shared with me, since they were based on many years of experience in the furniture industry.

Many of the dealerships were run as family businesses, with the husband taking care of the operational side, and the wife taking care of the design side. A number of these women were very smart and well respected in the industry. So I approached several of them and said, "I want to set up an advisory committee, and I want you to be a member." They included Laurie Landau, whose family operated an Ethan Allen in New Jersey; Joyce Chesnik in Houston; Hilda Flack in Memphis, Tennessee; Iris Tapplitz in Pittsburgh; and Carol Feldman in Atlanta. Not only did I rely on them for advice and ideas about our product styles, but I also invited them to join me on some of my business trips, such as when I visited suppliers in Italy (as I'll explain later).

I also came to spend more time with the company president, Clint

Walker. Clint and his wife, Janet, would come to play tennis with us in New Rochelle. He was a down-to-earth, soft-spoken New Englander, and we got along well together.

My efforts to get up to speed on the Ethan Allen system and culture were just beginning when tragedy struck Nat Ancell. Late in 1973, Nat's wife, Edith, died, a devastating experience for any husband. Soon thereafter, Nat himself suffered a health emergency that sent him to the hospital for several weeks and that required additional months of recovery at home. As a result, effective leadership of Ethan Allen was turned over to other executives, particularly Clint Walker, Pat Norton, Tom Swanston, and Phil Caroselli. I came to know all of them well and found them very supportive of my ideas and appreciative of my contributions to the business. I developed a particularly close relationship with Harold Golderberg, one of the senior merchants who worked for Phil Caroselli. All the merchants involved in buying accessories and rugs reported to him, and as our business grew, Harold would travel with me to Italy and other countries to look at products.

One of the first tasks I took on was building our international supply chain for accessories and other products. Initially, the main countries that Ethan Allen dealt with were Italy and Belgium. Through Nat Ancell and other contacts, I got to know Maurizio and Roberto, two young men who had just started a business called InterExport, based in Florence. I made a deal with them to become a buying agent for KEA, and through the 1970s I traveled to Italy three or four times a year, driving from Rome to Florence, Venice, Milan, and other cities, sometimes even sleeping in the car.

In a similar way, I contacted Banque Lambert, owned by members of the Rothschild families and shareholders of New Court Securities. They connected me to a well-known Belgian family named Lano who were rug producers in the Ghent region. They, too, became long-term suppliers to KEA.

Working with merchant suppliers sometimes posed unexpected

challenges. For example, I met an Italian man named Silvano Salvadori who owned a small company that made beautiful furniture out of brass, steel, and other metals. I liked Silvano's products, so I was distressed when he told me, "I've got financial problems. A customer in Florida owes me a lot of money and can't pay up. I'm afraid I'm going to have to shut down my business."

I didn't want to see him go, nor did I want to lose a good source of products. "What do you need to stay afloat?" I asked.

"Fifty thousand dollars would do it," he replied.

Luckily, one of the first things I'd done after launching KEA was to create a relationship with Chemical Bank, the bank that served Ethan Allen. I'd met with their banker, Don Wilson, and hosted him on a visit to KEA's headquarters in Larchmont. When I asked about arranging a million-dollar line of credit—a pretty big request for a fledgling business with just $100,000 in capital—Wilson okayed it, so long as Ethan Allen supplied what was called a "cold-comfort letter." This was a letter confirming that Ethan Allen intended to continue doing business with KEA, although no guarantees were offered. Nat Ancell wrote the letter, and Chemical Bank provided the line of credit.

This enabled me to give Silvano a loan to keep his company alive. Over the coming years, he became one of KEA's most trusted and valuable suppliers. And years later, Don Wilson of Chemical Bank served on the board of Ethan Allen.

Other countries in Europe became sources of various types of merchandise for KEA. For example, we bought chandeliers from Spain, crystal bowls and other products from a region of Germany close to the Czech border, and metal objects made in Holland using raw materials imported from Indonesia.

Next, I turned my attention to building our supply chain in South Asia.

Ethan Allen had been buying crewel fabric from Kashmir for some time, but the supply was still unpredictable. The problem was that the local producers were not properly controlling the quality of raw materials or the standards of production. So in 1974, I journeyed to Kashmir to tackle the issue directly.

Over a cup of coffee, I discussed the matter with Ibrahim Shahdad, a brother-in-law of Farida's. "All the people I meet say that the way crewel fabric is produced here is something that can't be changed," I said. "But I'd like to set up a more organized system for it. Can you suggest someone who might be interested in managing this for me? Is it something you would consider doing?"

Shahdad was dubious. "You know, I just graduated from law school," he said, "and I really have no business background. I'm starting a criminal law practice."

"That's perfect," I said. "I want somebody who's got common sense, who's a doer, and doesn't know much about business. Give it a year and a half. If it doesn't work out, you can always go back to the law. Those criminals are not going to go away."

Shahdad accepted my offer. We set up a company called Budshah Enterprises, named after a famous Kashmiri king of the sixteenth century who had helped bring arts and crafts from Iran and Central Asia to Kashmir. Then we went to visit the most successful local crewel merchant to get a feeling for how he did business. We found him sitting on a wooden platform in a large hall, smoking a hookah and inspecting bundles of fabric as they were delivered by the local cottage workers who'd produced them.

Afterward, I said to Shahdad, "Ibrahim, you have to do everything that fellow does. Get rid of your suits and ties, and start wearing a *shalwar kameez*. Then we'll build you a wooden platform to sit on, and you'll run your business just like a traditional crewel merchant." And that's what we did.

Just as with Italy and Belgium, I got into the habit of visiting Kashmir every three or four months to see how the business was doing. I was pleased with our progress, but I still thought we were missing opportunities to improve and expand our operations. So on one visit, I asked Shahdad, "Where does the wool come from?"

"We buy it in the local market," he said.

"But where does it come from?"

"Rajasthan in India."

"In that case," I said, "you should go to Rajasthan and figure out what you can do to ensure a steady, reliable supply."

I asked similar questions about the dyes and the cotton fabric used in making the embroidery. I learned that the dyes came from Bombay, and the cotton came from a village called Panipat near Delhi. I urged Shahdad to visit all three places.

He followed my advice, and little by little he tracked down the manufacturers who were producing all these raw materials. He made deals with them directly, bypassing the middlemen with whom he'd previously dealt. Now we had control over our supplies, which meant our production processes could be more reliable and predictable. What's more, we saved money because we were one of the biggest customers for these materials. These improvements enabled us to expand our business, selling crewel not just to Ethan Allen but to other furniture makers, and gradually becoming the largest crewel merchants in Kashmir.

We didn't stop there. Further inquiries told us that most of the artisans who produced our crewel were villagers who worked mainly during the winter, when it was too cold to work in the fields. They got their supplies of raw materials from us through individual agents who would travel to Srinagar, pick up bundles of fabric and other supplies, and carry them back to the villages, all by bus. This was a recipe for delays, inconsistency, and inconvenience, both for us and for the craftspeople.

I suggested a simple solution: "Ibrahim, why don't we buy a van and take the supplies to them?" We did that, and on the return trips we transported the finished fabrics to our warehouse in Srinagar. This system made life easier for the workers and also greatly increased their productivity—a classic win-win.

Ibrahim also became involved in helping me manage the flow of rugs from India. I'd fly into the Varanasi airport periodically to meet with Mr. Hai, who was our main supplier, and Ibrahim would accompany me.

Eventually, I became aware that there was a problem with Mr. Hai. In addition to shipping us rugs to sell to Ethan Allen retailers, he was selling rugs to other US importers through deals that I'd arranged for him—which meant, according to our agreement, that he owed KEA 5 percent of his revenues. But the money never arrived.

I put up with it for a year or two, during a period when demand for Indian rugs was so high that I didn't want to rock the boat with our main supplier. But then the market turned, and supply began to outstrip demand.

On one of my trips to India, Mr. Hai met me with a car at the Benares airport. He mentioned that his driver had lost an eye in an accident but was a fast driver.

"Let him sit in the back seat," I said. "I'll do the driving." I'd had practice on plenty of bad roads, and I preferred to be behind the wheel myself.

As I drove, we talked about economic conditions. "How is the rug business?" I asked.

"Not good, not good," Mr. Hai said, shaking his head. "Many of my friends are having their orders cancelled."

"What about *your* business?" I said.

"Our business is good, very good. You are keeping us very busy!"

"Well, I am thinking of cancelling some of my orders with you."

Mr. Hai looked stricken. "That would destroy me," he said.

"Well, you know, trust is a two-way street. You've never paid me the 5 percent you owe me. Maybe I have no choice but to cancel my orders. Think about it."

Ibrahim and I continued our inspection tour, and later that evening Mr. Hai came to us. "I've been thinking about what you said," he told me, "and I think we should pay you."

"Okay," I said. "Here is what I want you to do. Get a tin trunk, and put in it half of the money you owe us, in cash." I don't remember the exact amount now, but it must have been the equivalent of about $10,000. "Give the trunk to Ibrahim, and he will take it to Kashmir."

This plan made Ibrahim very nervous—he didn't like the idea of carrying that much cash. But I persuaded him to pack it in a large suitcase, and the money arrived safely with him in Kashmir. Most of it was given to charity. A couple of months later, Mr. Hai himself traveled to Kashmir with the rest of the money.

We continued to do business with Mr. Hai. The important thing is that the message got around among the other merchants in the region: Farooq Kathwari is a patient man, but his patience has some limits.

In 1975, I decided it was time to begin exploring the possibilities of doing business in China. I got a visa to attend the international trade fair in Canton (now known as Guangzhou) and caught a train from Hong Kong, where KEA already had a small presence. On the train, I sat next to a European businessman who put himself forward as an expert on China and the Chinese. As we departed the Hong Kong station, I noticed him speaking loudly and rudely to the conductor. When I asked him about it, he declared, "That's the way you have to treat these people—it's the only language they understand!"

Later that day, we crossed the border into the People's Republic. The government agent on the train gave us a long lecture about the Cultural Revolution and distributed copies of the famous "Little Red Book" containing the sayings of Mao Tse-tung. (I still have my copy.) After this, the tone of my European acquaintance changed. He became very quiet and respectful, almost deferential. "What about treating the officials rudely?" I asked.

"It's different here," the man replied. "Here you have to be very careful, or they'll throw you out. That's why I don't dare try to negotiate with them. I just take the price they offer. That's the way things are."

I was puzzled. It seemed to me that the Chinese people on both sides of the border were very much the same. I decided to take the man's advice with a grain of salt and draw my own conclusions.

I settled down in the Tung Feng hotel, the main one then available in Canton for foreigners, adjacent to the grounds of the trade fair. One afternoon, during the daily four-hour rest break that started at noon, I noticed a group of Chinese men playing badminton in the hotel courtyard. I went down there, took off my shoes, and started playing with them. (I'd been captain of the badminton team in college back in Kashmir.) We struck up a conversation, and I discovered that several of the players were important figures in Chinese government and business—for example, representatives of the China Arts and Crafts office and the China National Native Product and Animal By-Products agency, which dealt in goods made with wool and cotton.

I told them what my German acquaintance had told me about not being able to negotiate with the Chinese, and they all laughed. One of them explained, "It's true that we are not authorized to negotiate with foreigners. But we can make you an agent. Once you have this title, we can give you a certain percentage as an agent's fee—5 percent, 8 percent." Armed with this simple tip, I arranged to become an agent for Chinese companies and so made KEA eligible for a discount on everything we purchased from China. Over time, China grew into a significant source of products for us.

Meanwhile, back in the United States, I had built a small support team working out of KEA headquarters in Larchmont. My first two employees were Bert and Floyd, both from the Caribbean, who worked with me for years. Later they were joined by Jack Moll, who became my first plant manager. They would drive a truck to the piers to pick up shipments of goods from overseas (occasionally I did the driving).

Then we'd prepare the products for delivery to Ethan Allen's distribution centers. In some cases, this involved a fair amount of work. For example, the metal tables that Silvano Salvadori made for us in Italy arrived unassembled. So my workers and I would screw the parts together, install the glass tops, and then wrap the finished tables for shipment—all to the tune of about a thousand tables per month.

In time, the size of my team grew to about ten, and when we ran out of space in Larchmont, I rented a second space in Port Chester. During the seven years that I ran KEA, it grew into a $10 million business—although the products we sold, mostly to Ethan Allen, had a retail value about three times as great.

• • •

NAT ANCELL RECOVERED his health and returned to Ethan Allen after three years on the sidelines. He continued to run the company until 1980, when he and Ted Baumritter, his co-founder, decided to sell it.

In 1979, a St. Louis–based conglomerate named Interco offered to buy Ethan Allen. Interco had originally been built by acquiring apparel companies, such as Florsheim, Converse shoes, and the London Fog company. They then decided to branch out into furniture. After some negotiations, they made a deal with Nat and Ted to buy Ethan Allen for about $150 million. Soon thereafter, they bought two other major furniture makers—Broyhill Furniture Industries and Lane Company—thereby becoming, for a time, the largest furniture-producing company in the United States.

Having sold Ethan Allen but retaining his position as CEO, Nat renewed his invitation to me to join the company's leadership team. Once again, I held back. "I appreciate the offer, Nat," I told him, "but I like what I'm doing, and with my family in New Rochelle, I'm not eager to move to Danbury."

Nat pressed me to change my mind. So I told him, "I don't really want to join Ethan Allen. But if I ever did, it would have to be in your job." I thought this would end the conversation.

We were sitting in Nat's office at the time. Nat called Clint Walker, the company president, whose office was next door, and asked him to join us. "C.W.," he said, "I just asked Farooq to join Ethan Allen, and he said he would only do it if he could become CEO. What do you think of that?"

Clint had a low-key, understated style. He simply smiled and said, "Well, maybe Farooq has a point."

Nat smiled back, then turned to me. "Farooq, I cannot promise that if you join Ethan Allen, you will become CEO one day. But you will have that opportunity if you prove yourself."

This was a big concession from the man who had shaped the company from its founding. "You don't need to promise," I replied, "but keep in mind that, if I do join you, that will be my ultimate goal."

So now we began discussing in earnest the possibility of my joining Ethan Allen. We decided that I would sell KEA to Ethan Allen (which meant, of course, to Interco as well), for about $2 million—a hefty sum at that time. I remained president of KEA, but now I was also an executive of Ethan Allen.

There was a bit of fallout from this move. Pat Norton, the senior vice president of sales, resigned to join the La-Z-Boy furniture company. He'd hoped to become CEO of Ethan Allen one day, and my arrival in the executive suite made him conclude that the chance of this happening was slim. Norton soon became chairman and CEO of La-Z-Boy, which he successfully grew into a chain of stores somewhat similar in concept to Ethan Allen.

Meanwhile, Nat Ancell asked for my help in dealing with a series of businesses that were struggling.

The first was a business called Ethan Allen Contemporary, based in Florida. This was the company's first attempt to diversify its portfolio beyond the colonial American style on which its success had been based. I visited with the man who was running the company, a highly experienced merchant named Mr. Sperling. He would visit the annual furniture show at High Point and pick out contemporary styles to sell at two large stores, one in Palm Beach and the other near Fort Lauderdale. An enormous warehouse, also in Fort Lauderdale, serviced both retail locations.

I quickly concluded that the company had expanded too quickly to support the level of demand. Within a week, I closed one of the two stores, having managed to find someone who was willing to rent it from us. I also got rid of the oversized warehouse and replaced it with a much smaller facility.

Back in Danbury, I ran into Nat Ancell. "What do you think I should do with the contemporary business?" he asked me.

"I've already done it," I told him and explained the moves I'd made.

Nat was surprised. "Why didn't you discuss these ideas with me?" he asked.

"You said, 'Go and take care of it,' and so I did."

Nat wasn't used to having his team members act so decisively. But he endorsed my decisions, because he could see they made good sense. The incident was an illustration of our differing management styles. An entrepreneur at heart, I made decisions by my gut and moved quickly once I had a feeling for a situation. This approach ruffled some feathers within the more traditional, hierarchical management system that characterized Ethan Allen then.

The second challenge was a group of three furniture makers Nat had purchased, all of which were struggling financially. One was Knob Creek, a maker of decorative furniture and upholstery with two plants in Morganton, North Carolina, that had been founded by a dentist named Jerry McBrayer. A second was Kling Furniture, based in western New York, which made cherry furniture that it sold to Ethan Allen as well as to other companies. The third was Kenmar, an upholstery maker located in East Palestine, Ohio. All three purchases had been part of a long-standing Ethan Allen strategy to continually expand its manufacturing capacities.

I looked closely at the three businesses and realized there was nothing fundamentally wrong with any of them. But operating them separately meant wasteful spending on duplicate administrative, sales, and managerial costs. I combined the three companies under the Knob Creek name and found ways to trim the excess staff. Having to let go of fifty to sixty people was difficult, and we did our best to minimize the pain by offering generous severance terms. These steps saved the companies and enabled them to be productive and profitable again.

The last challenge Nat presented to me was the Ethan Allen Hotel, located near the company headquarters in Danbury. In the back of his mind, Nat had the idea that the company might one day develop a chain of hotels, but he never got around to doing it—and in the meantime, although the hotel was handy for out-of-town visitors to Ethan Allen, it was losing money. I worked with the hotel's managers to improve their marketing and merchandising methods, and we turned it around. We also expanded it by one hundred rooms and added a large conference/banquet center with room to host more than five hundred people. Today, the hotel is still in business, and it is an important landmark in the Danbury area.

These tasks gave me additional exposure within Ethan Allen. They also gave me practice in taking on troubled businesses and using innovation to improve the bottom line. As a result, I grew in both self-confidence and in credibility among my colleagues.

■ ■ ■

DECEMBER 23, 1980, was one of the coldest days of the year in upstate New York—a good twenty degrees below freezing. I remember it well, because that was the day when Farida and I, and our three children, first set eyes on what would become our family farm.

It happened like this. That fall, Charlie Flood and his wife, Kristin Gamble, both associates of mine at New Court Securities, had invited us to visit their house near Hudson, New York. Farida and I were charmed by the area, and we decided we'd like to own a place of our own nearby. We spoke with a real estate broker, who initially showed us a house that the Rockefeller family was interested in selling. (They were, and are, major landowners in the area.) That house was a little small for us, so I told the broker, "You know, I like to take on projects. Maybe you can find me a bigger place that I can put my own stamp on."

The broker soon called us back to say, "If you like projects, I have a farm you might want to see."

The farmhouse the broker showed us had been built in the 1850s. It was owned by the Giambalvo family, who'd immigrated from Italy and moved from Brooklyn to the town of Livingston during the Great Depression. Since then, Mario and Santo Giambalvo, together with their sister, had operated the two-hundred-acre farm, which included a barn that housed dairy cows, coops for chickens, and orchards where some six thousand trees produced pears, plums, cherries, and apples. We met the Giambalvos in the farmhouse, which was terribly cold that day—the kitchen had a wood-burning stove, and there was a kerosene heater in the living room, but those were the only two sources of warmth.

When it comes to making business decisions—including buying a house—I operate more from instinct than from analysis. We sat with the Giambalvos and chatted. "I'm interested in buying the farm," I said, "but why do you want to sell it? What are your plans?"

They said, "We want to continue to live around here. We've already built another house nearby, and that's where we plan to move."

I said, "Will you work with me, then?"

They agreed. The Giambalvos were willing to give me a mortgage to purchase the farm, and help us run the property in the future. Farida and I decided to keep our home in New Rochelle and use the farm as a part-time residence.

The following spring, we were ready to move into the farm when Farida's heart problem took a turn for the worse. She was suffering from shortness of breath and other symptoms, and her doctors recommended open-heart surgery to open or replace her mitral valve. Farida was admitted to Mt. Sinai Hospital in New York, and the mitral valve was opened. (Thirty years later, she would have a second round of open-heart surgery during which the mitral valve was replaced.)

The outcome was good, but of course open-heart surgery is always a major physical trauma. We delayed our move to the farm by four or five weeks, and Farida's parents came to stay with us. In retrospect, I wish we'd put off the move even longer. The journey to Hudson and the adjustment to the new home were stressful for her, although she quickly came to love the farm. We spent several weeks there in the spring of 1981, and ever since then it has served as our home for large portions of the year.

Charlie Flood introduced us to a skilled local carpenter and jack-of-all-trades by the name of Tom Rowe, who helped us renovate and upgrade the farmhouse—installing central heating, adding a second bathroom, and otherwise improving it to modern standards.

The Giambalvos had shut down the dairy operations of the farm. But we kept the fruit orchards going, in part because most of the work on them was done by outside workers that the Giambalvos hired and supervised. Santo and Mario also did general maintenance and caretaking of the property—cutting the grass, trimming the trees, keeping the fences in repair, and so on. Children of the Depression, they were very careful about husbanding resources, an attitude I appreciated.

Soon after we moved in, I asked Santo, "What sorts of improvements would you like to make around the farm?"

"Well," he replied, "there's a watering hole and a natural spring that the cows used to drink from. I've always wanted to turn it into a pond."

"Let's do it," I said. "Do you know anybody who's good at building ponds?" We brought in a skilled local man who built two small dams on our property, creating beautiful ponds, the larger one fully three acres in size. It was the kind of project that would be difficult to do today because of the need for extensive environmental studies, but back then the rules were less stringent.

We also worked with Tom Rowe to transform the old dairy barn into a house. Tom brought in a couple of workers to strengthen the structure (it had been tilting badly to one side) and convert the connected silo into a four-room annex, including a circular staircase. We originally planned to use the renovated barn as our guesthouse, but we liked it so much that we now use it as our main home, with the original farmhouse accommodating guests.

The farm became an important element in our family life, especially in the upbringing of our children. They loved the freedom of being able to play outside in the world of nature, just as children used to do in Kashmir when I was growing up. Our oldest son, Irfan, in particular loved the outdoors—in fact, Mario Giambalvo used to refer to the farm as "Irfan's farm." We stocked the two largest ponds with fish—mostly bass and carp—and Irfan had wonderful fun fishing there.

After Santo and Mario passed away, their daughter Kathy and her husband, Bob van Campen, began taking care of the farm for us. Another valued part of our family life was Gisele, a woman from Haiti whom we hired to help care for our kids. She came to live with us—in New Rochelle during the week, in Hudson most weekends and for longer periods in the summer. Gisele was with us for some thirty-five years. She's now retired.

At some point in the early 1980s, I spotted an old World War II Jeep on a nearby farm, with a sign: "For sale—$750." I bought it, had a mechanic restore it to working condition, and painted it bright blue. Since then, it has played an important role in our life on the farm. Our kids, and more recently our grandkids, have loved going for rides in the Jeep. As I'll explain later, I've also taken many other guests on Jeep excursions—including important dignitaries who visited the farm to discuss international affairs.

At the time we bought the farm, the nearby town of Hudson was economically depressed, but today it has become a center of tourism and artistic activity. It's close to the historic estate Olana, once the home of Frederic Edwin Church, a notable painter of the Hudson River School. Although many farms continue to operate in the area, especially growing fruit, Hudson also attracts lots of visitors from New York City who spend weekends taking walks in the beautiful country-side and visiting the local art galleries and antiques stores.

As I told the real estate broker, I like taking on projects. I certainly kept myself busy with projects during the 1980s.

For example, in 1980, I purchased a building in Larchmont and turned it over for renovation by my friend Lou Grasso. I renamed it the Clock Tower Building and turned it into a nice office building. Later, I bought another space in Larchmont—a plot that used to hold an A&P supermarket until it burned down. I built another successful commercial building there.

I also got involved in residential real estate. For example, I purchased the building that had once housed the Roosevelt School in the Wykagyl neighborhood of New Rochelle. Irfan had actually attended the school, but it was closed, and the property was put up for sale by the town of New Rochelle. I bought it and converted it into fifty-eight condominium units. We sold 70 percent of them the first week they were on sale, which made it a very successful launch. The Grasso family was involved in the renovation work on all my projects. The properties in Larchmont are maintained for me by Giuseppe "Nino" Bellantoni and Libardo Baron, who have worked with me for more than thirty years.

Occasionally, my projects included a social mission. There was a time when the Muslim community in Westchester was struggling to find a place in which to hold services and operate their Sunday school.

They asked me to help and even named me president of the Westchester Muslim Center. I helped them think through their requirements and eventually located an ideal location—a former Greek Orthodox Church in Mount Vernon. The church had been closed and the building sold to a businessman who dreamed of converting it into a casino. But his plan never materialized, and since the building had lost its religious exemption, there were now close to $400,000 in real estate taxes due on the property.

I went to the mayor of Mount Vernon and described the situation. "We'd like to buy this property and put it to good use again," I said, "but we can't afford to pay the back taxes. Can the town give us a note—a mortgage—for the amount owed, and we'll repay it over time?" Mount Vernon agreed to this arrangement. My friend Lou Grasso converted the building from a church into a mosque, which included, among other changes, the removal of two large cement crosses in the front entrance of the building. The Westchester Muslim Center continues to operate successfully in that location to this day.

We also undertook a different kind of "project"—an annual family trip to Kashmir. Farida and the children would spend six or seven weeks in Kashmir, and I would join them for seven to ten days. This tradition began in 1979, when my brother Tariq joined me and Irfan on a hike to the Kolhai glacier, located in the northwest Himalayas at an average elevation of over 15,000 feet. In subsequent years, various groupings of family and friends participated in similar hikes in various locations around Kashmir. I always made a point of taking a dip in one of the glacial lakes (though sometimes for no longer than twenty or thirty seconds—those lakes are really cold!).

Our son Omar actually named his own son Kolhai in memory of those trips. We called ourselves the Kashmir Mountaineering Club, and we made up certificates with hand calligraphy by our daughter, Farah, for distribution to all those who participated in our hikes—as well as some "honorary" members, like my mother.

Our trips to Kashmir were also occasions for family and cultural bonding. Farida spent time with her parents and siblings, and our children got to know their cousins as well as the traditions of Kashmir. While we are patriotic Americans, we are also deeply proud of our Kashmiri heritage and happy to have been able to nurture that connection through all these years.

. . .

DURING THE FIRST HALF of the 1980s, a kind of tug-of-war developed between me and Nat Ancell regarding my role with Ethan Allen. I had the important responsibility for all the non-furniture products sold at Ethan Allen stores—the "coordinates," as we called them. But Nat wanted to give me an even bigger role at the company, though with limited authority, which I was reluctant to accept. I liked being my own boss and an entrepreneur, and I didn't think that fitting into a corporate hierarchy suited my style. In particular, it was hard for me to feel free and empowered as long as Nat himself—a dynamic leader with a strong personality—insisted on remaining at the helm of the business he'd founded and nurtured through all these years.

As a result, Nat, Clint Walker, and I engaged in a long-running debate about exactly how I should be fitted into the company's plans. I have a copy of a letter that Clint wrote to Nat about me and my role at Ethan Allen. It's dated January 31, 1981. It reads, in part:

> When Farooq sold his business to Ethan Allen, he thought he would be coming to Danbury to understudy you and within a reasonable time would take over the reins as chairman, providing he was capable of doing the job.
>
> It was the lure of running a big business that induced him to give up the adventure of running his own business. In my opinion, and I feel strongly about this, he is a doer. He gets things

done with little or no help from anyone. He is also a damn good businessman and [has] a track record to prove it. These are the very qualities you need in a chief executive. In the interest of time, I will skip all of Farooq's other good attributes, although I can list them for you at a moment's notice.

The problem, you see, as you probably know, lies in you rather than Farooq, and unless you can discipline yourself to give Farooq a clear area of responsibility, and then keep out of it, any attempt to fit Farooq into our Danbury executive organization will fail . . .

You're too old to change your habits, so am I, so let's cut through all the ifs and maybes. Farooq is a damn good international trader, and we should be casting our nets far afield. If you were to give Farooq the total responsibility for developing an overseas market for EA products with all the freedom in the world to wheel and deal without your backstopping him, I think we might just possibly be offering him something that would be big enough to satisfy his appetite. There is business to be done, and we are not even scratching the surface. Let him select his targets after he surveys the potential. Let him put his organization together and develop his forecasts, his budget, his timetable, etc. . . .

Of course, neither you nor Farooq may think what I am proposing would be wise. If so, I have nothing further to offer, other than to hope we can offer Farooq a compensation arrangement that will keep him with us in KEA, a business that would, in my opinion, fare poorly without his services. I have tried to be constructive in my criticism of you, Nat, in the same spirit you have tried over the years to be helpful to me.

Sincerely, Clint

I grew up in the Himalayan region of Kashmir, where
my grandfather (right) was a successful merchant and
my father (left) was an attorney and political leader.

In 1948, political turmoil turned our family into refugees.
We made our home in the mountain city of Murree, Pakistan,
where my mother and father posed for this picture.

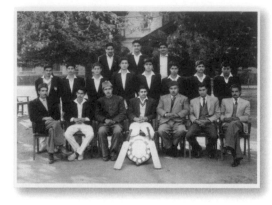

As a young man, sports was my first love. I am in the center of this photo, leading my college cricket team, which was one of the best in Kashmir.

During periods of turmoil, the Indian government, which ruled much of Kashmir, would require young people to take military training. Here I am in western India, one of two Kashmiris chosen to receive advanced training as part of the National Cadet Corps.

As a popular leader of sports teams at Sri Pratap College, I was given my own office. Here I am meeting there with a professor and a fellow student.

With the help of my father and many other people, I was able to come to America in 1965 to study at New York University's school of business.

My father's friends, Gerald and Mimi Levy from Brooklyn, became close friends of mine as well. Here they are hosting a visit from my grandfather (left).

A rarely-used provision of Kashmiri law allowed Farida and me to get married by telephone. Here is a portrait of Farida in her traditional Kashmiri bridal gown.

When she joined me in Brooklyn, Farida quickly adopted American customs. Here she poses proudly with our first car, a brand-new 1968 Mustang.

Farida and me, two young immigrants with high hopes for their new life together in New York.

As our family grew, we began taking annual trips to stay in touch
with our Kashmiri roots. Here I am hiking in Kashmir with family
friend S.S. Ali (left) and my children, Irfan, Farah, and Omar.

A vacation snapshot that captures
some of the remarkable beauty of
mountainous Kashmir.

I enjoy sharing my passion for mountaineering with friends. I joined Gary Wendt, CEO of GE Capital, on an expedition to Africa's fabled Mount Kilimanjaro.

With Farida during our
Kilimanjaro journey.

Ancell and Walker Honored

Nathan S. Ancell, Chairman, and Clinton Walker, Vice-Chairman, each received an unexpected award of their own at the Innisbrook Dealer Conference. Mr. Farooq Kathwari, President, presented each of them with a bronze plaque which read in part: "In recognition of these many years of dedicated leadership from the Ethan Allen Family."

When I became an executive at Ethan Allen, I was lucky to follow in the footsteps of great leaders. Here I am honoring company founder Nat Ancell and president Clint Walker.

When I was appointed president of Ethan Allen, my family joined me at the celebration in Phoenix, Arizona—from left, Omar, Farah, Farida, and Irfan.

Team-building is one of my most important—and enjoyable—duties. Here I host a gathering of Ethan Allen retailers at our family farm in Hudson, New York.

Many of Ethan Allen's wonderful people have become lifelong friends. In this picture, I honor one of our most distinguished retailers, New Jersey's Phil Esposito, with whom I love to go boating.

Shirley Parker is a longtime associate at Ethan Allen's workshop in Maiden, North Carolina, one of the many experienced team members who help make our company great.

Ethan Allen is proud of the high labor, environmental, and product quality standards upheld at our plants outside the U.S. Here I am greeted by team members at our facility in Silao, Mexico.

Our family farm in Hudson, New York, has been the site of many wonderful gatherings of family and friends. We love taking the blue Jeep on rides around the property.

Our eldest son Irfan was especially fond of outdoor life. Here I am enjoying a horse-back ride with Irfan and his sister Farah during a family trip to Kashmir.

Irfan's untimely death is the greatest tragedy
our family has suffered. Here we are visiting
his gravesite in Afghanistan with my father
and Farida's mother.

Two years after my first visit to Irfan's gravesite,
I found the area being refurbished and cared for
thanks to the efforts of a family friend.

My quest for a peaceful solution to the Kashmir problem led to many intensive meetings with Pervez Musharraf, the mercurial president of Pakistan.

I founded the Kashmir Study Group to develop practical solutions to the Kashmir problem. Its members included distinguished scholars, experts, and government officials. Back row: Rodney W. Jones, Thomas P. Thornton, Ainslie T. Embree, and Edward Sutton (briefly a KSG member). Front row: Howard Schaffer, me, William Phillips Talbot.

Ambassador Frank Wisner has long been a partner in my efforts to promote peaceful conflict resolution, and has also served as a member of the Ethan Allen board.

My friendship with Ambassador Howard Schaffer dates back to my student days in Kashmir. Years later, he visited me at our family farm.

I've always kept the American government informed about my private efforts to promote peace in the Kashmir region. Here I pose at a White House event with Farida (far right), President and Mrs. George W. Bush, and Indian Prime Minister Manmohan Singh and his wife.

I was honored to serve as a member of President Barack Obama's advisory board of Asian Americans and Pacific Islanders.

Members of the Task Force on Extremism in Fragile States, established in 2017 in response to a request from the US Congress. From left: Nancy Lindborg, president of the US Institute of Peace; Michael Singh, managing director of the Washington Institute; me; former Secretary of State Madeleine Albright; former New Jersey governor Thomas H. Kean; and Stephen J. Hadley, former national security advisor.

After enjoying the honor of ringing the opening bell of the New York Stock Exchange, Farida and I visited the floor of the exchange with four of our grandchildren: Samantha, Zavier, Gabriel, and Kolhai.

Farida and me enjoying a weekend visit to our family farm.

Our cats have long been cherished members of the family. Here I am with Abyssinian "temple cat" Tass.

The elegant Pashmina is an Egyptian Mau cat who joined us after the death of Tass.

A family gathering at our home in New Rochelle. Back: Kolhai held by Omar, Nadia, Farida, Farooq, Gabriel held by Farah, Robin. Front: Zavier, Samantha

I think Clint's letter captured the situation very well. But it was hard for Nat to embrace this reality. The friction between Nat and me gradually increased.

Feeling torn, I sent a letter of resignation to Nat in 1982, saying, in effect, "My being an officer of Ethan Allen just doesn't work for me. Let's go back to our old arrangement, with me running a separate business as a joint venture with you."

Nat agreed to accommodate me. We set up a new company that I called IFO Enterprises, in honor of my three children—Irfan, Farah, and Omar. As we had done with KEA International, I owned 60 percent of IFO Enterprises, and Ethan Allen owned 40 percent. The new company would supply "coordinates" to Ethan Allen, just as KEA had done. However, Nat insisted that I retain an official title within Ethan Allen as well—in fact, he used the opportunity to announce that I had been promoted to executive vice president. This was a very unusual arrangement, of course, and Nat didn't even bother clearing it in advance with the parent company, Interco.

I also mentioned to Nat that driving back and forth from Danbury to New Rochelle was way too much for me. Nat responded by saying that he'd been thinking of buying a new car, and he suggested I take his older, big-finned classic and hire a driver. I hired Alberto Arias in 1983, and he is still driving me today, thirty-five years later.

As Clint Walker had recommended, I did make a number of moves to expand Ethan Allen's international presence during these years. I made an agreement with a well-respected German company called Musterring to open a series of Ethan Allen design studios in Germany. Successful stores were launched in Berlin, Frankfurt, Dusseldorf, and Munich to much fanfare.

I made a similar deal with Perrings Home Furnishing, a family business then headed by Ralph Perring. He arranged to open three Ethan Allen studios in England.

Perring had served as Lord Mayor of London, and he invited me to the mayor's official residence to attend a meeting of the carpenters' guild, an ancient organization of English furniture makers. It was a gala event, with the guild members wearing special robes and proposing a series of toasts for dignitaries from the Queen on down. When a new member was inducted into the guild, the ceremony was worthy of someone being elevated to knighthood.

When I was asked to make a few remarks as an honored guest, I said, "Lord Mayor, I always used to wonder how a small country like Britain could run the whole world. Now I know. Seeing how the cabinetmakers' guild is run like a grand military operation, I finally understand how you were able to manage colonies all over the globe." They all laughed, but my insight into the British character was a serious one.

During the early 1980s, Ethan Allen also won a $30 million contract with the US State Department to furnish the official residences of American diplomats overseas. And I improved and expanded sales of Ethan Allen furniture through the US Navy exchange stores, traveling to open galleries at naval bases in Yokosuka, Japan; Guam; Pearl Harbor, Hawaii; Rota, Spain; Naples, Italy; and Puerto Rico. Our company's presence around the world was steadily expanding.

Despite all these successes, the ambiguous relationship between me and Nat Ancell continued to chafe. I was eager to try my hand at really running a big company, and to do it without having the company founder looking over my shoulder. On more than one occasion during the early 1980s, I offered Nat my resignation, only to have him refuse to accept it. But he also couldn't bring himself to turn over the reins.

The turning point finally came in 1985. Nat Ancell called me into his office one day and said, "Farooq, I know you've wanted to be in charge of Ethan Allen for a long time. The day has come. I'm going to name you president and chief operating officer. I'll remain as CEO."

"I'll accept on one condition," I said. "I want everyone else in the company to report to me. I'll report to you." It was important, I thought, to have very clear lines of responsibility. It would never do to have company officers—most of them Nat's longtime friends and associates—going to the CEO with complaints or requests every time I made a decision they didn't like.

At first, Nat balked. "How can I agree to that?" he said. After so many years in the captain's seat, he found it hard to accept the idea of no longer having his hand in every major decision made by every company department.

"If you want me as president," I said, "that's what you'll have to do."

To his credit, Nat agreed. A new era in my life, and in the story of Ethan Allen, was about to begin.

7

TAKING CHARGE

IN 1985, I BECAME the president of Ethan Allen. I found myself the leader of a company in need of transformation. It had a business model and a collection of product offerings that had been very successful for decades but that needed to reflect changing times. Sales had stagnated, and long years of growth had slowed. It was a warning of difficult times ahead.

Ethan Allen was not the only company in this position. Many successful organizations that had been founded one or two generations earlier were in the same situation. A changing world demanded innovation, and delivering that innovation to Ethan Allen was my mandate.

But as almost everyone in business knows, driving innovation at a tradition-bound company is one of the biggest challenges a leader can face. I also had to expand my personal skills. Through years of experience, I had gained expertise in choosing attractive products, responding to customer tastes, developing supply chains, and managing logistics. Now I had to learn the finer points of working with manufacturing, with our marketing and advertising experts, with staffers in finance and human resources, and with many others in various departments.

One of the things I quickly realized was that the company's traditional structure, which had evolved over several decades, was no longer viable in a far more competitive business world.

At the time I became president, Ethan Allen had some 250 stores, almost all run by independent owners. Most of these owners were skilled, experienced, and dedicated businesspeople. But they were also fiercely independent and wedded to their own ideas about what Ethan Allen ought to stand for. They made their own merchandise choices, devised their own marketing plans, and ran their own ads—often sending contradictory messages about our brand. In an increasingly mobile society integrated in many complex ways, it no longer made sense for Ethan Allen to have dozens of different brand images.

We also had thirty manufacturing plants scattered around the country, from New England and North Carolina to Ohio, Oklahoma, California, and elsewhere. This made the logistics of warehousing and shipping products needlessly complicated and costly. It also meant we were spending extra money to maintain separate management systems for dozens of operations that were run almost like independent companies. It was a system that had expanded piece by piece through acquisitions over the decades rather than having been planned with an overarching strategy in mind.

I realized we would have to transform these systems to meet the demands of a new era. I began formulating a new partnership model for our dealer network that would combine discipline, unity, and control with entrepreneurship, creativity, and transparency. I also began thinking about how to simplify and consolidate our array of production facilities without damaging the tradition and continuity that Ethan Allen stood for.

But I knew that before I could transform our business model, I had to first establish a personal connection with the people I was now about to lead.

This process had already begun over the previous years. I'd gotten to know many of the people of Ethan Allen during my time as president of KEA and while I was the executive vice president responsible for Ethan Allen's accessories and imported products and for developing our international business. Most of them had been supportive of me and very receptive to the new ideas I'd offered regarding product styles and marketing concepts. But now I had to find ways to forge bonds with people who hadn't yet had a chance to work with me.

I knew this might be a challenge in some cases. I was a man with an unusual name from a faraway part of the world now in charge of an iconic American brand. Many of our team members lived and worked in some of the most socially conservative parts of the United States—places like the Green Mountains of Vermont and the Appalachian hills of North Carolina. Some came from families with Ethan Allen roots that went back two or three generations. I knew if I was going to lead them successfully through the changes the company needed to make, I had to start by winning their trust. I had to reach out to Ethan Allen people of every background and show them that I understood their interests and concerns. Only by making this kind of personal connection would I be able to convince them that the transformation I had in mind would be beneficial, in the long run, not just for Ethan Allen but also for them.

One of my first speeches as company president was delivered to the workers at our factory in Vermont. Clint Walker, who had been my predecessor as president and was now serving as vice chairman, had become a good friend of mine. He introduced me to the audience. Some knew me, but many were meeting me for the first time. I imagine that a few may have been wondering what this man from halfway around the world was really like. So I carefully planned my speech to highlight what we had in common rather than our obvious differences.

I praised the beauty of the Green Mountains for which that corner of New England is so famous. It was easy to offer this praise with great sincerity—those mountains really are beautiful, as any visitor will tell you. Then I added, "Being here makes me feel truly at home—although I must say that the Green Mountains are small hills compared to the Himalayan mountains I hiked as a boy back in Kashmir!"

After this drew the laugh I hoped for, I went on. "Of course, one thing I'm sure we mountain people can agree on is that most of the world's problems are created by all those flatlanders!" This got thunderous applause. Suddenly I was "one of them," and my job of winning their support had become much easier.

My remarks about being a "mountain person" weren't just talk. I identify deeply with the people of the Himalayas among whom I'd grown up—people with a profound respect for nature and for other human beings. From my boyhood hiking those beautiful, snowcapped slopes, I remember the three simple words of greeting habitually exchanged by travelers who would encounter one another in the mountains: "*Takda? Kher? Razi?*"

Translated roughly into English, they ask about three fundamental necessities of life: "Are you well? Is your family well? Are you contented?" Health, family, contentment—a set of values that I think translate well from the mountains of Kashmir to any setting in the modern world.

I've seen the same values among my colleagues in America's highlands, including the Northeast Kingdom of Vermont, the Blue Ridge Mountains of North Carolina, and other places in the United States.

The way I talked with the people of Ethan Allen about personal experiences and values like these helped them understand that I aspired to become a colleague and teammate. Hearkening back to my days as the captain of the cricket team, my number-one goal would be to make the people around me more skilled, more productive, more committed to our shared success, and more satisfied with their work.

Armed with these attitudes, I gradually won the friendship and support of almost everyone at Ethan Allen, including any who might once have mistrusted me. To this day, when I visit our factories, warehouses, and other facilities—as I frequently do—our rank-and-file people greet me with remarkable warmth and friendliness. They share news about improvements they've made in their operations; show me the latest pictures of their children or grandkids; and ask me smart, thoughtful questions about the initiatives we are working on back at headquarters. I can't keep track of all the generous cards, letters, and even gifts they've sent me over the years—all designed to show me how much they appreciate my efforts on behalf of our beloved Ethan Allen and how fully they've accepted me as a member of the family.

Perhaps the most interesting challenge for me was the Ethan Allen dealers. As I've explained, they were independent businesspeople who were used to running their own shows. Many had owned and managed Ethan Allen dealerships for decades or even generations. They knew a lot about the furniture market and industry—in many cases, much more than I did. So it's understandable that some of them were reluctant to accept me as the new leader of the company, especially when they realized that I had strong ideas about how Ethan Allen needed to change. But they all saw me as an entrepreneur, which represented a potential bond between us.

At the time I became president, I was aware of the challenges I might face in winning over the support of the dealers. We had a track record together that had shown me how independent-minded they could be—and how important it was for me to earn their trust and respect.

A year earlier, in 1984, I'd bumped heads with some of the leaders of our very strong dealer group on the West Coast. I had met most of them before when presenting them products on behalf of KEA, but this meeting in San Francisco was the first time I'd joined them in my role as executive vice president of Ethan Allen.

After exchanging greetings, I started the meeting by briefly describing some of the projects I'd been working on back on the East Coast and explaining the company's strategic objectives for the coming year.

The dealers asked one or two questions, but basically they seemed satisfied with my presentation.

Then the question that was on all of their minds was asked. It came from Howard Jacobs. He owned a string of successful stores in Orange County, which made him a big customer and an influential person within Ethan Allen. (And, as I mentioned earlier, he was married to Sookie, the daughter of Ted Baumritter, who was the co-founder of Ethan Allen along with Nat Ancell, as well as being Nat's brother-in-law.) Jacobs was an unofficial leader of the West Coast dealer group, viewed by some as a likely successor to Nat as CEO.

For all these reasons, Jacobs viewed me with bit of suspicion, and his style at that San Francisco meeting was rather confrontational.

"It's all well and good for you to come here and tell us about the company's strategies for next year," Jacobs said. "But what we want to know is, What are *you* going to do for *us*?"

I understood where he was coming from, and I had no desire to offend him or the other dealers. But I also knew I had to be clear about the need for all of us—dealers and everyone else at Ethan Allen—to begin thinking and acting like a team. With that in mind, I responded to his challenge this way: "Howard, I'm going to work very, very hard to make sure we've got the best products, the strongest merchandising programs, and the best support we can provide. But then, with all due respect, I'm going to ask—What are *you* going to do for Ethan Allen? I hope you are going to do things right—to perform to your utmost to help make the whole company as successful as possible. If you don't, you're going to hear from me! And the same goes for everybody in this room."

I was well aware that this was the first time Howard—or any other dealer—had heard a message like this from anyone in Ethan Allen leadership other than Nat Ancell himself. There was a moment of silence. Howard stared at me in disbelief. The other dealers glanced at one another, then back at me.

And then they laughed—not with disrespect, but with sheer surprise at my nerve. Here I was, this young fellow with less experience and a shorter history in the furniture business than any of them, telling them that it was my turn to make demands of them! It was so unexpected that they found it funny.

But then we started talking about what I really had in mind—and their laughter turned to nods of understanding and agreement. They could see that I had the company's best interests at heart, and that I was right to say that we all needed to work together to achieve the best results.

From that moment on, the potential conflict between me and Howard Jacobs was defused. Jacobs and I became friends, and my relationship with the West Coast dealers was on solid footing.

Soon thereafter they said to me, "We hope you'll try to come west to attend our future meetings, at least once or twice a year."

"I will, on one condition," I replied.

Again, this drew a laugh from the group. *We're inviting you, and you are setting conditions?* "What's your condition?" they asked.

"It's a good condition," I answered. "I promise you will like it. You know that my wife, Farida, and I grew up in the beautiful mountains of Kashmir. Now we are here in America, and I know that many of the most spectacular sights in the country are out here in the West. So I wonder why we are meeting here in a hotel room in the city. I'll join your meetings if you promise to have them someplace special, where we can all enjoy the beauty of this part of the world."

They liked my idea. In future years, we had dealer meetings in places like Yellowstone National Park in Wyoming, Pike's Peak in Colorado, and the resort city of Banff in Alberta, Canada.

Later, our dealer groups in the mid-Atlantic, Midwest, and Southwest latched on to the idea. They moved their meetings from locations like airport hotels to beach towns in Florida or the Bahamas, or to culturally rich cities like Santa Fe and New Orleans. We not only accomplished a lot of business at these meetings but we also boosted the morale of all our team members and their families.

Meetings like these also helped me develop strong relationships with our dealers. For example, one of our biggest dealers was Royce Baker, who owned successful Ethan Allen stores in Colorado and San Diego. Royce and his wife almost adopted me and Farida, hosting us on many delightful visits, getting to know our children, and offering me all kinds of valuable business advice. I became a close friend and boating partner of Phil Esposito, a New Jersey dealer, and I developed similarly close friendships with dealers from Texas, the mid-Atlantic states, and other parts of the country. They were all tough, entrepreneurial people, but they liked me because they could see that I was a straight talker and a fair-minded individual. Lifelong friendships were often the result.

Another thing I'd done to develop a strong relationship with our dealers was to begin modeling for them how our stores could be improved and modernized.

As a tool for doing this, I used the company-owned Ethan Allen store near our headquarters in Danbury, Connecticut. This was at the time the only store we'd built from scratch to be managed by the company itself. (We had three other company-owned stores then—in Detroit, Minneapolis, and Washington, DC—which we'd taken over when their owners had run into financial difficulties.) During my time as executive vice president, I'd begun thinking about the need to remake our retail stores to better fit the tastes and styles of modern customers, as well as to reflect a national brand built around Ethan Allen products.

So in 1984, during a flight back from the furniture market at High Point, North Carolina, I said to Nat Ancell, "Why don't we completely redesign our Danbury store and turn it into a model of what a contemporary Ethan Allen store could be? Then we'll invite all our dealers to visit it and take inspiration and ideas from what they see."

At first, Nat was dubious. "The dealers already travel twice a year to the furniture show at High Point. They might not be in the mood to make another trip."

"If we make the Danbury event a big enough deal, they'll *have* to come," I responded.

"Okay," Nat said. "Take your idea and run with it."

I set about reorganizing the Danbury store. I installed a new management team, and we replaced the old retail fixtures with modern, state-of-the-art displays and updated the furniture styles, lighting, rugs, decorative objects, and other accessories with the very latest looks. I then announced to dealers around the country that we would be hosting company-wide gatherings in Danbury to which all our dealers would be invited, each taking place just before or after the High Point markets in the fall and spring. So if dealers still wanted to attend High Point, they could do so—and then extend their travels to include a visit to Danbury. There was a bit of grumbling, but most dealers were curious and willing to cooperate with the plan.

When the dealers saw what we'd done with the Danbury store, many of them were won over. Some said, "We didn't think Ethan Allen could do this." For the first time, they could see the full aesthetic potential of Ethan Allen furniture when paired with thoughtfully selected complementary products—lamps, vases, rugs, pictures, sculptures, wall hangings. We'd brought in skilled designers to work with merchandising experts to create showrooms that embodied particular attitudes rather than having been thrown together based on someone's whims. The dealers marveled at the difference this made. They could see how much easier it would be to sell their customers back home on a complete roomful of attractive merchandise, all of it chosen and arranged to produce a harmonious, dynamic effect.

This initiative was an important first step in the transformation of Ethan Allen from a manufacturer into a modern, world-class retailer. Bringing the dealers to Danbury had started the process of unifying the company and enlisting the dealers' support behind the need for reform.

Now, as president of Ethan Allen, I needed to rally the whole organization around some even more sweeping changes.

Over the decades, like most successful organizations, Ethan Allen had grown complex and somewhat bureaucratic. We were operating some thirty manufacturing plants and seven distribution centers; we had a team of around one hundred account managers working with our hundreds of independent retailers; and we had twenty vice presidents overseeing different parts of this complicated machine. All these divisions had become siloed, operating independently from one another in ways that sometimes conflicted, each under the direction of leaders who ran their businesses exactly as they saw fit. The sense of camaraderie, teamwork, and unity that I had relished during my years as a cricket captain—and which had made my leadership successful—seemed to be lacking.

I set about changing this. I wanted every Ethan Allen employee to feel like a member of the team, not a cog in a complicated bureaucratic machine. So I took some unprecedented steps to help make that happen.

For example, an important new policy I announced was that, henceforth, Ethan Allen dealerships should sell *only* Ethan Allen products—not the hodgepodge of goods from a variety of sources that our independent dealers had previously stocked. If Ethan Allen was one company with one strategy and one consistent brand, it needed to look and feel that way—and that meant carrying a consistent array of attractive, modern products that, together, would constitute the Ethan Allen style.

Some of the dealers rebelled at the idea. They feared it would squash the creativity of their staffers who worked with customers to select furnishings to suit their individual style. "Remember that we employ hundreds of interior designers," these dealers protested. "Their role is to provide customers with unique, creative solutions. Limiting them only to Ethan Allen products just won't work. They need more options!"

I heard the concerns, and I understood them. In fact, one of my goals was to enhance the importance of our designers—to empower them and make them even more valuable members of the Ethan Allen team.

To begin making this happen, in 1986 we hosted an all-expense-paid trip by some six hundred Ethan Allen designers from across North America to attend a summit meeting at our headquarters in Connecticut—the first such meeting we'd ever held. Many of these designers had worked with our dealers for decades. Now they had their first opportunity to see a designer-curated gallery filled with nothing but Ethan Allen products, and they liked what they saw. As a result, they embraced our plan to develop a unified and distinctive Ethan Allen style based on a consistent array of company-wide products. Many went home and served as effective ambassadors on behalf of the plan, winning the support of dealers who'd previously been dubious about it.

The summit meeting also gave us an opportunity to greatly improve our training of designers. Previously, most of our training was limited to presentations by our field representatives who would visit local stores to offer product knowledge and a smattering of design ideas. These were supplemented by occasional regional sessions. Now we brought together designers from around the country to attend training sessions by top experts, to learn about current trends in color, texture, and style, and to offer feedback to our headquarters team about product ideas. We called this "Ethan Allen College." The level of professionalism and creativity of Ethan Allen designers sharply increased as a result of these new training opportunities.

We've held our designers' summit every year since 1986, and it remains an enormously popular event. We provide the designers with news about the latest product and style ideas coming out of Ethan Allen, and we gather their feedback and suggestions about concepts we can develop in the near future. We also recognize and honor designers who've achieved the most for their customers during an evening of Academy Award–style presentations. Nurturing and tapping the creativity of our designers is one of the best ways we've discovered to ensure that we're creating products that speak directly to the interests of our customers as well as millions of potential customers whom we hope to attract.

My interest in building a sense of teamwork and shared purpose didn't stop with our designers. At a business meeting in Danbury, I'd met a journalist named Judith Cutright. I asked her to join Ethan Allen to develop a quarterly video communication program for us to share with our network. The videos were shown at our manufacturing plants and at our dealer stores.

One day when I was visiting our plant at Beecher Falls, Vermont, an associate got my attention. "I saw the video showing how you invited six hundred designers to visit the Danbury headquarters," he said. "It's a great idea. But why not include the factory workers too?"

I liked the idea. So I invited five thousand rank-and-file team members from Ethan Allen facilities all around the country to visit us at our corporate headquarters in Danbury—at company expense, of course. Some of our longtime employees, who worked at rural locations in places like Oklahoma and Texas, had never been on an airplane before. But we persuaded them to make the journey, and they came to attend get-to-know-you sessions with all our top leaders in groups of three hundred or so at a time. We shared our ideas about improving the company, listened to the team members talk about the things they loved about Ethan Allen and the things they'd like to fix, and we enlisted their support as change agents for the quiet revolution we were mounting.

In these meetings I talked a lot about the importance of teamwork and even shared some stories about the leadership lessons I had learned while playing cricket. I also said a couple of things that made our corporate leaders a little nervous. For example, I declared, "The most important job of any leader is to make the people around him or her better. If your leader doesn't do this, you have a right to revolt!" Some managers were shocked to hear their president seemingly fomenting revolution among the ranks! But I sincerely wanted everyone at Ethan Allen to feel empowered to produce positive change—from the bottom up, if necessary. The goal was not to promote needless dissent, but to make the whole company stronger—and over time, that's what happened.

. . .

UNFORTUNATELY, BRINGING CHANGE to a big company isn't all about making persuasive speeches and inspiring the enthusiasm of employees. Sometimes, overcoming obstacles to reform can involve actions that are difficult, even painful.

I've mentioned the fact that, over time, Ethan Allen had developed a series of siloed departments that operated almost like independent businesses, under the guidance of managers who were accustomed to having their own way. It's human nature for people who've accumulated power to be reluctant to surrender it.

One of the early management challenges I faced came from a particular vice president (I'll call him "Jim"). For a number of years, he'd been running a large part of our manufacturing operation in a very independent fashion—and according to many of his colleagues, the decisions he made weren't always ethical or based on the best interests of Ethan Allen. Instead, Jim was using his power to reward cronies, punish those who tried to thwart him, and to line his own pockets. He reportedly even used his knowledge of some secrets of higher executives in the company to pressure them into letting him have his own way without restrictions. In short, he was treating his corner of Ethan Allen almost like his personal fiefdom.

In "the old Ethan Allen," Jim would probably have been allowed to hang on through sheer inertia until he reached retirement age. I realized I couldn't let that happen if I wanted my message of company-wide change and revitalization to be taken seriously. So I went to his office and confronted him. I was accompanied by Jim's superior, a vice president I'll call "Lou," who was one of the people Jim had reportedly been manipulating through intimidation.

"Jim," I said, "I've heard a number of disturbing things about the way you've been running your operation here." And I mentioned several of the stories I'd been told about inappropriate actions Jim had taken. "I'd like you to tell me your side of what's going on."

"I don't have to tell you a thing," Jim replied.

I responded in a quiet, patient tone. "Jim," I said, "I'm sure there are a number of issues involved here. We need to discuss them so we both know where we stand."

"I don't have to tell you anything," Jim repeated. "I've already discussed things with Nat Ancell and Clint Walker."

"Jim, I'm president now. I'm going to give you one more chance. I want the full story, and I want it now."

"The answer is no," Jim said again.

"Then, Jim, you're fired," I said.

Jim was genuinely shocked. "You can't fire me!" he declared.

I said, "Jim, I don't think you fully comprehend that I'm the president of this company now." I turned to Lou, and I noticed that he was visibly shaking—despite the fact that he officially outranked Jim. Jim was known to carry a gun, which was more common back then than today.

"Lou," I said, "Jim has five minutes to leave the office. Get whatever backup you need. If he refuses to go, call the police."

Jim left the meeting fuming. Exactly as I'd expected he would, he immediately called Nat Ancell. He figured that Nat would immediately reverse my decision.

Crucially, Nat reacted the right way. As I heard later, he quickly told Jim, "Farooq is our president. If he has fired you, then you are out."

Within days, there was a new executive running Jim's department— and doing so with honesty and integrity.

Confronting Jim had been a risky move on my part. Its success laid down an important marker. From that moment on, it was understood that Ethan Allen was serious about changing its culture and its ways of doing business.

Not everyone at the company was able to change with the times. Those who couldn't adjust to the new regime had to depart—though very few were forced out as unceremoniously as Jim was. Over my first three years at the helm, about 70 percent of Ethan Allen's top managers ended up retiring, recognizing that the company's culture was changing in a way they would find difficult to accept.

The ones who remained became the core of the new Ethan Allen, many of them rising to leadership positions as the company's transformation created fresh opportunities.

■ ■ ■

I CONTINUED TO PRESS AHEAD with the complex process of changing Ethan Allen. I said to my associates throughout the company, "It's time to forget the old slogan, 'If it ain't broke, don't fix it!' Sometimes you have to fix things even when they're not broken. And now is one of those times."

We'd already begun the process of creating a unified business model and brand message that every part of the organization—including all our dealers—would stand for and spread. But more needed to be done. To win support from my associates, I adopted another old saying, this one the motto that founding father Benjamin Franklin is said to have shared with his fellow revolutionaries: "We must, indeed, all hang together, or most assuredly we shall all hang separately."

One innovation in the new Ethan Allen—perhaps the most controversial—was to change our traditional pricing policy. We had previously treated the network of Ethan Allen dealers like a number of separate businesses, separated by geography. Prices varied greatly from one region of the country to another. There was a practical reason for this approach. As I've mentioned, our products were being built in some thirty separate production centers, most of them in the Northeast. We also operated eight national distribution centers, while each local dealer also had a smaller warehouse of its own. All these factors affected product pricing. The closer a dealer was to our manufacturing centers, the lower the cost of freight, and therefore the lower our suggested prices. These price differences led to variations in the suggested prices paid by customers around the country, as well as to varying profit margins enjoyed by our dealers.

I decided that this should change. I thought it would be more appropriate to have one suggested price nationally. (The "suggested price" formula is legally required to avoid running afoul of anti-trust laws that forbid price fixing.) So at one of our national meetings, I stood before the dealers and announced, "As part of our effort to create a credible national brand, we're going to create one suggested price nationally. We'll deliver the products to you at one cost, whether your stores are based in Florida or Maine, California or Texas."

The result was perhaps the most serious dealer rebellion I ever faced. The dealers who were likely to enjoy an overall price reduction—chiefly those in the western states—were pleased with the proposed change. But those who'd been winners under the old system—mostly large dealers in the eastern part of the country—were unhappy about losing their advantage. A number of them decided they weren't going to accept my decision without a fight. Thirteen dealers from the eastern half of the United States, in cities like New York, Boston, Philadelphia, Washington, Atlanta, and Chicago, formed an association they called "The Group of 13." After some strategizing among themselves, they summoned me to a meeting in a rented conference room at the airport in Pittsburgh. I showed up at the time appointed, prepared to respond as best I could. I knew that my future as the president of Ethan Allen might be on the line.

When I arrived, I found that Dan Brown, our largest Ethan Allen dealer with stores on New York's Long Island, had been appointed spokesman for the group. Brown was a tough character; he had served in military intelligence during World War II and earned his stripes interrogating prisoners of war. I found the thirteen dealers sitting along one side of a long table, with Brown in the center. A chair for me was sitting on the other side of the table. I thought it looked like a court martial.

Dan Brown spoke first. "Thanks for coming, Farooq. I think you know that we respect you as a person and a leader. But we seriously question your judgment and fairness in trying to impose the new single-suggested-price policy on all of us dealers. The only way you can charge the same price for products delivered to any dealership around the country is to charge more to people like us, who currently benefit from our proximity to the factories and the warehouses. We'll have to pay more so that people elsewhere can pay less. That's just not right, and we can't accept it." Brown's colleagues around the table were nodding in agreement.

"Now I'd like to call on my fellow dealers in turn. They each have some comments to make and some questions they'd like to ask you." But before he could launch the discussion on that basis, I interrupted him.

"Dan, I would like to hear from everybody. But I'm not going to answer each one separately. Let's go around the table and let each dealer say his piece. Then I'll respond on behalf of the company." I wasn't about to let myself be worn down by getting into a debate against thirteen opponents. So each of the dealers made a brief statement, all of them basically repeating variations of the theme that Dan Brown had introduced—the unfairness of introducing a new pricing policy that would harm them financially.

When they were done, it was my turn to reply. "You know, I understand what you are saying," I began. "It's not easy for those who have enjoyed an advantage to find that it is going to be taken away from them. It's not surprising that you are unhappy about it.

"It's also human nature to feel that a benefit you've experienced through good fortune is something you deserve. This is the way of the world—those who have the most usually come to believe they somehow earned it completely on their own. The truth is that it's not the case. The one hundred stores that we have west of the Mississippi play a big role in the success of Ethan Allen. They buy a lot of our furniture, and the money they spend helps support our manufacturing. If those dealers did not exist, our business would be much smaller, and our production costs would be much higher—which would hurt your bottom line.

"We've got to be able to create credibility for the Ethan Allen brand nationwide. That requires mounting sales efforts that are consistent across the country, backed by advertising campaigns that reach every community. Yes, you folks are advertising by yourselves and reaching a few local customers. As big dealers, you have an advantage right now. But over the long term, as competition keeps getting tougher, you're going to lose that advantage. We need to be a national business that is strong everywhere and that treats everybody fairly. The better we do out west, the better you will do here in the east.

"I'm convinced that these are realities that Ethan Allen must deal with if our company is going to survive and thrive in the future. So we simply have a choice to make between two ways: your way or my way. As far as I am concerned, Ethan Allen is going to go my way. I'm not going to change. That leaves it up to you to make up your minds."

After a long silence, Dan Brown spoke first. "I may leave the system," he announced. One other dealer gave the same response—our biggest dealer in Atlanta. All the others decided to stay with Ethan Allen—to take a chance on the new national network we were creating, in which the entire company would speak with one voice and contribute to a shared future of success or failure.

To win—in business or in any other competition—one must also be willing to lose. In this case, I'd taken a chance, and I'd won. It was a victory for Ethan Allen, because our new way of doing business led to greater long-term profitability for our dealers and for the company.

In the meeting, I'd spoken about my plan for the future with seeming confidence. But in reality, the task of converting Ethan Allen into a more unified business did not come easily. The change to a one-price system required us to look hard at our logistics methods, and to find ways to improve our warehousing and transportation systems so that the costs of delivering products to different regions of the country could be made more consistent as well as affordable. It took time to develop and implement the necessary changes; but today, Ethan Allen has one of the best logistics networks of any national retailer in our industry.

The two dealers who decided to drop out of our network would both go bankrupt within a few years—while most of the dealers who stayed with Ethan Allen would thrive. This result confirmed my instinct about the importance of a unified national system for retailing success in the modern era.

Over time, we introduced one more essential change to the relationship between Ethan Allen and its dealers. As dealers retired— particularly those who didn't have a family member poised to take over the business—we started buying the stores and running them out of our Danbury headquarters.

Of course, changing the traditional system of independent dealers, which had grown and expanded for decades since the 1930s, would not be a fast or easy process. We had no desire to drive away families that had been involved with Ethan Allen for years. So when stores are being well run and managed, we are happy to allow them to continue to be independently owned. However, when the time comes that the owners are ready to retire or move on to other activities, we work with them to buy their stores and convert them into Ethan Allen–owned properties. This process began in the mid-1990s and it is still continuing today.

It's important that this process of transferring stores from individual ownership to company ownership be done in a way that is fair and respectful to the entrepreneurs who have helped build Ethan Allen over the decades. So I painstakingly developed a formula, through consultation with our dealers, to determine a fair market price for the assets we purchase. Using this formula saves time, trouble, and cost for everyone involved. Most of our store owners who are ready to sell find they don't need to hire outside brokers or bankers to represent them. In almost every case, I sit down personally with the family members— we've usually known one another for years—and we calculate a deal that is reasonable and fair. Everyone walks away reasonably satisfied.

•   •   •

BACK IN 1985, when Nat Ancell gave me the job of president of Ethan Allen, he did not completely understand the degree of change that the company needed to survive and thrive into the twenty-first century. Of course, he realized that Ethan Allen sales had stagnated, that profits had stalled, and that the specter of new competition was steadily increasing around him. But he wasn't convinced that dramatic changes were needed. Nat thought that a small adjustment here or there would suffice to set Ethan Allen on a strong course for the future.

The partnership we'd forged between Ethan Allen and KEA had demonstrated to Nat Ancell that I was a determined change agent— someone who was able and willing to accept the need for sweeping modernization of a business model that was in danger of becoming irrelevant and ineffective. I wasn't satisfied with "tinkering around the edges" so that Ethan Allen could eke out survival for a few more decades. I wanted to do what was necessary to help the company be a leader in the world of home furnishings for generations to come.

When I took over the president's chair and launched the change initiatives I've described in this chapter, Nat soon realized what he'd gotten himself, and his company, into. And, to his credit, he recognized the value of what I was doing and gave me his full support. This reaction made it easier for other members of the Ethan Allen family to accept and support me, and to join me in building the new company culture and business model I envisioned.

Within a few years, as my change initiatives took shape, the company fortunes began to improve. Little by little, metrics regarding customer service and client satisfaction began to climb. Soon it was clear that the Ethan Allen brand had turned a corner. By 1988, I'd been named chairman and CEO as well as president. The new Ethan Allen was well on its way.

8

MONEY MATTERS

ALL THROUGH THE LATE 1980S and the early 1990s, as we were rein-venting Ethan Allen's operations on many levels, we were wrestling with financial challenges that made our initiatives more urgent—and more complicated. In fact, Ethan Allen was caught up in the complex, aggressive, high-powered financial world of that era as symbolized by characters like Gordon Gekko, the cigar-smoking, Rolex-wearing cor-porate raider in the movie *Wall Street*. The steps we took to survive in that world make for a remarkable story.

As I've explained, when I became president of Ethan Allen in 1985, the company was owned by a conglomerate called Interco. Based in Clayton, Missouri—a suburb of St. Louis—Interco had purchased a number of furniture businesses, including such well-known brands as Broyhill and Lane. Their goal was to become a dominant company in the world of furniture. In pursuing that goal, they faced competition from other companies such as Masco Corporation, which had pur-chased Drexel, Thomasville, and other furniture businesses.

The theory behind conglomerate building was that the executives who owned and ran the corporations could apply their business and financial smarts to make the companies they bought better run and more profitable. Interco applied this thinking to Ethan Allen. They would send executives to our quarterly board meetings—a typical thing for a conglomerate to do with one of its holdings. They'd also been keeping track of Nat Ancell's planning for succession, since he was in his late 70s by then. So I'm sure Interco had approved Nat's choice of me as president.

In the spring of 1988, Interco's plans for continued growth were complicated by an unexpected outside assault. The corporation received a hostile takeover bid from two young men from Washington, DC. Steven and Mitchell Rales, brothers in their thirties, were in the process of building a conglomerate of their own under the name of Danaher Corporation. Using large sums of borrowed money, they were following the classic pattern—buying up companies from a wide variety of industries and trying to maximize the profits from each. Now the Rales brothers set their sights on Interco, believing that, under their management, the company could become more lucrative than ever before. They offered $2.47 billion for the entire corporation.

Interco's management had no desire to sell. They hired the well-known investment firm of Wasserstein Perella & Company to counsel them on dealing with the bid. Wasserstein Perella advised Interco that they should pay a huge dividend to their shareholders, which would help stave off interest in the Rales brothers' offer. In those days, one of the weapons used to fight hostile takeover bids was to increase the debt of the company, which would make it less attractive. So they took on debt, which they used to pay the dividend.

Naturally, as an executive at a firm owned by Interco, I followed these financial maneuverings with interest. Seeing that our parent company was taking on high debt, I said, "Interco is going to need money. This may create an opportunity for me. Perhaps Interco will consider selling off parts of their empire as a way of raising cash. If so, this might make it possible for me, along with other investors, to take ownership of Ethan Allen from Interco."

To explore this idea, I reached out to two of my associates from New Court Securities, both of whom were now working at Chemical Bank, which was the banker for Ethan Allen—Roger Widmann and Richard Smith. (Roger who had introduced me to Nat Ancell in the first place.) I said, "There may be an opportunity for a group of us Ethan Allen managers to purchase the company. I'd like you to do an evaluation of the possibility."

After they analyzed the financial situation, they offered this diagnosis: "It's not going to be easy, but it's possible."

My next discussion was with Nat Ancell, who at that time had the titles of chairman and CEO of Ethan Allen. I said, "Nat, let's go to St. Louis and tell Interco we want to buy the company."

We arranged a meeting with Harvey Saligman, the chairman of Interco, and Ron Aylward, the vice chair. In his usual, very direct style, Nat said to them, "We have decided to buy Ethan Allen, and you've got to sell it to us."

They replied, just as bluntly, "It's our company, and it's not for sale."

Before the conversation could degenerate into an argument, I interjected my voice. "Obviously, we understand you've got to make the decision," I said, "but we believe a sale might make sense for both parties." And I briefly outlined the kind of deal we had in mind.

Saligman and Aylward listened carefully and said, "Okay, we'll think about it and get back to you."

Nat and I returned to New York. The combative tone of the meeting had made our relationship with the leaders of Interco a bit awkward. In a few days, Saligman called me up and said, "We'd like to talk to you about the situation at Ethan Allen. We're thinking that maybe the time has come for Nat to retire."

I said, "Let's all have a face-to-face discussion about it." I knew that Nat would not be pleased with this development—although it was clear to me that eventually he would have to step down from his leadership role.

Nat and I returned to St. Louis for another conversation with Saligman and Aylward. Harvey Saligman got right to the point. "Nat, we believe it makes sense at this stage for you to retire and let Farooq be the chairman and CEO."

Nat said, "No, I'm not going to retire."

They said, "Nat, you know, we understand how you feel as the company co-founder. Of course you have an emotional investment in the business. You've done a great job, but the time has come for a change. You should step down."

He said, "I refuse to retire. But let me talk to Farooq. Can you give us a few moments to speak privately?"

So Saligman and Aylward left the room. Nat turned to me and said, "Farooq, what do you think?"

I said, "Nat, don't put yourself into a position in which they'll fire you. I don't want to get this job from them. I want it from you. You'd better retire. Otherwise, it's going to be bad."

Nat simply shook his head. "No, I'm not going to do it."

Saligman and Aylward came back in. They had made up their minds. They said to Nat, "Today is Wednesday. If by Monday morning you don't send us a letter of resignation, you're going to be terminated, and you'll have to leave the office."

Nat said nothing, except to tell me, "Okay, Farooq, let's go home."

He didn't say a single word to me on the entire flight home. It was clear he was upset, hurt, and angry—both with the leaders from Interco and, to some extent, with me.

That Saturday, I was scheduled to go to San Francisco to meet with the West Coast dealers, including Howard Jacobs, Royce Baker and his wife, Kitty, and important dealers from Los Angeles, Seattle, Phoenix, Las Vegas, San Francisco, and other cities. I decided to use this meeting as an opportunity to tackle the looming problem.

I said to the dealers, "All of you have become good friends and supporters of mine. Now I face a big decision that could affect your future as well. I want your opinion. I would like to see us try to buy Ethan Allen from Interco, and I would like you, and all of our dealers, to be partners in the purchase. Are you willing to pursue this opportunity with me?"

They said, "Yes, we all support you."

Then I told them, "Nat may be part of this buyout too." I didn't tell them that by Monday he could be terminated.

I took the red-eye flight back home to New York, feeling very bad about what was going to happen on Monday.

Arriving home on Sunday morning, I called Nat. Nat said, "You know, I've been giving this problem a lot of thought. Come over. I'd like to talk to you."

When I got to Nat's house, before he could say what he had on his mind, I said, "Nat, I have been thinking a lot about this problem too. I've decided I'm not going to take the job of chairman and CEO without your involvement and support."

He said, "Well, I've made a decision also. I've decided that I'm going to do exactly what you tell me to do."

I was happy Nat had come to terms with the fact that his days as chairman and CEO were coming to an end. "In that case, Nat, I think you should take the title of chairman emeritus. Step aside voluntarily rather than letting yourself be fired by Interco."

"That's settled, then," Nat said. "But now you've got to take care of me. Make sure I get to keep my company car, that I have use of an office in Danbury, and that I get a fair financial settlement."

"Of course," I replied, relieved that the only remaining issues revolved around money—since money issues are usually easier to resolve than issues of power, prestige, and control. "You can be sure I'll take care of you, Nat."

Then we talked about how to handle the next steps. "Tomorrow morning, I'll call the Interco people in St. Louis and ask them not to make any moves or issue any public statements. We have a dealer meeting scheduled in Danbury. Let's use that as an opportunity to take command of the situation." And then Nat and I worked out exactly what we would say.

On Monday morning, Nat took the floor in front of our dealer group and said, "I have an important announcement to make. I've made the decision that now is the right time for me to step down as chairman and CEO of Ethan Allen. And the obvious person to fill those roles is our president, Farooq Kathwari. An orderly transition along these lines has been planned for some time. I'm very pleased to be able to turn over the company we all love to a leader who has proven to be so talented." Nat went on to give a very detailed speech to the dealers about Ethan Allen's strategic and business prospects and offering a vision for the company's future—a vision that matched the one I'd been advocating, point by point. His endorsement of my ideas was an important act that made the leadership transition much easier than it might otherwise have been.

Later that morning, an official press release with the news was sent out to the media by the Ethan Allen headquarters. It noted that, at age 44, I was unusually young to be serving as president, chairman, and CEO of a major publicly owned corporation.

Of course, I was pleased by the messages of congratulations and support I began to receive. But I was even more gratified by the fact that Nat Ancell had handled what could have been an awkward situation with grace and generosity. Nat continued to use his office and staff in Danbury for about three years, quietly supporting me as I continued the task of transforming Ethan Allen.

Having built a great company, Nat Ancell deserved to go out with his head held high—and that's exactly what he did.

. . .

MEANWHILE, THE ISSUE OF ownership of Ethan Allen and the hostile takeover bid facing Interco remained unsettled. Interco's position had been that Ethan Allen was not for sale. But a week after Nat's retirement, Saligman called me up. "We've talked to advisors about your idea," he said, "and we've come to the conclusion that your idea is a good one. We'll sell Ethan Allen to you."

I was delighted. But then he spelled out the terms he had in mind. "After a great deal of discussion, we've determined that the price we want is $600 million, and we believe that the deal should be closed in six weeks. We're going to announce that the company is for sale, and if any other parties want to compete with you, they'll be permitted to offer bids of their own. Your job as chairman and CEO will be to help sell the company to the highest bidder—whether or not that bidder is your group."

My immediate reaction was that the proposed price was absurd. This was the 1980s, when prices for companies were being driven sky-high through the use of debt. And the Rales brothers were being supported by Drexel Burnham Lambert, the famous "junk bond" kings who had pioneered the aggressive use of high-yield debt to finance high-priced company takeover bids. But even under these circumstances, $600 million seemed way too high.

I called up Roger Widmann and Richard Smith at Chemical Bank, and they confirmed my instincts: "Six weeks is impossible, and the price they're asking doesn't make sense. Nobody's going to do it."

Still, at least we had our foot in the door. Now we had to figure out a way to quickly hammer out a deal that made sense to us and that the people from Interco would be willing to consider. At the same time, I had to address the sensitive issue of being a potential buyer of the company while also managing its possible sale to someone else. Our plan was to combine a substantial amount of investment funds from me with a smaller amount from a group of other people associated with

Ethan Allen—a number of my fellow executives and some of our independent dealers.

I had met Jack Welch, CEO of GE, and I knew Mike Carpenter, CEO of Kidder, Peabody, which was owned by GE Capital. So I called up Mike and explained the situation. Mike asked a few pertinent questions and suggested that I go to meet Gary Wendt, the chairman and CEO of GE Capital.

Wendt was a tough executive with a great history of success. He and I hit it off right away. "Let's see what we can do," he said. Wendt put a team together that reviewed the Ethan Allen financials. Three weeks later, they asked me to attend their Credit Committee meeting at GE Capital in Stamford and suggested I bring along one or more of the company's senior executives. I did not have a senior financial executive at that time, so I took the vice president of manufacturing.

We had an in-depth discussion about the past, present, and future of Ethan Allen. After we'd been talking awhile, one young analyst for GE Capital asked me, "Suppose we put together a deal that enables you to buy Ethan Allen. Imagine how you will feel a year or two from now. What do you think will be the problems that keep you awake at night?"

I responded, "You know, I usually sleep pretty well. But if anything is going to keep me awake at night, it will be if you all try to tell me how to run the company. If that's what you want to do, let's not make a deal."

After a long moment of silence, Gary Wendt spoke up. "Good answer!" he said. He respected the independence and self-confidence that my response had shown. (Wendt and I went on to become lifelong friends. In 1994, he invited Farida and me to join him in climbing Mt. Kilimanjaro in Tanzania, one of the most memorable experiences of our lives, and just one of many expeditions and adventures I've been able to enjoy with Gary Wendt.)

By the end of the day, GE Capital had agreed to set up a structure under which they would provide my team with $550 million in cash. I would own 30 percent of the company, while GE would own 70 percent—but I would control 51 percent of the voting shares, unless my team couldn't meet the financial covenants.

"Go buy the company," they told me.

I hadn't approached Chemical Bank to serve as a financial partner in this deal, but I did ask my contacts there to recommend a good attorney to help me. They introduced me to Jim Carlson, then a young lawyer. He became not only a fine advisor but also a long-term friend. He currently serves as a director of Ethan Allen. We decided to bid $475 million for the company. The rest of the $550 million that GE Capital had promised would be set aside for business purposes.

Meanwhile, other would-be buyers had begun to circle. The Rales brothers continued to be interested in making Ethan Allen part of their growing Danaher Corporation conglomerate. A team from the investment bank of Salomon Brothers visited the company, doing reconnaissance for another potential bidder. The president of Masco Corporation, which I mentioned earlier as a rival of Interco in the furniture business, visited us from Detroit and urged me to throw in my lot with them. In the interests of full disclosure, I had to let all these parties know that we were working on a bid of our own. Most of these potential buyers wanted me to be part of the transaction.

One important factor in our favor was that the overwhelming majority of Ethan Allen's independent dealers supported our bid. Many sent messages to convey their feelings—for example, a letter I've saved from Royce Baker, owner of three Ethan Allen stores in San Diego, California. Writing on behalf of seven other members of our West Coast dealer group, Royce declared, "We have great confidence in your present management staff," and he expressed his willingness to invest personally in our bid. This support meant a lot to me. It also signaled to Wall Street and to the business world in general that those who knew Ethan Allen best believed that the company's future would be brightest under the leadership of our team.

About three weeks later, the day arrived when bids were due. We had to visit the offices of Interco's lawyers and give them the details of our bid in a sealed envelope. I'm not sure how many other bidders there were—two or three, I believe. But late that night, we heard from the lawyers: "Congratulations," they said. "You submitted the winning bid."

We didn't have much time to celebrate. The Rales brothers went to the Delaware court and got an injunction to stop the deal. They wanted to meet with me again to determine whether they'd missed any information. They again asked me to partner with them. We went through another bidding process. About thirty days later, it was confirmed that our team was the highest bidder.

Nailing down the complexities of financing the purchase now became our highest priority.

Because Interco now needed cash, their advisors told them that to avoid paying taxes, it would be better for them if we bought the company using a note guaranteed by a letter of credit and kept the $475 million in a bank as a deposit. Interco began discussions with banks, searching for one that would give them such a letter of credit. And since the highest-rated banks in 1988 were Japanese, not American, those were the banks they began negotiating with.

But a month later, Interco came to us and said this plan was defunct. Their lawyers had told them that under the plan, if Ethan Allen went bankrupt, they might lose the note. So they proposed having Interco itself provide the financing for the deal. "We'll give you the same terms that GE offered," they said, "except that we cannot give you majority voting rights."

"I understand," I said, "but that's a deal breaker."

The Interco people said, "All right—give us some time to figure out what we can do." I agreed to do that. A few weeks passed, then three months. Meanwhile, our deal with GE Finance was on hold.

The world, however, was not on hold. And during this time, conditions in the markets had changed. In September 1988, the Securities and Exchange Commission charged Drexel Burnham Lambert with insider trading, stock manipulation, and fraud. Partly as a result of the downfall of the junk bond kings, in the early months of 1989, a number of other highly leveraged companies got into financial difficulties. The inflated market for corporate control began to deflate a bit. I realized that it was probably no longer necessary for us to pay the original price of $475 million to get control of Ethan Allen.

I began looking into financing options other than GE Capital. I had met with Sandy Weill and Jamie Dimon, then respectively the CEO and president of Smith Barney. I was also talking with Walter Shipley, CEO of Chemical Bank. Shipley suggested that I travel with him in his company plane to a resort in West Virginia, where the bank was holding its annual retreat. Right there, next to the tennis court, we began discussing the parameters of a new deal. The dealmakers included a fellow by the name of Jimmy Lee, a well-respected financial wizard; Bill Harrison, who later became the CEO of J.P. Morgan; and Roger Widmann. We decided that Chemical Bank would also invest in the company. So would Smith Barney. GE indicated that they wanted to remain a partner. And there was another investor, brought in by Chemical Bank—a private equity firm known as Castle Harlan, co-founded by John K. Castle, onetime president and CEO of Donaldson, Lufkin & Jenrette. Within a week's time, we put together a partnership among all these folks. They would give debt, equity, senior debt, and unsecured debt totaling $400 million, and we would make a purchase offer of $350 million. The remaining money would be retained to help finance our operations and the initiatives we hoped to undertake to restart the company's growth.

Based on this financial package, we were able to buy Ethan Allen in the spring of 1989.

As with many companies in those days, the purchase price we paid for Ethan Allen was financed largely with debt. In fact, fully 90 percent of the value was borrowed, leaving us with just 10 percent equity. Of that debt, $150 million was in the form of high-risk securities—junk bonds—that carried a hefty 15 percent interest rate. What's more, these bonds carried a note saying that if in one year the bondholders were unable to sell the debt, the interest rate would rise to 18.25 percent.

The reduced price we paid for the company later caused a bit of a complication for us. Distressed about the fact that we ended up paying more than $100 million less than our original offer, the leaders of Interco sued their own investment bankers for giving them flawed advice about the sale of Ethan Allen. As the case went on, the attorneys for the investment bankers called me in for a deposition, suspecting that, as Ethan Allen's president, I might have been privy to inside information that I'd kept secret from the world—and especially from the other bidders.

Over two days of testimony, I was grilled about every detail of Ethan Allen's finances and about the complicated process of bidding for and ultimately buying the company. The lawyers were unable to find any evidence that we'd been less than forthright about the company's circumstances, so the lawsuit ended up going nowhere.

Many of the people who made possible our purchase of Ethan Allen are still active in the business world. In fact, late in 2017, I ran into Jamie Dimon, now chairman and CEO of JPMorgan Chase, at a public meeting. We waved at one another, and Jamie called out, "1989, Smith Barney, five hundred million dollars."

I replied, "Eighteen percent, and we paid you back every dime."

"Yeah, you did pay it back!" he responded with a laugh.

■　■　■

AS OF MAY 1989, the management and investor team I led now owned Ethan Allen. We named the ownership group Green Mountain Holding Corporation in honor of Ethan Allen's Vermont heritage. Green Mountain's official headquarters was the former bowling alley in

Larchmont, New York, that I had bought years earlier to house the offices of KEA International.

To finance my personal share of the purchase price, I'd mortgaged everything I had—our family home, the farm, and the other pieces of real estate I owned. I also threw in all the cash I had from other sources, such as the sale of our New Rochelle condominium building the year before. So I was making a significant financial bet on the future of Ethan Allen. If our efforts to turn the business around had foundered, not only would the company have suffered but so too would my personal finances, along with those of my business partners.

Among other responsibilities that came with my new leadership role, I had to name four directors to serve on the company's board. The directors I nominated included Kristin Gamble, who'd worked with her husband, Charlie Flood, at New Court Securities, the Rothschild's firm, with me; she now lived near the farm that Farida and I had purchased. I also selected Ed Meyer, chairman of Grey Advertising, and Horace McDonell, CEO of Perkin-Elmer Corporation.

Chemical Bank, GE Finance, and Smith Barney each had the right to name a director. Another major investor, John K. Castle of Castle Harlan, was also given a seat. It turned out that Castle was quite a character—very smart and highly respected, and with a towering ego to match. He also named Clint A. Clark, founder of the Children's Place retail chain, to a director's seat.

In October 1989, I went with bankers from Kidder, Peabody and Smith Barney on an overseas trip in an effort to sell our Ethan Allen bonds to foreign investors. We visited London, Edinburgh, and had a very promising meeting in Tokyo—only to return home late in the month to the news that the New York Stock Exchange had suffered the greatest single-day crash in its history. With markets in a tailspin, the notion of selling high-risk bonds flew out the window. So the interest rate on our debt shot up to more than 18 percent. For the next couple of years, Ethan Allen would be responsible for interest of over $50 million per year—while our expected company profits were around $40 million.

Fortunately, a provision we'd negotiated helped us continue our business. When the interest rate on the $150 million in unsecured debt to GE Capital and Smith Barney increased to 18 percent, we had the option of paying it not in cash but in the form of a payment in kind—which meant that the interest was added to the principal. This let Ethan Allen survive, but it made the amount of debt we were carrying even greater.

This economic backdrop made the strategic transformation of the company even more urgent. "We've got to modernize this company fast," was the message I shared repeatedly with my leadership team. "If we don't, we have no chance."

■ ■ ■

ONE KIND OF CHANGE I'd long realized we needed was a revitalization and modernization of our product styles.

Prior to the mid-1980s, Ethan Allen had always focused on early American furniture—English-inspired designs from the colonial period, typically made in cherry or maple woods. In fact, this style of furniture had largely dominated the entire US industry for decades. Pressure was now mounting to develop a new look for the American home.

Styles in home decor developed over time, following a pattern that is roughly similar to the pattern we see in other areas of design.

Consider, for example, the way Americans dress themselves. In the 1700s and early 1800s, most people made their own clothes at home, mostly following simple, traditional patterns. Only the wealthiest 1 or 2 percent could afford to be "fashionable," buying store-bought clothes that imitated trends launched by designers in world capitals like London and Paris.

The advent of mass-produced clothing and national retail chains in the late 1800s led to the rise of department stores. These made basic, attractive clothing in simple styles available to millions of people. And while these styles evolved over time, most Americans continued to shop for clothes in the same way as late as the 1970s, updating the family wardrobe once or twice a year during a visit to a local store like Sears, Macy's, or J. C. Penney.

The 1970s marked a dramatic change in this pattern. New kinds of clothing stores reflecting fresher, more varied styles began to make their appearance in malls and on Main Streets all over America—the Gap, Banana Republic, and others. Millions of middle-class Americans who had once been satisfied with clothes that were functional and followed the same basic styles worn by others now began to seek out clothes that expressed a sense of personal identity and flair.

In the years since then, the multiplication of style options and the expansion of retail choices have only increased. Foreign-based companies like Zara and H&M have begun to pop up in American malls; online stores have made even more style choices available to millions.

This general evolution in the direction of ever-increasing choice, variety, and creativity has occurred in other areas of consumer life, from automobiles to food. And by the 1970s, the same trend came to home decor. Early American furniture was no longer the dominant style. More and more consumers, especially younger ones, were eager for different styles of home furnishings—contemporary, European-inspired, Asian-accented, and so on.

Making matters worse for us, to many in the rising generation of people launching families and decorating their new homes, the name Ethan Allen had begun to sound a bit stodgy and old-fashioned. If we didn't modernize our offerings, we ran the risk of becoming irrelevant.

Ethan Allen responded to this challenge with new lines of products that modernized our look and began to attract a whole new generation of consumers. While I am not a trained designer, I have a good sense of evolving styles. I set about educating myself so that I could play my part in bringing a more up-to-date design sensibility to Ethan Allen. Otherwise we could find our sales and profits dwindling as our traditional customers grew older and were not replaced by younger ones.

Over time, our team members developed what we called "classic design with a modern attitude." In 1991, we launched a style program called American Impressions, inspired by the Mission-style furniture of the late 1800s. This was quickly followed by American Dimensions, a more modern yet classical look. In both cases, we used "American" as part of the title to symbolize the transition we were making from Ethan Allen's past to its future. Each of these new attitudes was designed to be relevant to the tastes and values of an emerging set of customers while maintaining the commitment to quality materials, design, and workmanship that have always made Ethan Allen one of America's most admired and desirable brands. Other new looks have followed.

At times, we still get glances of pleased surprise when people look at one of our catalogs, our website, or a showroom display after years away: "Wow—is *that* Ethan Allen?!" But those looks of surprise are becoming rarer. More and more consumers now recognize that Ethan Allen is a source for high-quality home design in a range of styles that almost anyone can appreciate and enjoy. And that includes younger customers who we hope will be shopping with us for decades to come.

. . .

AT THE SAME TIME, we set about remodeling our company image to keep pace with the new attitude instilled in our products. For example, the traditional Ethan Allen logo had used an Early American–style typeface and the color green, evoking the colonial period and the state of Vermont. We updated this with a new logo that used a modern type style in a vibrant shade of blue. The new logo was unveiled at a big dealer conference in Manhattan, which featured a performance by a troupe of singers and dancers from Broadway. It was then featured on the external signage of a grand new flagship store that we opened on Third Avenue and 65th Street in the heart of New York's most fashionable retail neighborhood. This was showy behavior for a company once considered rather staid.

We also needed to update the look of our storefronts. For decades, our stores had different names, reflecting the fragmented nature of our dealer network: Carriage House; Georgetown Ethan Allen; Restful Ethan Allen. Beginning in the 1990s, we began changing this so all the stores would have the same Ethan Allen name.

We also wanted them to have the same design appearance—just as every Apple, Target, or Nordstrom store displays the same logo and has a similar look and feel. In 1991, I met with a number of architects who offered ideas about how to redesign the Ethan Allen store exteriors. Their proposals were expensive, and none of them excited me. Then Joyce Chesnik, our dealer in Houston and a member of my advisory committee, introduced me to an architect named Joel Brand. His concepts were appealing, so I invited him to a meeting in Danbury in February 1992. We were joined by a few of our independent retailers from the New York area, including my good friends Phil Esposito and Bill Landau, as well as Lou Grasso, my New Rochelle–based contractor.

We all agreed that Brand's sketches were attractive, so I said, "We want to redesign our Danbury store along the lines you propose by this April—two months from now."

Brand was a bit shocked. "It will take me that long just to finish my architectural drawings," he said.

I turned to Lou Grasso. "What do you think, Lou? Could you start work in Danbury using Joel's sketches while the finished drawings are being developed?"

"I can do that," Lou replied.

"Then let's do it," I said. Later that day, I called the mayor of Danbury to ask for an expedited demolition permit, and the project was under way. I worked closely with Lou over the next two months to keep the cost of the renovation project under $100,000—a figure we believed most of our dealers would be able to afford.

By April, the Danbury storefront was finished, and we invited our dealers to come and see it. They were suitably impressed. But some were reluctant to invest the money in redesigning their own storefronts. So we made an extraordinary financial offer to those dealers. "If you're ready to join us in adopting the modern new look of Ethan Allen," I said, "we're willing to lend you the cash you'll need to implement the changes in your property. We can advance you $100,000 at an interest rate of 10 percent."

Nowadays, of course, 10 percent would be a high rate of interest to pay for a property improvement loan; but in the late 1980s, it was an unusually *low* rate. And remember that we ourselves were paying more than 18 percent on the cost of capital. Thus, we were *losing* money on every loan we made to the dealers. Not that they were aware of the fact; we didn't widely publicize the interest rate on our bonds, because the news would have made the dealers very nervous about the future of Ethan Allen.

Still, convincing individual owners with a strong emotional attachment to their traditional look took a lot of persuasion and diplomacy. In the fall of 1992, I got our long-standing Chicago dealer Ron Emanuel to redesign his storefront in a prominent shopping area in Skokie. Soon thereafter, we held a dealer gathering in Chicago's famous Drake Hotel and showed them a powerful video highlighting customers' positive reactions to the new look. By the time the meeting ended, ten more dealers had decided to make the switch.

The following spring, dealer Royce Baker redesigned the exterior of his San Diego store. Again, we ballyhooed the change during a subsequent dealer meeting, this one at San Diego's beautiful Coronado Hotel. This won over another twenty to thirty converts. And in the fall, we launched our new design center in Atlanta during a meeting at the Ritz-Carlton hotel in Buckhead, Georgia.

Thanks to efforts like these, within three years' time, more than 70 percent of the Ethan Allen stores had been converted to the new look—which helped bring in streams of new customers and increased revenues.

We also needed to change our approach to advertising. Prior to the 1980s, there had been limited national advertising for Ethan Allen in shelter magazines like *House Beautiful*. Its sole purpose was brand building. For a comparison, think of the brand-building television ads by automakers like Ford or BMW, which are supplemented by very different ads run in local markets by specific car dealers. In the same way, individual Ethan Allen dealers were accustomed to running their own ads in local newspapers, magazines, and on TV.

The result was a cacophony of messages as each dealer created a unique message that had no clear relationship to those of other dealers. It also led to a disparity between the larger dealers and the smaller ones. The biggest dealers with the strongest revenue flows were able to afford much more local advertising, while the smallest dealers could run few or no ads. I moved to replace this with a much larger, stronger, and more coherent unified national advertising program that would benefit all our dealers, not just the richest few.

But the shift to national advertising required an expensive investment. Ethan Allen was dealing with a significant burden of debt at this time, which meant that finding a large amount of money to launch a new advertising program wasn't easy. We even borrowed almost $30 million to launch our first big national ad campaign. To take such risks, we had to be very sure of the long-term value of the strategies we were pursuing. We were; and over time, the bets we placed paid off. By 1992, Ethan Allen sales were on the rise. The company's growth trajectory, which had stalled for a number of years, resumed its climb.

. . .

OUR TURNAROUND STRATEGY for Ethan Allen was working. But the massive, expensive debt we'd taken on—first to purchase the company, then to invest in its reinvention—was still hanging over us. In early 1993, we decided it was time to raise some money to pay off that debt. The solution was to go public again—to raise cash through an initial public offering (IPO). This strategy of taking a company private, then going public again, was common in the 1990s, a time when the market for corporate control was very dynamic.

One of the first things we did was identify a lead underwriter—an investment bank that would manage the IPO process for us. SEC regulations required an independent lead underwriter, which eliminated both Kidder, Peabody (then owned by GE) and Smith Barney, which had equity in the company. So we retained Morgan Stanley to take on that role. We set up a meeting with a highly regarded young banker from Morgan Stanley in the Manhattan office of Ed Meyer, chairman of Grey Advertising and a member of our board.

The meeting was just a few minutes old when this banker brought it to a screeching halt. As our entire team waited to hear his recommendations for a strategy regarding the Ethan Allen IPO, he looked around the room and declared, "We've studied your numbers and your business circumstances, and we've determined that Ethan Allen cannot go public."

I broke the stunned silence. "Why not?"

"Because once the debt you're carrying is balanced against the revenues and profits you're generating, there's no value left. According to the numbers, Ethan Allen is not a going concern."

This was a pretty serious determination. In effect, he was saying Ethan Allen needed to file for Chapter 11 bankruptcy.

All of us in the room were well acquainted with the serious financial challenges Ethan Allen faced—in fact, we'd been working day and night for years to overcome them. But we were shocked to hear this outside banker blithely declare that our efforts had achieved nothing. As for me, I was angry.

"We asked you here to give us advice about going public, not to tell us that the company we've been building has no value. You're fired. And I'll have nothing to do with you, because you're absolutely wrong in your conclusions."

The next day, I called up John Birkelund, my old CEO and mentor from New Court Securities. By this time, Birkelund was heading the investment bank of Dillon, Read & Company, and he'd been following the fortunes of Ethan Allen.

I asked, "John, do you believe in me and in Ethan Allen?"

"Of course," he replied.

"I appreciate your saying that," I said. "We've been dealing with some tough financial circumstances, but we've made a lot of progress. Now we want to go public to raise the money we need to get out from under our debt. We hired Morgan Stanley to help us handle the process, but they refused to do it, because they are worried about our prospects. They're wrong to be worried, but it's only fair to tell you about their opinion—because I'd like to ask you and Dillon, Read to take us public as our lead underwriter. Will you consider it?"

"Of course I will," Birkelund replied. I arranged to have our financial data delivered to Birkelund and his team, and after they studied the numbers—the same numbers that Morgan Stanley had examined—they agreed to do it. Dillon, Read became our lead underwriter, and Smith Barney and Kidder, Peabody took secondary roles.

In March 1993, our IPO was announced in a small story in *The New York Times:*

Ethan Allen Interiors Inc., a manufacturer and retailer of home furnishings, made an initial public offering of stock on Tuesday.

Underwriters led by Kidder, Peabody & Company priced the 7.35 million common shares at $18 a share. The shares closed yesterday at $20.25 a share, up 25 cents for the day. The stock is trading on the New York Stock Exchange under the symbol ETH.

(Actually, as I've noted, the IPO was led by Dillon, Read; Kidder, Peabody was a secondary underwriter.)

Ethan Allen Interiors was the new public name adopted by the entity that had previously been known as Green Mountain Holding Company. We still use that name today. I had the honor of ringing the ceremonial bell that marks the opening of trading on the New York Stock Exchange. Most important, the IPO raised a reasonable amount of money that we could use to pay off our high-interest debt. Many of our independent dealers also profited from the IPO, because they were investors in Ethan Allen, and therefore got some of their money back when we went public.

The big, risky bets we'd been making ever since I took over the company were finally paying off.

■ ■ ■

I EXPLAINED PREVIOUSLY how part of our strategy for reinventing Ethan Allen was to gradually buy out many of the independent dealers who owned and ran our stores around the country. This process continued and accelerated in the mid-1990s, as increasing numbers of our longtime dealers decided they were ready to retire. Whenever this happened, I would meet with the dealer and his or her family, and offer a fair price for the store or stores based on the formula we'd developed. In most cases, this led to a deal that everyone found satisfactory.

Now let me explain in a little more detail how this process fit into our business and financial strategy.

One of the things we did as we took over a growing number of stores was to give roles of increasing prominence to the designers who were the creative force behind our retail operations. When I examined what was happening at a given dealership, I often found that the lead designer was the smartest and most effective manager at the location. When Ethan Allen took over the store, it often made sense to elevate that designer to the manager in charge of operations. It was a bit like taking a talented, ambitious major in the army and promoting him or her to the rank of general. In most cases, this decision paid off handsomely. The designers were pleased and excited to be granted this new level of authority and influence, and they used it to make the stores more dynamic, attractive, and successful.

We also took advantage of the transition from independent ownership to company ownership to rethink the physical locations of many stores. Some were in locations that had once been highly successful but had gradually become less popular over time—places where the traffic had diminished and where fewer and fewer shoppers could be found. When we took over those stores, we sold the property and used the proceeds to move to new locations—for instance, to the new so-called lifestyle centers where traffic-generating stores like Whole Foods were beginning to open up. In this way, we were repositioning Ethan Allen to be ready for a new era of retailing.

In developing a new, growing chain of retail stores that we owned along with our manufacturing operations, we were transforming Ethan Allen into a vertically integrated company—one that controls the whole value chain, from production to customer sales. This was an unusual strategy. In fact, conventional wisdom today states that it's generally better to break up vertically integrated operations and to outsource as many operations as possible. This is why, for example, companies like Nike and Apple outsource their production processes through outside manufacturers rather than owning their own factories. This system is supposed to provide a level of flexibility and low costs that protect the profitability of the firm.

However, we've found that the mathematics of designing, producing, warehousing, shipping, and retailing our own lines of goods works well for Ethan Allen. In fact, even when a particular retail store is not highly profitable, owning and managing it is beneficial to our overall finances. In our case, the retail side gives business to the wholesale side.

In other words, having our stores attract customers to buy our furniture enables us to keep our factories running.

This was the business model we were building and perfecting as we integrated more and more of our retail outlets within the overall Ethan Allen umbrella.

During the decades that followed our 1993 IPO, Ethan Allen generated some $2 billion of free cash, which enabled us to pay down our $400 million in debt. We also purchased back almost $600 million of our stock, enriching our shareholders; paid out almost $400 million in dividends; and invested almost $800 million in capital expenditures.

Ethan Allen was firing on all cylinders.

9

HEARTBREAK

FROM HIS EARLIEST DAYS, our oldest child, Irfan, was a very bright, lively, engaged child—someone who enjoyed life to the fullest, taking a passionate interest in a wide array of subjects. He loved outdoor activities of all kinds, including sports. The old tennis court that we refurbished in the backyard of our New Rochelle home became a popular hangout among the local kids, and Irfan spent countless hours volleying balls back and forth with his sister and brother and friends from the neighborhood.

Irfan also had a deep love of nature, so when we bought our farm in 1981, he was absolutely thrilled. He loved to fish in the ponds we built. His love of the outdoors persisted into his teenage years. When he was old enough to take on summer work, I offered to give him a job at Ethan Allen, but he preferred taking on jobs that let him spend his days outside, building things with his hands. A natural musician, Irfan became a skilled guitarist after just a year or two of practice, able to play both classical guitar pieces and rock tunes by groups like Led Zeppelin.

Irfan was also a smart and successful student. For a short time, he attended a public elementary school in New Rochelle called the

Roosevelt School, and then he was selected to attend a public school for high-achieving students. Later, he transferred to Iona Grammar School and then moved on to Iona Preparatory School. Both schools had been founded by the Congregation of Christian Brothers, a worldwide religious community within the Catholic Church. Having attended Catholic-run missionary schools back in Pakistan and Kashmir, I felt comfortable having Irfan educated in these Christian settings—in fact, many of his teachers were priests, and he enjoyed taking part in religious classes that included intensive Bible study.

Farida and I later learned that Irfan took special pleasure in friendly debates about theology with his teachers and fellow students at Iona. His classroom study of the Bible as well as his private reading of the Koran turned him into an unusually thoughtful, introspective young man. He was also sensitive and altruistic—the kind of young person who takes his allowance and gives it to help the poor rather than spending it on himself.

A bit of Irfan's personality can be glimpsed in a meditative poem he wrote that earned him an A in Miss Sweeney's tenth grade honors English class:

Me

Who am I? What am I? Where am I?

Am I important? Or am I not?

Am I a king sitting upon his throne?

Or am I the peasant at his feet?

Is my head hollow, or is it solid, like a stone?

Am I dust made incarnate?

Or just a lump of meat?

Of all the questions that could be, and of the answers I cannot see,

I do know one thing . . .

And that is that I am Me.

During the 1970s and 1980s, when Irfan's character was being developed, I was working very hard, particularly during the period when I was running two businesses. Like many businesspeople, I put in long hours during the week and even on the weekends. But I was luckier than many other ambitious executives. Starting in 1973, my main office was in Larchmont, quite close to our home. That meant I was able to spend almost every evening with my family, except during the international trips I made each quarter.

Once we had the farm, we spent about half our weekends there as a family, participating in outdoor activities and simply enjoying being together. Having grown up in the mountains of Kashmir, Farida and I shared the philosophy that children need free time to roam, explore, and develop themselves, rather than having every minute scheduled with music lessons, tutoring sessions, and other prescribed activities. For many years, we didn't even have a television at the farm. "Let them grow up slowly and enjoy playing in the woods," we often said. And Irfan in particular took full advantage of this opportunity.

We also made the most of our chances to travel together as a family. Sometimes the children attended Ethan Allen dealer meetings that were organized as "family meetings." For example, in 1985, when I became president, Nat Ancell suggested we hold our national conference at the famous Biltmore Hotel in Scottsdale, Arizona. More than four hundred of our dealers and their family members attended, as did Farida, Irfan, Farah, and Omar.

Most years, we took two family trips. One trip would be to a destination somewhere in the United States or Canada—a place like the Grand Canyon, Williamsburg in Virginia, Banff National Park in Canada, the islands of Hawaii, or Disneyland.

The other trip we took most years would be to our family's homeland in Kashmir. At first, we traveled back to Kashmir and stayed with family members in their homes. Later, when annual trips to Kashmir had become our regular habit, we built a house of our own in Srinagar, where Farida and the children would stay for several weeks every summer. I joined them there for as much time as I could take away from the office, an average of ten days or so. Starting in the late 1970s, with our children getting bigger and stronger, we began spending part of our summers taking hiking trips in the Himalayas, calling ourselves the Kashmir Mountaineering Club.

As a dedicated outdoorsman, Irfan loved these trips to the mountains. And as he grew older, these trips also helped him develop a deeper and more sophisticated understanding of his Kashmiri heritage—including its social and political aspects. During our travels, he spent time talking with the people about their lives. He developed friendships with a number of his Kashmiri cousins, who would accompany us on our hikes.

As time passed, he could see the unhappiness of the people of Kashmir. He realized how deeply they desired to be free, even though their understanding of what "freedom" meant was limited. And he developed a sense of sympathy and concern over the plight of Muslims deprived of the right to govern themselves. I'm sure the knowledge that I'd been involved all my life in peaceful struggle in support of this right helped strengthen Irfan's conviction that this was a worthy cause.

Irfan's growing sense of political engagement during the 1980s also took place against the backdrop of the Soviet invasion of Afghanistan. This was a matter of complicated geopolitical conflict that few people at the time fully understood—and that many people continue to misunderstand to this day.

The war between invading Soviet forces and a collection of local insurgent groups in Afghanistan ending up lasting over nine years and taking the lives of hundreds of thousands of people. It originally started as a result of a power struggle among the rulers of Afghanistan. The country's Communist party had seized control of the nation in a 1978 coup led by Nur Mohammad Taraki. A year later, Taraki was killed on the orders of a political rival, Hafizullah Amin, who took power in his place. This provoked intervention by the Soviet Union, then led by Leonid Brezhnev. The Soviet army deposed Amin and installed their favorite, Babrak Karmal, as the new president of Afghanistan.

Armed groups who were opposed to the Soviet intervention quickly formed, mainly in the Afghan countryside. Collectively known as the mujahideen, these groups launched a rebellion against the Soviet-backed government. Foreign powers around the world also denounced the Soviet intervention. In January 1980, the nations of the Islamic Conference called for immediate withdrawal of the Soviet troops, and the UN General Assembly passed a resolution making a similar demand.

Soon vast amounts of military aid, equipment, and training began to flow to the insurgent groups in Afghanistan. This support was paid for mainly by Pakistan, by a number of wealthy Arab nations, such as Saudi Arabia, and by the United States, mostly through covert action by the Central Intelligence Agency. The Americans viewed the conflict as an opportunity to combat the Russian influence in Afghanistan and as an indirect way to get revenge on the Soviets for the long, costly struggle against Communism that the US itself had experienced in Vietnam. Thus, the conflict in Afghanistan quickly became a "proxy war" between the USSR and the US.

Over the next nine years, this long, brutal war produced enormous consequences. Millions of Afghans became refugees and fled to neighboring countries, including Pakistan and Iran. Tensions between East and West reached new heights, leading to the American-led boycott of the 1980 Olympic Games in Moscow as well as an answering boycott of the 1984 games in Los Angeles. The US funneled up to $20 billion to the mujahideen, with some of the funding continuing during the Afghan civil war that followed the withdrawal of Soviet troops in 1989. And some experts believe that the leadership vacuum in Afghanistan left in the wake of the war—combined with the accumulation of weapons and military expertise by the mujahideen, thanks to US support—helped lead to the rise of al-Qaida and, eventually, the tragedy of 9/11. It's a classic example of the unintended consequences that can arise from well-intended but poorly conceived actions by a government that doesn't really understand the societies in which it intervenes.

In this painful, prolonged struggle among warring political powers, countless idealistic young people got caught up. One of them was our son Irfan.

As Irfan followed the news about the fighting in Afghanistan, he became strongly convinced that the Soviet invasion was an evil act that must be opposed—peacefully if possible, but by force of arms if necessary. Remember that Farida's family on both her father's and her mother's sides had come from Afghanistan to Kashmir, and Irfan himself had met some of these family members during our trips to Kashmir. So there was a link between our family and the struggle in Afghanistan. Irfan began talking about this battle with friends and family members and even wrote an essay about it for one of his high school classes.

In taking a position in support of the mujahideen, Irfan was embracing his fellow Muslims, who viewed the cause of repelling the foreign invaders as a religious struggle as well as a political one. But he was also following the lead of our own President Ronald Reagan, who declared, in a famous 1983 speech, "To watch the courageous Afghan freedom fighters battle modern arsenals with simple handheld weapons is an inspiration to those who love freedom."

Hearing about the twin struggles for freedom by two groups of Muslims—those in Kashmir and those in Afghanistan—strengthened Irfan's determination to be some kind of political or social activist. Simply learning about problems wasn't enough; he felt a responsibility to take concrete actions to help stop atrocities and support movements toward freedom around the world. And his growing sense of Muslim identity fed this feeling. He'd developed a strong conviction that Islam should be a religion that is not governed by priests or imams enforcing a prescribed dogma but rather a faith based on the freedom and equality of all believers.

For all these reasons, Irfan was increasingly interested in studying and possibly practicing Islamic law, seeing it as a way of promoting his vision of a free, just, and equal Muslim world—the vision that he believed captured most accurately the original spirit of the Prophet Mohammad.

. . .

IN 1989, IRFAN GRADUATED from Iona Prep. He briefly attended McGill University in Montreal, but he didn't like it very much. So he decided to take a semester off. He returned to New York and enrolled in some classes at Iona College, right near our home in New Rochelle.

Our family had taken its annual hiking trip in Kashmir in the summer of 1989. Unfortunately, it would be the last such trip for a while—because in 1989, after a period of peace, fighting broke out in Kashmir again.

As with many aspects of the ongoing conflict in Kashmir, even describing exactly what happened is difficult. Each group in the region has its own version of the story, complete with its own vocabulary. So, for example, the militant Muslim groups that organized in response to contested elections held in 1987 are called "freedom fighters" by their supporters—which include the government of Pakistan. By contrast, those who oppose these groups, including the government of India, describe them as "Islamic terrorists."

What is clear, however, is that in Kashmir, as in many societies riven by long-term strife, there is a vicious cycle at work. When militancy erupts on one side, fighting begins, leading to a strong reaction from the other side. In the case of Kashmir, many members of the Hindu community, who made up about 10 percent of the population, began to flee the region. Some say they left because they felt threatened by local Muslims; others contend they emigrated because of encouragement by the Indian-controlled government.

In any case, both India and Pakistan responded to the political turmoil in ways that were not helpful. The Indian army launched a harsh crackdown in Kashmir, while the Pakistani government provided guns to young rebels in the region, fueling further fighting. Within months, some twenty thousand Kashmiris had been killed. The Indian government imposed martial law and launched a house-to-house search for Muslim militants, subjecting innocent people to humiliating searches and forcing them out of their homes. Our own relatives shared stories about this happening to them, which left Irfan fuming over the injustice of it all.

I shared many of Irfan's feelings, although I was focused more on the cyclical nature of the conflict than on a one-sided story of Indian repression and Muslim suffering. As a prominent Kashmiri-American, I was strongly motivated to do what I could to try to resolve the conflict. For this reason, I listened carefully when I was approached with the offer to serve as president of a newly formed Kashmiri-American Council, whose goal would be to advance the two causes of human rights for all and the political freedom of Kashmir.

However, my ears pricked up when one of the members of the group, in an effort to persuade me to accept this role, proudly declared, "We've already received plenty of funding that we can use to publicize and promote our work."

"Where has this funding come from?" I asked.

"We can't tell you that," was the reply.

This didn't sound right to me. I asked for a day to think about the offer. When I met with the organizers again, I respectfully declined the position of president, and in fact I informed the group that I would be unable to support them in any fashion.

Instead, I helped form a body called the Committee for Solidarity in Kashmir. It was co-chaired by me and a Kashmiri Hindu, and it attracted members from both the Muslim and Hindu communities of Kashmiri-Americans.

We held a meeting in Danbury, Connecticut, in which the two religious groups engaged in a heated discussion. After listening for a while, I intervened. "If we insist on taking sides with either India or Pakistan, we'll never find common ground. Instead, we need to focus on the welfare of the people of Kashmir." I urged the Muslim members and the Hindu members to meet in separate rooms for a while, to discuss whether they could accept this core principle. After about two hours, both groups emerged from their separate conferences and reported that they were ready to forge an agreement. On this basis, the committee issued statements and published newspaper ads calling for a peaceful resolution to the Kashmir conflict and the creation of a government that would be free of discrimination or bias.

I also met with a delegation from India. The delegation was led by Atal Bihari Vajpayee, who later served several years as the prime minister of India. It also included Rafiq Zakaria, a prominent Muslim political leader whose son, Fareed Zakaria, was then beginning his career as a distinguished American journalist. We talked about the dire circumstances in Kashmir, including the flight of Hindus and the imposition of martial law by the Indian government, which had led to the imprisonment of many Muslim leaders. I also had several meetings with Dr. Karan Singh, the former "head of the state" of Kashmir who was now serving as the Indian ambassador to the US. These were positive meetings that underscored the fact that leaders of goodwill could be found on all sides of the conflict—but they led to no immediate solution.

During this same period, the fighting in Afghanistan continued, despite the fact that the Soviet army had withdrawn its troops in 1989. The departure of the Russians had led to a new phase of fighting in

Afghanistan, with the mujahideen now battling against what they called the "puppet regime" that held nominal control of the country. The leaders of the Democratic Republic of Afghanistan had long been supported by the Soviets and in fact were heavily armed with weaponry supplied by the USSR. With the Soviet Union itself tottering— remember, the Berlin Wall fell in 1989, signaling the beginning of the end of the Communist empire—this pro-Russian government at Kabul was weakening. By the early 1990s, the mujahideen were increasingly optimistic about their chances of seizing control and installing a religiously conservative Islamic regime.

Undoubtedly both the Kashmir conflict and the drawn-out war in Afghanistan weighed heavily on Irfan's mind in 1990 and 1991, as he tried to decide the next step in his studies, his career, and his life.

In 1991, my old schoolmate, Justice Ali Nawaz Chowhan, came to visit our family in New York. As I've recounted, when I was child back in the 1950s, I lived for a time in the Pakistani city of Rawalpindi, where I attended a school called St. Mary's. I'd known Ali Nawaz Chowhan when we were classmates together at St. Mary's. Over time, he had become a prominent attorney, jurist, and legal educator back home in Pakistan. His career in government would ultimately include an appointment as a justice of the International Court of Justice at The Hague and gain him respect as a human rights leader.

During his visit with us, Ali Nawaz learned about Irfan's interest in the law. As they conversed, he also discovered that Irfan was unsure about what to do next in his life and that he was increasingly preoccupied with the problems being faced by Muslims around the world.

Ali Nawaz believed he might have a solution. "You know," he said, "we have an international university in Islamabad. It has a fine program focused on Islamic law. Why not come to Pakistan for a semester or two and study law there?" The idea, Ali Nawaz later explained to me, was that being in school in Islamabad would encourage Irfan to concentrate on his studies.

Irfan liked the idea, and the powerful influence of Ali Nawaz enabled Irfan to be accepted by the university, even though the official time for submitting an application had passed. In September, Irfan flew to Pakistan to begin his studies. (It was not Irfan's first trip to Pakistan. He had visited the country twice before—once with our family when we went to see my sister and her husband, who was a senior UN official stationed in Pakistan, and once on his way to attend a conference on Kashmir.)

A few uneventful months went by, and then, in December 1991, I decided to travel to Islamabad myself to see how Irfan was doing. What I found was disturbing. The university, I learned, was a hotbed of political discussions—with the conflict in Afghanistan at the top of the list. Every corner of the school seemed to be filled with students arguing about what was going on in Afghanistan. Many were furious at the history of outside interference in the country, and quite a few were giving speeches declaring that it was the duty of every serious Muslim to contribute to the fight against the lingering Russian influence. (I've noticed there always seem to be plenty of people announcing that it is the duty of *other* people to risk their lives in the battle against evil— not so many taking up the cause themselves.) These rabble-rousers were calling the battle by the mujahideen a noble example of what the Koran calls jihad. It's a common misunderstanding of the word, which really refers to the spiritual struggle that a person wages within himself, not the physical battles involved in warfare. But many militant Muslims use the word "jihad" in this way, thereby giving their favorite political cause the aura of religious blessing.

To my dismay, I realized that, rather than sheltering Irfan from talk about jihad, we'd inadvertently thrust him into the middle of it. Now, with 20/20 hindsight, I could see our error—but it was too late to correct it.

I spent several days with Irfan at the university. Ali Nawaz also arranged for the two of us to spend one night together in a cottage up in the mountains. Huddled together for warmth, we stayed up late having a long father-son talk.

I shared my worries. "Irfan, your main job is your studies. It upsets me to see you so preoccupied with politics and war."

"You don't need to worry about me, Dad," Irfan responded. "What's happening in the world is important—you know that, too. I am just trying to figure out what I can do to help."

"That's why I'm worried," I said. "I want you to come back to America with me."

Irfan shook his head. "No, Dad, I need to be here. It's our job to help people who are less fortunate than us. Unless we do what we can to help others, our lives are meaningless."

"If you feel that strongly about it," I said, "I'll go to Afghanistan and help the people in their struggle. It would be better for me to go than you, with your whole life ahead of you."

But nothing I said could change Irfan's thinking.

I returned home without Irfan, feeling very concerned. Still, nothing alarming happened for a while. Irfan visited us at home for a couple of weeks during the end-of-year holiday, and everything seemed normal. A couple of times during Irfan's visit, I thought about taking his passport from him and hiding it, which would have prevented him from returning to Pakistan. But I realized that would be the wrong thing to do. A young man must make his own decisions—especially a strong-minded young man like Irfan.

He returned to Islamabad in January 1992. During the first few months of the year, the newspapers reported intensified fighting in Afghanistan. Farida and I were praying that Irfan would stay focused on his studies.

As far as we knew, all was well—until the phone rang on April 10. It was Ali Nawaz, delivering the message we'd been dreading—the worst message that any parent could receive.

. . .

DAYS LATER WE LEARNED the circumstances of Irfan's death.

April 4 through 7, 1992, had been a long weekend for the students of the international university—a celebration of the Islamic festival of Eid, marking the end of the holy month of Ramadan, with its fasting. That's when one of Irfan's college friends said, "Let's take the weekend to visit Afghanistan. We can see for ourselves what's happening there and maybe do something to help." A group of four boys agreed to make the trip—one from Bangladesh, one from Pakistan, one from Jordan, and the American, Irfan.

They traveled to Afghanistan and made their way to a hillside in the mountains near the provincial capital of Jalalabad, where they joined an encampment of mujahideen fighters. The mujahideen welcomed them; they were accustomed to being visited by foreigners coming to offer support.

Irfan and his friends had only been at the camp for a few hours when government soldiers launched a mortar attack on the mujahideen fighters. Irfan and two of the other students were killed by the shelling. Only the boy from Pakistan survived to tell the tale—he had left his friends sitting together while he went off to fetch some food. His brief absence was what saved his life. He returned to the university a few days later and told the authorities what had happened. They contacted Ali Nawaz, and he called us in America.

I was not at home when the call came—I was in North Carolina attending a furniture fair. Farida received the news and called me. I flew home immediately, and our daughter, Farah, met me at the airport for our heartbroken reunion.

Later we learned a little more of the story. After the mortar attack, the mujahideen brought the bodies of Irfan and the two other boys to

an area known as Torkham, which is near the border between Afghanistan and Pakistan. All three boys were buried there.

Ironically, it all happened just one week before the pro-Soviet government in Kabul decided to give up the fight and relinquish power,
thereby ending the fighting in Afghanistan.

I was tempted to travel immediately to Pakistan—to attend a
memorial service that had been scheduled at the university, and then
to visit Irfan's grave across the border. But on reflection, I realized
that it was more important for me to stay at home with the rest of our
family. Irfan's sister, Farah, then seventeen years old, and his fourteen-
year-old brother, Omar, were devastated by the news—as was Farida.
We spent the next few weeks staying as close together as possible,
while hearing of events in Pakistan from long distance. Farida's father
and her brother-in-law Ibrahim Shahdad traveled from Kashmir to
attend the memorial service in Islamabad, where Ali Nawaz and others gave eulogies.

In time, we held our own memorial service at our home in New
Rochelle. Our friends and family gathered around us, as did many of
my colleagues from Ethan Allen. Irfan's friends from the community
and from the schools he'd attended came out in force, along with many
of the teachers who'd appreciated his lively intellect and his sensitive
personality. There was little that anyone could say to comfort us in a
time of such shattering grief. But the presence of so many people who
loved us and who cared for Irfan was deeply meaningful.

Those first few weeks after receiving the news were a time of shock
and devastation. Much of the time, Farida and I were simply going
through the motions of life—living mechanically while keeping, as
best we could, the most painful emotions at bay.

Only gradually did we begin the real, long-term work of grappling
with what had happened, and with the terrible questions: How? Why?
What did it mean? And was there something we could have done differently that might have spared us this unimaginable tragedy?

One of the ways I personally tried to deal with the event was to begin reading the Koran more seriously than I'd ever done before. I knew that this holy book was the source of many of the ideas and ideals that had motivated Irfan in the final months of his life, and I decided I wanted to understand it better—perhaps feeling that, in so doing, I could somehow get a little closer to the beloved child I would no longer be able to communicate with in life.

One of the most painful things I had to cope with was my intense anger with some of the people around Irfan—friends, teachers, and advisors who had influenced his thinking, often not in a good way. I kept remembering the passion in Irfan's voice when he spoke about jihad, and I was filled with bitterness toward the people who had filled his head with such thoughts, many of them people who refused to lift a finger themselves on behalf of the cause they talked about so freely.

I was especially angry because the more I studied the Koran, the more I realized how badly the concept of jihad is misrepresented in today's world. In true Islam, the greatest jihad is the struggle for control of oneself—control of your emotions and your personal conduct. Jihad is reflected primarily in treating people fairly, respecting the dignity of every human being, and contributing generously to charity. But today the term "jihad" is used mainly in reference to violence. This is a tragic misunderstanding that has led to much suffering.

Irfan was a serious student of the Koran, and he understood the right interpretation of jihad. Yet somehow he got caught up in the Afghanistan conflict. When he made his fatal journey to that troubled country, his goal was to help people facing injustice. He believed that Islam, like every great religion, teaches us that all people will be judged by their Maker on their actions in life. Did you do your part to support those who are suffering and oppressed, or did you stay comfortably on the sidelines? Irfan took this question very seriously, and it led him to his death.

In reflecting on these matters, I thought about my own life when I was as young as Irfan. He and I had a lot in common. Like Irfan, I believed passionately in human rights, and I cared deeply about the injustices my people were experiencing. Like him, I felt compelled to speak out about these issues, and like him I took chances that exposed me to serious danger. There were times when I could easily have lost my life just as Irfan did.

Why did I escape the fate that Irfan suffered? I believe the Koran provides an answer. The scriptures tell us that we all must leave at an appointed time. It will not matter where we are, either in high buildings or hiding underground—when our appointed time comes, then death will take us. We come from God, and we return to God, and the time is not of our choosing.

This explanation leaves the specific reasons for a person's early death mysterious. Yet I find it somewhat comforting. If God makes the choice for us, then our part is to accept that choice and to carry on faithfully with our duties.

When a tragedy like this strikes a family, each member has his or her own painful journey to take. Irfan's brother and sister have had a difficult road to travel, and both have had their lives changed by the loss they suffered.

At the time Irfan was taken from us, Farah was about to finish high school and was in the process of applying for colleges. When she had to decide which college to attend, she came to the conclusion that she didn't want to go too far from home. Farah attended Barnard College at Columbia University, where she studied political science. And during her years there, she would sometimes call her mother and me at night to talk about how homesick she felt. I would say, "You know, I like driving at night." And I would drive down to Manhattan to pick her up and bring her home to sleep in the comfort of her own bed, surrounded by her loved ones.

Farah went on to become passionate about social engagement and human rights, just as Irfan had been. After graduating from Columbia, she pursued graduate studies at the University of Chicago. Then she returned home to the New York area, where she started her family. Today she is the mother of two beautiful little children and an active leader on behalf of progressive political causes in Westchester County.

Omar had been especially close to Irfan, and so he was hit very hard by our loss. For two or three years, he was withdrawn and silent, dealing with the hurt in his own way. Gradually he recovered, and he has gone on to be a very sensitive and thoughtful husband and father to two beautiful children. I think that Irfan's life inspired Omar with a sense that caring for others is the most important thing we can do. He seems to be living his life in accordance with that belief.

Nature has been a powerful source of healing for all of us. Earlier, I mentioned the African journey that Farida and I took in 1994, which included an ascent of Mount Kilimanjaro with our friend Gary Wendt. The next year, I took a six-day rafting trip with Farah and Omar from Lake Powell in Utah to Nevada, through the Grand Canyon. Both of these trips provided us with the kind of healing energy that only a deep connection to the natural world can offer.

A similar impact on me has come from two beautiful animals that have been an important part of our lives—an Abyssinian "temple cat" named Tass, who lived with us from 1991 to 2005, and an Egyptian Mau cat named Pashmina, who joined us after Tass's death and is part of our family to this day. Both cats have been beloved companions, joining me on morning walks and waiting to greet me when I return home in the evening. Little by little, their presence has helped soothe the ache I feel when I think about the loss we suffered, which nothing in the world can ever fully heal.

As for Farida, she has lived with a grief no mother should have to experience. I must say that she has been stronger than I have been. She has been the rock that kept our family together, even at times when my hurt and anger came close to making me want to break down in despair. Seeing how Farida has dealt with our tragedy has made me admire her more than ever.

. . .

AS I'VE SAID, IN THE immediate aftermath of Irfan's death, I resisted the temptation to travel to Pakistan, choosing instead to stay home with family and close friends. But in December 1992, Farida, Farah, Omar, and I made the journey to the place where Irfan lost his life. My father and Farida's mother also traveled from Kashmir to be with us on this trip.

Traveling from Pakistan into Afghanistan was not easy or safe at that time. Our trip was facilitated by a Mr. Hashmi, a friend of my father's who lived in Rawalpindi. He had met Irfan and visited with him at the university. Some of my father's friends intervened with the Pakistani army and with the Afghan rebels to arrange for us to cross the border into Afghanistan, despite the fact that we had no papers giving us permission to make such a trip. Both groups of soldiers had heard about Irfan's death, and they escorted us respectfully to the place where our son was laid to rest.

Irfan's grave was on a hillside—a somewhat neglected place that Irfan shared with the bodies of many other young people killed in the fighting. In accordance with custom, the graves were all unmarked, but we'd been told where Irfan lay, and so we could pay our respects.

It was sad to see how this gravesite, where the hopes and dreams of so many families had come to an end, had become lonely and barren in appearance. Mr. Hashmi sensed our feelings about this. "I want to do something about this place," he told us. "I'll take the responsibility of caring for this whole gravesite. I'll enclose it with a fence and plant trees to make it a more suitable resting place for those who have died."

I appreciated this offer very much. "What about the people in the village nearby?" I asked. "Is there anything we can do for them?"

"It's a poor place, with no access to drinking water," Mr. Hashmi told me.

"Let's help them with that," I said. Mr. Hashmi and I made plans to carry out these two projects. With my support, he made plans to bring water to the village by extending a nearby supply pipe. He also refurbished the gravesite, building a fence around it and planting trees and flowers to make it a beautiful, peaceful place, as I saw when I revisited the place by myself two years later.

Irfan is lovingly remembered by many people here in America. Brother Devlin, who was Irfan's headmaster at Iona Grammar School and now teaches at Iona College, visits with me and Farida about once a year to reminisce fondly about Irfan. Soon after Irfan's passing, my colleagues at Ethan Allen thoughtfully planted a tree at our headquarters in Danbury, with a plaque that still bears his name. Farida and I have endowed the honors program at Western Connecticut State University in Irfan's name, and in 2015 the college gave its Alumni Hall the new name of Irfan Kathwari Honors House.

Farida and I also established the Irfan Kathwari Foundation. It supports a variety of worthwhile causes, including, for example, providing scholarships for the children of Ethan Allen employees. Every year, some forty to fifty students are selected based on criteria originally established by a committee of scholars led by my dear friend, the late Ainslie Embree. Ainslie was one of the world's leading experts on South Asia, a longtime professor at Columbia University, and, as I'll explain in the next chapter, an important member of our Kashmir Study Group.

Choosing the students to receive an Irfan Kathwari scholarship was one of Ainslie's favorite activities every year. He once told me, "Most of the students I work with are PhD candidates with degrees from prestigious colleges whose dream is to be a university professor. It's a wonderful change to get to know high school students from Vermont, North Carolina, or Oklahoma whose dream is to become a nurse, a bookkeeper, or an elementary schoolteacher."

Losing Irfan changed all our lives in profound ways. But perhaps the single most powerful change for me has been a deepening of my desire to use my time, energy, and talent in support of peace and reconciliation among peoples. The best memorial to Irfan that I can imagine would be a world in which no young people ever have to lose their lives in war.

10

PEACE IS THE MISSION

IN THE YEARS FOLLOWING Irfan's death, our family drew even closer. Farida and I devoted much of our time and attention to caring for Farah and Omar, who'd been devastated by the loss of their brother. At work, I was also deeply engaged in the ongoing challenge of reinvigorating Ethan Allen.

At the same time, I became increasingly involved in worldwide efforts to promote peace, alleviate human suffering, and seek solutions to violent conflicts. This engagement with the world helped me come to terms with my own grief while also helping me maintain a sense of balance and purpose in my life.

I found no shortage of people and communities around the world that are in desperate need of help in dealing with the consequences of bigotry, hatred, and oppression. One person I got to know was Alisa Majagic, a Bosnian Muslim whose hometown was destroyed during the ethnic fighting that resulted in the breakup of what had once been Yugoslavia. Alisa, then nineteen years old, spent more than two months in a concentration camp at Trnopolje with her family. Among other consequences, this meant that Alisa's education was halted, since her papers had been lost, and many of her teachers had been killed.

When I met Alisa, she had come to the US through the efforts of a number of nonprofit groups, including Catholic Charities and the Fellowship of Reconciliation, a pacifist organization. Alisa had been introduced to the Westchester Muslim Center, where I had served as president. Seeing an opportunity to help, Farida and I offered to sponsor Alisa. She lived with us while attending Mercy College in Dobbs Ferry. The college awarded her a full scholarship to study international business. In 1995, I traveled to Bosnia at the invitation of Prime Minister Haris Silajdžić. I saw the remains of the local furniture industry, which had been destroyed in the fighting, and I met Alisa's parents. Later, we helped them visit the United States for Alisa's graduation, and they stayed in our home.

We've kept in touch with Alisa over the years. Today, she is a financial executive based in Atlanta, and we're very proud of her. Farida and I feel strongly that helping Alisa helped us just as much as it helped her.

I also devoted time to supporting, learning from, and working with organizations dedicated to the causes of peace, freedom, and assistance for the most vulnerable among us, including the Council on Foreign Relations, the International Rescue Committee, the United States Institute of Peace, the Center for Strategic and International Studies, Refugees International, the World Conference of Religions for Peace, Freedom House, and the Institute for the Study of Diplomacy at Georgetown University. But no single cause received more of my time or attention than the continuing tragedy of my birthplace, Kashmir.

In the previous chapter, I discussed the outbreak of hostilities and violence in Kashmir in 1990. In the decade that followed, this led to the death of some hundred thousand people from the region. In response, I co-founded the Committee for Solidarity in Kashmir, made up of Kashmiri-Americans of both Muslim and Hindu faiths. The committee members found common ground and issued a number of statements calling for a fair settlement of the Kashmir issue, but the communal conflicts in Kashmir continued to fester.

Throughout the early 1990s, I made a deliberate effort to stay in touch with community members and leaders on all sides of the issue, searching for opportunities to reduce the hostilities. Many people mentioned the fact that my family's loss had given me unusual credibility as a spokesperson for peace efforts. Having experienced the tragedy of war firsthand, I was in a position to challenge those on both sides who promoted conflict as a way of pursuing their own goals, such as political power. I could speak with authority on behalf of the families who'd lost children, pleading for greater humility, tolerance, and forgiveness rather than escalating resentment and hatred.

In 1994, my conversations led to a potential breakthrough. Saleem Shervani, a member of the Indian parliament and a former government minister, visited me at our family farm in Livingston. He urged me to increase my personal involvement in efforts to resolve the Kashmir conflict. Shervani followed this up with a conversation with Rajesh Pilot, the Indian minister for Kashmiri affairs in the government of Prime Minister Rao. On behalf of the government, Pilot asked me whether I would undertake a mediation effort. He invited me to visit with Indian leaders, and he approved of my intention to meet with leaders from Pakistan and the Kashmir region in hopes of launching a dialogue that might break the cycle of violence.

My first stop on the journey was in Delhi, where I met with Rajesh Pilot. I told Pilot it was important for me to speak with the leaders of the Kashmiri separatist movement, several of whom had been imprisoned by the Indian government. Pilot agreed and asked me whether it would be helpful for him to arrange a military escort to protect me during my trip to the area of conflict.

"No," I replied. "Having an escort from the Indian government would make me more of a target for violence." So I set out for Kashmir on my own.

I met with several political and religious leaders of the Muslim community. They included the nineteen-year-old son of Mirwaiz Farooq, the religious leader who had officiated at my telephone marriage to Farida and had later been killed in the ongoing violence in Kashmir. Then I traveled to Jammu, where three of the most senior leaders of the movement—Shabir Shah, Abdul Ghani Lone, and Syed Ali Shah Gilani—were being held in prison. I was accompanied by Ibrahim Shahdad.

It was not easy to arrange a meeting with such high-profile political detainees. When I made the request, the superintendent of the prison challenged me: "By what authority are you seeking this meeting?"

"I've come all the way from America at the request of the prime minister of India himself."

"That may be," the superintendent replied, "but no one has informed us about it."

"Go ahead and call the prime minister's office in Delhi," I responded. "They will confirm my story."

My air of authority persuaded him to change his tune. "Show me your papers and fill out this application. If everything is in order, we'll provide you with a cell in which you can meet with these three prisoners for a couple of hours."

In a little while, the superintendent escorted me to a small cell, just large enough for three chairs. Ibrahim Shahdad stayed behind in the superintendent's office. Shah, Lone, and Gilani were seated in the cell—Shah sitting on the floor—waiting to meet me. Before the door was slammed shut, I turned to the superintendent. "Can you please have some tea sent in for us?"

The superintendent looked surprised. "What is this, a hotel?" he muttered. But in a few moments, a guard brought us the tea.

I explained to the three Kashmiri leaders that I was there to learn about their position on the Kashmir issue so that I could communicate it to the leadership in India and Pakistan in hopes of beginning to find some common ground. "The situation now is a disaster," I said. "The Indian government is running the state under military law, and violence is causing great suffering on both sides. What would be your plan for a solution?"

All three leaders were quick to respond with a simple, "We want freedom for Kashmir."

"I understand," I replied. "But what exactly do you mean by 'freedom'? Who will rule Kashmir? What kind of government will be created? Who will qualify to be a citizen of the new nation? And what will its borders look like?"

There was silence for a few moments. Then one of the leaders replied, "We don't have answers for any of that. But once the Indians leave, we'll decide." And the others nodded.

I shook my head. "That's not much of a plan," I said. "The Indians have thousands of soldiers and police in Kashmir, and they claim the right to govern the region. They're not simply going to pack up and leave because you ask them to. As for the Pakistanis, after I leave here, I'm going to be speaking with the prime minister, Mrs. Bhutto, and her senior team. But I don't think it's realistic to believe that the Pakistanis are going to solve your problem. They also claim the right to rule the region. The only result is that your children are dying."

These leaders were not accustomed to having someone challenge them with real-life facts on the ground. They were used to simply speaking in slogans—"Free Kashmir," "India Get Out"—without addressing the serious challenges involved in converting those slogans into actual results.

"What about the UN plebiscite?" one of the leaders asked. "The world agreed many years ago that the people of Kashmir should vote on their own future. We should demand that the plebiscite take place and that the result be honored." Again the other two leaders nodded in agreement.

"You know very well that's not going to happen," I said. "There's a good reason why the plebiscite never took place. The Hindus, mostly in Jammu, would vote to stay with India. The Muslims in the rest of the region would vote to join Pakistan. Both India and Pakistan claim the right to rule all of Jammu and Kashmir, and neither one is prepared to give up that claim. And remember that independence was not even one of the options in the plebiscite mandated by the UN. So no matter how the people voted, at least one regional power would reject the plebiscite and continue the fighting. The idea that a plebiscite will solve anything is not realistic."

The leaders couldn't argue with my points. But neither would they budge from the unrealistic positions they held. We talked for close to an hour and a half. They understood that I wanted to help, and they encouraged me to continue. They said they would support my efforts, even while remaining silent in public.

My conversations with other Kashmiri leaders outside the prison were similar. None of them offered a realistic plan for the future of the region. I also met with many members of my family, some of my classmates, and my university professors to get their perspectives.

I returned to Delhi and reported these findings frankly to Rajesh Pilot. Then I went to Islamabad, where I met with Prime Minister Benazir Bhutto, Foreign Minister Shahryar Khan, and several of the country's top military leaders. I also met with other political leaders and participated in discussions at one of the country's leading think tanks. These conversations helped many influential people know who I was and the mission I'd undertaken.

I took the opportunity of being in Pakistan to make another visit to Afghanistan again accompanied by Mr. Hashmi. As before, we were able to cross the border without any traveling papers, thanks to the help of the local tribal leaders. We paid our respects at Irfan's gravesite, which Mr. Hashmi and the tribal leaders had improved with a wall and many newly planted trees. It was a sad visit for me, of course. But it was also a reminder of why my efforts to improve the chances for peace in South Asia and around the world were so important.

I came away from my meetings with the regional leaders with a deeper understanding of the vast gulf separating these leaders from any real solution for Kashmir. The Indians believed that somehow their military rule would break the will of the separatist movement and convince millions of unhappy Kashmiris to accept Indian control. The Pakistanis believed that their continued support of the Kashmiri dissidents would somehow convince India to abandon the region. Both positions were driven, ultimately, by the mutual hostility of India and Pakistan, with limited concern for and understanding of the people of Kashmir.

. . .

I RETURNED HOME CONVINCED that the most important thing I could do for Kashmir was to try to change the debate—to refocus the discussion on some meaningful options rather than on empty nationalistic slogans.

I also realized that no one person, no matter how influential, could succeed in bringing about such a change. So I decided to create an organization that would serve this purpose. In a nod to my grandfather and his associates, whose Kashmir Reading Room had been a catalyst of the freedom movement in the 1930s, I gave the organization a similar name: the Kashmir Study Group (KSG).

The first person I called about joining the group was Howard Schaffer, the American diplomat I'd met during the Kashmiri uprising of the mid-1960s. He not only agreed to serve but also suggested that I contact a number of other notable experts and leaders he'd met over the years. They included Ainslie Embree, one of the world's foremost scholars on India and the other countries of South Asia; Robert G. Wirsing, a leading expert on South Asian security matters; Ambassador William Phillips Talbot, a scholar on the Indian subcontinent who had previously headed the South Asia Bureau at the US State Department; and Professor Joseph Schwartzberg, a noted South Asian historian from the University of Minnesota. Three politicians also joined the group—Congressman Gary Ackerman, from the New York City borough of Queens, who was chairman of the India caucus in the House of Representatives; Congressman Robert Torricelli from New Jersey (later a member of the Senate), who chaired the Pakistan caucus; and Congressman Jim Leach of Iowa.

Eventually, we put together a distinguished roster of members that included world-famous scholars, presidents of think tanks and nonprofit organizations, five former US ambassadors, and other impressive individuals, all with deep knowledge of the history and politics of South Asia. Most had spent years in the region. (For a complete list of KSG members, see Appendix B.)

Dr. Rodney Jones of Policy Architects International agreed to serve as secretary—an important job, because it involved drafting many of the reports and documents that KSG would issue. I undertook the role of chairman, thinking, as an entrepreneur and the chief executive of a leading business enterprise, I might be able to drive the organization toward concrete, practical actions rather than being simply a "debating society." I was also the only member of the group who came from the Jammu and Kashmir region—a deliberate choice, since I was eager to avoid making KSG seem like a political organization or a lobbying group representing anyone with a vested interest in the conflict.

I thought there was a good chance that our US-based group could be seen as an evenhanded, honest broker in the quest for a solution. Our own US government had tried to play such an unbiased role from the start of the conflict. The US had been one of the countries that proposed the idea of a plebiscite through a resolution of the UN Security Council, nominating Chester W. Nimitz, the American admiral who headed the Pacific Command during World War II, and a Czecho-slovakian diplomat named Josef Korbel to oversee the plebiscite. (As minister of law and finance in the Pakistani-administered region of Kashmir, my father had occasion to meet both of these notable leaders. Korbel wrote a book on the Kashmir issue called *Danger in Kashmir (Princeton University Press, 1955)*. Years later, his daughter, Madeleine Albright, served as secretary of state in the Clinton administration, and she and I became friends. To this day, whenever we see one another, she likes to remind me of the fact that our fathers met in Kashmir many years ago. (In fact, she often refers to me jokingly as a member of her family.)

The Kashmir Study Group was officially launched in 1996, and in 1997 seven of our members undertook a three-week trip to India, Pakistan, and Kashmir. The goal was to speak with and learn from people in the region who represented a wide range of backgrounds and perspectives on the Kashmir conflict—an essential foundation for any effort to develop a peace proposal with a chance of being approved by all the interested parties.

The result was a report titled *The Kashmir Dispute at Fifty*, published in 1997. It provided a detailed, objective, and authoritative overview of many of the basic facts regarding the Kashmir problem, including unbiased explanations of the official and unofficial positions held by people and groups from the region itself as well as from India and Pakistan. It also provided a set of twelve recommendations regarding short-term confidence-building measures and other steps that we believed should be taken to help create a climate in which positive, mutually respectful dialogue leading to a long-term solution could take place. The report received significant positive publicity and quickly earned KSG a role as an informed voice for moderation and compromise on the Kashmir problem.

Earning this kind of recognition had been one of my main goals in launching KSG. Embarking on my first foray into the world of global diplomacy, I applied my business background to the challenge. Any expert in marketing will tell you that an organization seeking to influence human behavior needs to achieve two things—to be *known*, and to be desired. That's true whether the organization produces consumer goods—like clothes, soft drinks, or furniture—or political and social concepts that are competing in the marketplace of ideas. So we deliberately marketed KSG to the worlds of politics, academia, and media, seeking to be known and desired by key leaders and opinion-makers in those worlds. We soon built a reputation as an important participant in the debate over the future of Kashmir.

One result was that KSG was invited to take part in a number of conferences sponsored by organizations such as the United States Institute of Peace, the Carnegie Endowment for International Peace, and the Stimson Center, a well-known Washington think tank. Another result was that I was sought out by leaders who shared our goal of breaking the stalemate that had blocked a solution to the Kashmir dilemma for so long.

One of these was K. K. Nayyar, a former vice admiral of the Indian navy, who had known my grandfather—in fact, he used to visit with our family when he traveled to Kashmir. We encountered one another at a think tank meeting focused on the Kashmir issue. After consulting with Atal Bihari Vajpayee, the Indian prime minister, and his leadership team, Admiral Nayyar was authorized to invite KSG to serve as "coordinator and facilitator" for meetings between India and Pakistan regarding the Kashmir question. "Why don't you organize an initiative," the admiral asked me, "that will let us discuss some options in a quiet, low-key way?" After consulting with my KSG colleagues, we agreed to play this role.

By this time, the urgency of a solution to the Kashmir problem had become even greater, with India and Pakistan having conducted tit-for-tat tests of nuclear bombs in May 1998. The risk that these two countries armed with the most destructive weapons in history might come to blows over the disputed region was a truly frightening one—the reason that President Bill Clinton would soon refer to the line separating the two parts of Kashmir as "the most dangerous place in the world."

In October 1998, with no public fanfare or publicity, KSG convened a meeting to begin a dialogue about the future of Kashmir. Those in attendance from the Indian side included Admiral Nayyar and Shilendra Kumar Singh, a diplomat who had served as ambassador to Pakistan and later retired as foreign secretary. The Pakistani government sent Khalid Mahmud Arif, a retired four-star general in the army, and Niaz Naik, a retired foreign secretary who had once served as ambassador to India. All of these were leaders who were highly respected in both countries. Members of KSG who participated in this meeting included Ainslie Embree, Howard Schaffer, and William Phillips Talbot, and me. Generally known as Phil, Talbot was a former US ambassador to Greece and a former assistant secretary of state for the Middle East and South Asia. A serious scholar of India, Talbot had lived in a Kashmiri village for a summer back in the 1940s.

We started the weekend with dinner at my family's home in New Rochelle, then climbed into cars for a drive to our farm in Livingston, New York, where the bulk of the discussions would take place.

The first day's conversations served as an illustration of why the impasse over Kashmir had persisted for so long. The representatives from India and Pakistan were mutually respectful and cordial, but they were also inflexible. Each side repeated the official talking points they had long been using to justify their own demands for control of the region and to blame the opposing side for the continuing unrest and violence. And when ideas for possible solutions were raised, they were the same tired, impractical ideas I'd heard mentioned during my meetings in the region—a plebiscite, or a complete withdrawal of one side or the other, rather than a realistic plan for peaceful coexistence.

That evening, Farida joined us at dinner, and at a certain point the conversation turned to poetry—an interest shared by several members of the group. General Arif recited a couple of poems in Urdu—the dominant language of Pakistan—and received some well-deserved compliments for the beauty of the poems.

I then turned to Farida, who is also a lover of poetry. "Will you recite for us?" She was reluctant, but after a bit of persuading, she consented, and beautifully recited a poem in our native Kashmiri language.

Unlike General Arif's poems, Farida's offering was met with silence. Finally, S. K. Singh commented, "Your recitation was lovely, but I didn't understand it." And the others around the table nodded in agreement.

"The reason is clear," I remarked. "You gentlemen are very knowledgeable and well educated, but you don't know the Kashmiri language. And so it's not possible for you to understand Kashmiri poetry. In the same way, it's not really possible for you to understand the experiences and aspirations of the Kashmiri people. Perhaps this helps explain the difficulties we had today in finding common ground during our discussions of the future of Jammu and Kashmir—especially the Kashmiri-speaking region."

As I made this comment, I saw nods of agreement around the table. It was one of those seemingly small moments that can sometimes produce a spark of understanding—and, with luck, a movement toward positive change.

It was also a moment of realization for me. I became aware that the leaders of the Kashmir-speaking areas had done a poor job of communicating their story to the peoples of India, Pakistan, and the world. They talked a lot about Kashmiri independence without acknowledging the fact that Jammu and Kashmir was like the former Yugoslavia—a collection of differing ethnicities, languages, and cultures stitched together by outside powers for reasons of their own.

The next morning, our conversations continued. For a time, there was no change—I kept hearing the same talking points repeated. After a while, I proposed a break, and I invited the two military men—Admiral

Nayyar and General Arif—to join me in a ride in our beloved family Jeep. We toured the farm, bouncing on the dirt roads, until we reached the farthest corner of our property. At that point, I shut off the engine and turned to my two guests.

"How long are we going to go on this way?" I asked them. "How long are we going to keep on arguing about our national pride, about this right and that wrong, while our children are choosing up sides and getting killed? What are we waiting for—another Lord Mountbatten to come along and settle the arguments for us, like he did at the time of the partition? We all know how well that worked out!

"Instead of waiting for someone else to save us, let's stop fighting and solve the problem once and for all. We all know that the main area of contention is the Kashmiri-speaking region. You both know what's possible and what's not. Let's start talking about an honorable, sensible solution that both sides can accept."

The two men listened in silence. Both of them had to admit my words rang true. And both agreed to contact their governments and request permission to begin a *real* dialogue about finding a way forward.

We drove back to the farmhouse, and Nayyar and Arif phoned their respective leaders. Both ministers said, "Go ahead and talk about it. Let's see what you can come up with." We then reconvened as a group, and after discussing a general framework, we agreed to delegate the task of drawing up the outline of a plan to Mr. Singh and Mr. Naik—distinguished diplomats of India and Pakistan, respectively—with the help of Howard Schaffer, the former US ambassador who was respected and trusted by both sides.

"Spend the rest of the day together working on a plan," I told them. "If it would be helpful, we can lock you up until you're finished! Meanwhile, the rest of us will relax and enjoy the farm."

By the end of the day, our three-man committee had drawn up a document that was the nucleus of what came to be known as the Livingston Proposal. It listed a series of steps designed to pave the way toward a resolution of the Kashmir problem that would be "peaceful, honorable, and feasible." Those three words are important—we chose them carefully and deliberately to define the characteristics of a plan that we considered essential in any realistic discussion about the future of the region.

It took several more discussions over the next two years to work out the details of the Livingston Proposal.* In the end, we laid out a number of specific recommendations, including the following:

· Establishing three self-governing entities—Kashmir, Jammu, and Ladakh—in the region then being administered by India. These entities would participate in a body that would coordinate issues of shared interest, such as internal trade and transportation.

· Establishing two entities—Azad Kashmir and the Northern Areas—in the region then being administered by Pakistan. These entities would participate in a coordinating body of their own.

· Establishing an All-Kashmir body to coordinate areas of broader interest, such as regional trade, tourism, environment, and water resources. This body would include representations from all five entities as well as from India and Pakistan.

According to the proposal, both India and Pakistan would agree to demilitarize the five entities while also taking responsibility for defending them. Additional details on borders, trade, and similar matters would be worked out among India, Pakistan, and the five entities. We summed up the plan by describing it as a way of reconstituting the former state of Jammu and Kashmir "as a sovereign entity or entities (but without an international personality)." In other words, unlike most nation-states, the new entities emerging in the Jammu and Kashmir region would not be able to enter into treaties or maintain their own

---

* See Appendix C, "Kashmir—A Way Forward" (2005).

armed forces. But for the first time, they would be sovereign—that is, self-governing.

Once the group of us meeting at the farm had hammered out appropriate language to capture these concepts, we went to my office at Ethan Allen headquarters in Danbury, Connecticut, and had the document typed up for delivery to the governments of India and Pakistan.

Over the next decade or more, the Livingston Proposal became the subject of widespread commentary and debate. It was also refined, modified, and updated by the members of KSG and is now generally referred to as the KSG proposal. We also asked Hurst Hannum, a professor of international law at the Fletcher School of Law and Diplomacy at Tufts University, to write a memo that outlined a number of specific options for concrete implementation of the general concepts outlined in the proposal.

In its various forms, the KSG proposal has continued to serve as a vital element in the ongoing quest for a lasting solution to the Kashmir problem.

■ ■ ■

IN THE SHORT TERM, the creation of the Livingston Proposal led to a flurry of hopeful activity. Within a few months, the governments of both India and Pakistan gave cautious approval to the framework it established, saying, in effect, "We accept the Livingston Proposal in principal—although important details must be worked out before it can be implemented." Then, in February 1999, in an important gesture of goodwill, Prime Minister Vajpayee startled the world by traveling to the Pakistani city of Lahore—just the third trip to Pakistan ever made by an Indian prime minister. Even more remarkable, Vajpayee journeyed to the historic site of the Minar-e-Pakistan, a tower built to commemorate the spot where the Pakistan resolution was passed in 1940—"the birthplace of Pakistan," as many call it.

Previously, the idea that an Indian leader would pay his respects there had been almost unthinkable.

The next month, I journeyed to India at the invitation of the government. Among other officials, I met with Ajit Doval, who was then in charge of Indian intelligence operations in Kashmir. Today he is India's national security advisor. I met with Mufti Mohammad Sayeed, who would later serve (from 2002 to 2005, and again from 2015 to 2016) as the chief minister of Kashmir—the title equivalent to "prime minister." I also met his daughter, Mehbooba Mufti, who has served in the same role since 2016. And I met with Narinder Nath Vohra, who was given the job of "interlocutor" by the government of Kashmir to communicate with separatist leaders. He served as governor of Kashmir from 2008 to 2018.

Then I traveled to Jammu and Kashmir, where I met with the current chief minister—Farooq Abdullah, who had been elected in 1996. He is the son of Sheikh Abdullah, and I'd met him back in 1964 when introducing journalist Richard Critchfield to a number of Kashmiri leaders. I also met with the local opposition leaders, whom the Indians referred to as "secessionists." All of them had heard of the Livingston Proposal, and though they would have preferred a plan that provided them with a stronger form of independence, they expressed tentative support for it. They'd begun to accept the fact that a feasible plan was better than one with no hope of ever being implemented—and, after all, the Livingston Proposal included the magic word "sovereignty," which appealed strongly to their community pride.

So I left Kashmir feeling that our proposal had the quiet, unofficial support of most of the regional leaders.

The next logical step was for me to travel to Pakistan. But before I could go there, a fresh complication related to the Kashmir conflict intervened. The so-called Kargil War erupted in a sparsely populated, mountainous district of Kashmir alongside the Line of Control that separates the areas administered by India and Pakistan. It was evidently caused by a combination of factors, including attacks by indigenous Kashmiri insurgents and by Pakistani militants who had infiltrated the region. The conflict lasted from May to July 1999, when Pakistani Prime Minister Nawaz Sharif, under pressure from US President Bill Clinton and other international leaders, withdrew his nation's troops from the area. This retreat caused Sharif significant political damage at home. It helped lead to the military coup that brought General Pervez Musharraf to power on October 13, 1999.

The Kargil War was a big setback for peace efforts in the region. It was particularly disappointing for me because I'd met with Sartaj Aziz, the Pakistani foreign minister, in New York just a short while before. On behalf of Prime Minister Sharif, Aziz urged me to continue the dialogue process and invited me to visit Pakistan. But then the coup took place. A year passed before there was further movement.

This time, I was contacted by a Pakistani leader, Niaz Naik. "I've explained your proposal for peace in Kashmir to General Musharraf, and he has encouraged us to reopen discussions about it." At his suggestion, I called Admiral Nayyar, and we had a meeting at our home in 2000, attended by the admiral, General Arif, S. K. Singh, and Niaz Naik, the former Pakistani foreign secretary and ambassador to India, who was of Kashmiri heritage. (In Pakistan, people like these, descended from ancestors who migrated out of Kashmir more than a century ago, are known as "older Kashmiris.") A fresh invitation for me to visit Pakistan was offered, and I made arrangements to visit India as well. I hoped I could serve as an emissary between the two countries. Of course, through all my dealings with these foreign governments, I kept the US State Department and the National Security Agency informed of my plans, and they made sure that the American ambassadors in the nations involved provided me with any support or guidance I might need.

It was the spring of 2001 when I met General Musharraf for the first time. While having claimed the title of "chief executive" of Pakistan, he was still commander-in-chief of the army, and so I met him in his military headquarters, where he was still wearing his uniform.

Musharraf's aides had evidently done their homework about me, because his first comment was, "Mr. Kathwari, you've been a chief executive for much longer than I have. What advice do you have for me?"

I replied, "Well, General Musharraf, for a CEO running a public company, the objective is to manage expectations. So I recommend that you do what I do: Promise less and deliver more, and then try to repeat that performance every quarter."

Musharraf received this suggestion with a thoughtful look on his face. "In that case, I can see that I've already made mistakes. I've promised too much to the people of Pakistan." This opening exchange created a bit of a bond between the two of us.

We soon moved on to discussing the Livingston Proposal. "You know, Mr. Kathwari," Musharraf said, "this plan that you have, it's tough. It would be very difficult for Pakistan to do." He was speaking about the elements of the plan that would require Pakistan to give up its dreams of ever claiming complete sovereignty over the Jammu and Kashmir region.

I responded this way: "Let me ask you a question, from one CEO to another CEO. Imagine that there had been a plebiscite back in 1948 or 1949 and that you were the leader of Pakistan back then. If Pakistan had lost the plebiscite, then what would you have done?"

"We wouldn't have lost!" he responded.

"That's not what I asked," I explained. "I said, *if* you had lost, then what would you have done? What is your honest answer?"

He paused, then finally admitted, "Going along with that result would have been very, very difficult."

I said, "General, that's the problem. The Indians feel the same way. Neither side is willing to give up what it claims. And the chance of either side seizing it by force is very small. So both sides keep fighting. The problem is that the Kashmiris are in the middle, and they are the ones doing the suffering. It makes me wonder: You claim you are concerned about the welfare of the people of Kashmir. But how are you showing it?"

Musharraf stared at me with a look of surprise on his face. I don't think anyone else had dared to speak that way to the great military leader of Pakistan. Finally, he replied, "I must admit that what you say makes sense. But what will you do next with this peace plan of yours?"

"I'm going to visit the leaders in Delhi," I told Musharraf.

"You know, we have no direct communications with India," Musharraf said. "I would like you to take a message from me to Prime Minister Vajpayee. And please do me a favor. Come back and tell me what the Indians say, even if their answer to my message is no."

"I don't know whether the prime minister will see me," I said. "But if he does, I'm willing to deliver your message." And I asked for a piece of paper so I could write out the message word for word, just as the general spoke it.

That evening, before I departed for Delhi, the chief of the Pakistani army invited me to his home for dinner with a group of his fellow generals. Over an elaborate eight-course meal—a strange experience for me, since I'd seen how Kashmir was suffering from major food shortages—we had a frank exchange about the Kashmir conflict.

"Mr. Kathwari," one of the generals told me, "your plan is based on the idea that we must give up our claims on Kashmir. But Kashmir is part of Pakistan."

"Do you really believe that?" I asked. All the generals nodded. "If that is so, then, with all due respect, why are you not fighting there? Instead, you are letting our children do the fighting—and the dying." They had no answer for me, but I could see that my point had hit home.

The next day, I traveled to Delhi, where I had a scheduled a meeting with Ajit Doval, the intelligence chief. He was deeply involved in the affairs of Kashmir on the Indian side. When he heard I had a message for the prime minister from General Musharraf, he said, "Please give it to me."

"No," I said. "I'll deliver it to Prime Minister Vajpayee, and only to him."

Doval shook his head. He said it would be very difficult for him to bring me into the prime minister's office. So I left Delhi and traveled to Kashmir, where I met with the local leaders. All of them were very anxious and concerned about the prospects of a major war between India and Pakistan, and they were eager to know about my interactions with General Musharraf.

Then I went back to Delhi, where I was met at the airport by the Indian security police. "You have to come with us," they said, "and no, we can't tell you where."

After a car ride, I found myself in the prime minister's office being greeted by Brajesh Mishra, then the national security advisor. "I understand you have a message from General Musharraf for the prime minister," he said.

"Yes," I replied.

"Well, the prime minister is sitting in his office next door. We know that you want to give it to him directly, but I am asking you to give it to me and let me take it to him. The reason is political. Members of our parliament, including those from the opposition party, already know that you've been here. They're going to ask the prime minister whether he has seen you. And once they ask that, they will ask about what the two of you discussed. And soon our efforts at quiet diplomacy will explode into controversy. It would be much better if the prime minister could honestly say that he has not met with you. So please, let me have the message, and I will read it to him."

I thought about what Mishra had said, and I said, "That's fair enough." So I handed the message to him, and he disappeared into the prime minister's office.

After twenty minutes or so, Mishra emerged. "We've officially received General Musharraf's message, and we need to think about it before we respond."

I departed. The next day, after a meeting with Richard Celeste, the American ambassador to India, I was greeted at my hotel by another contingent of Indian intelligence officers, who once again escorted me to the prime minister's office. Once again, Brajesh Mishra was waiting for me. "We have a response for General Musharraf," he said.

"I will write it down," I said. And I did.

The next day, I was back in Islamabad. Traveling between these countries was not easy at the time, but I was treated by both governments as an official diplomat. In Pakistan, I had an escort of motorcycle policemen who cleared my way to the government headquarters, where I was ushered into the office of General Musharraf.

"Did you see the prime minister of India?" he asked me.

"The good news is that I was able to deliver your message to the prime minister," I replied. "And as I promised, I've returned with his reply. The bad news is that his reply is not positive."

For years afterward, I refrained from revealing the messages I delivered—but I can disclose them now.

General Musharraf's message, in effect, said, "The government of Pakistan wants to resolve the Kashmir situation. We are willing to consider the proposal from the Kashmir Study Group as a path toward a resolution of the conflict. And we are willing to take steps immediately to try to reduce the militancy among those opposed to Indian rule in the region. Please let us know if you are ready to take the next step in this process."

Hindsight is 20/20. Looking back, I can see that the general's message, while well intentioned, had contained an error. That error led to its rejection by the Indian leader.

Prime Minister Vajpayee's response to General Musharraf said, in effect, "When you say that you are willing to try to reduce the militancy in the region, what that means is that you are unable to guarantee that attacks on the Indian forces will stop. Your intention, then, is to hold the peace process hostage to the actions of the militants, whom you support. For this reason, we cannot agree to take the next step."

As you can imagine, I was disappointed and chagrined at this outcome of my effort at shuttle diplomacy. Sadly, it was not the first time that an attempt to move toward a peaceful resolution of the Kashmir conflict had fallen apart due to mistrust on one or both sides—nor would it be the last.

Right after the terror attacks on September 11, 2001, the US decided to respond militarily by attacking Osama bin Laden supporters in Afghanistan. This resulted in thousands of refugees fleeing from Afghanistan to Pakistan. Refugee camps were established in many parts of the so-called tribal belt, particularly in Wana, the capital of Waziristan.

I was on the board of Refugees International, and I decided, along with two other board members—Jim Kimsey, founder of AOL, and Queen Noor of Jordan—to visit the camps in Wana. We went first to Islamabad, where we met with President Musharraf on December 7, 2001. He arranged a military helicopter to fly us to Wana, where the three of us toured the camps.

Later, after Kimsey and Queen Noor returned to the US, I met with President Musharraf and his foreign minister, Abdul Sattar, to discuss the steps needed to restart the discussions with India. Knowing that one of the big obstacles to talks was concern by Indian leaders regarding Pakistani support of militancy in Kashmir, President Musharraf asked me to convey to them that Pakistan would take immediate steps to curb its support for militancy.

I returned to New York on December 12 and called Brajesh Mishra, the Indian national security advisor. He was pleased by the positive news of my discussions with President Musharraf, and he promised to share it with the prime minister.

Before that conversation could happen, a terrible event intervened. That same day, December 12, an attack by gun-wielding terrorists on the Indian parliament resulted in fourteen deaths, including those of the five gunmen. Indian authorities blamed two Pakistani terrorist organizations, and the incident outraged Indian citizens and leaders and greatly heightened the tensions between the two nations.

Still, Mishra had presented my news to the prime minister. When Mishra called me the next day, he assured me that the prime minister was not blaming the government of Pakistan for the attack, and he expressed gratitude to President Musharraf for publicly condemning it. We then engaged in a detailed discussion of the possibility of talks over Kashmir. Mishra said that India was willing to proceed with talks, provided Pakistan took immediate steps toward stopping violence in the region—while understanding that the Pakistani government could not completely control events on the ground.

I pressed Mishra a bit. "Is India prepared to enter these talks with an open mind? Or are you still wedded to the clause in the Indian constitution that states that Pakistan-administered Kashmir must be given to India?"

Mishra replied with a series of significant concessions, which I carefully recorded in my notes. He said that India recognized that Kashmir "is a problem"; that the people of Kashmir are alienated; that the idea of Kashmiri accession to India was "questioned"; and that Pakistan must be a party to any discussion of a solution. Most important, Mishra acknowledged that "a sensible solution that meets Kashmiri aspirations is important," and that "people are more important than the constitution."

I was surprised, pleased, and moved by Mishra's words. I immediately called Pakistani Foreign Minister Sattar, and he, too, was pleased. In subsequent conversations, leaders from both India and Pakistan asked me to arrange for the Kashmir Study Group to provide ideas for helping the talks move forward. I set up a team of advisors made up of experts associated with KSG to play this role. I also kept the US government fully informed of my actions. On December 28, Donald Camp, a senior official at the National Security Council, called to tell me that Secretary of State Colin Powell was in touch with both

President Musharraf and Indian foreign secretary Jaswant Singh, hoping to calm both sides. A US emissary was planning to visit the region early in 2002 after being briefed on the KSG peace proposals.

For a few months, it seemed that this initiative might lead to a breakthrough. I continued to speak with leaders from Pakistan and India, as well as with American foreign policy leaders who were seeking a framework for negotiations. But a few months into 2002, these conversations broke down. It appeared that hard-liners in India, incensed over the terrorist attack on parliament, had dug in their heels. They insisted that India's leaders refuse to meet with their Pakistani counterparts without receiving significant up-front concessions—a demand that effectively precluded serious talks.

I was deeply disappointed by this setback. But I was impressed by the openness that the Indian government had expressed to me during our December conversations. This willingness to discuss a range of possible futures for Kashmir could serve as a foundation for meaningful negotiations with a real chance of forging a "peaceful, honorable, and feasible" solution, and a lasting peace.

• • •

OUR QUEST FOR A peaceful resolution to the Kashmir problem attracted the attention of an interesting international organization known as the Pugwash Conferences on Science and World Affairs— most often referred to simply as Pugwash. Headquartered in Rome, Pugwash was founded in 1957 by the physicist Joseph Rotblat and the philosopher Bertrand Russell in Pugwash, Nova Scotia, Canada. Its goal is to bring together scholars and public figures to work toward reducing the danger of armed conflict. Thus, the activities of Pugwash are rather parallel to those of the Kashmir Study Group, though of course they are much broader in scope. For its work, Pugwash won the 1995 Nobel Peace Prize.

In the early 2000s, the Pugwash organization contacted me about the work of KSG and offered its support for our efforts. The initial result was two meetings sponsored by Pugwash that were focused on the Kashmir issue—the first in Rome, the second in Geneva. The Geneva meeting attracted participants from both India and Pakistan, including a number of former military leaders, diplomats, and others with close ties to the governments of the two countries. It was important because the KSG concepts were discussed in detail, and because it created an opportunity for both the Indian and Pakistani political and military leaders to get to know me.

At the same time, tensions in the region enjoyed a temporary respite. The armies of India and Pakistan, which had amassed near their shared borders in a posture that threatened the outbreak of another war, were gradually drawn back, and the rhetoric on both sides was toned down. Then, in January 2004, Prime Minister Vajpayee accepted an invitation from President Musharraf to visit Islamabad. At the end of the meeting the two leaders issued a joint declaration stating their shared desire for an honorable solution to the Kashmir problem. Later that night, President Musharraf called me at home and told me that our crucially timed shuttle diplomacy had helped move the issue forward. He said Pakistani officials had been talking explicitly about the settlement concepts set forth in the KSG proposal.

Encouraged by these signs of progress, the Pugwash organizers in consultation with KSG proposed a conference that would bring together a diverse collection of leaders from the Jammu-Kashmir region and from the neighboring countries, including people representing many sides of the issue: pro-Indian, pro-Pakistani, and pro-independence, along with religious adherents of every sect as well as secular leaders. It had been fifty years since such a broad-based gathering of leaders from the region had occurred. The conference was scheduled for December 11–13, 2004, in Kathmandu, Nepal.

The Nepal conference included a number of separate sessions.

Perhaps the most significant one was attended by some thirty people from the Jammu-Kashmir region itself. Representatives of India and Pakistan who had journeyed to Kathmandu for the meeting were not included in this session. We wanted to create a forum in which the focus would be on the feelings and desires of the people most affected by the problem—the people of the region themselves.

Our first challenge was to set an agenda and a framework for the discussion—both items that had been left open during the planning process to avoid sparking controversies that might prevent the meeting from taking place at all.

I took the opportunity to open the conversation. "I know that proposing an agenda has the potential to create dissension," I said, "but it seems to me that there is an obvious agenda we can all agree upon. The agenda is simply to find a peaceful, honorable, and feasible solution to the Kashmir dilemma. Is that acceptable to everyone here?"

Everyone nodded their heads.

The next obvious challenge was to name a chairperson. Several people asked me to fill that role, and soon a consensus formed around my name.

"I'll be happy to act as chair," I said, "but only if certain conditions are met. First, let's agree that everyone at this table should be treated as equals. It doesn't matter whether you are a religious leader, a political leader, or a former government minister—all should be treated with the same respect.

"Second, I would ask everyone to speak 'from the bottom of their stomachs,' as the saying goes—in other words, to express your own deepest experiences and feelings rather than repeating political slogans or debating points.

"Third, let's all do as much as humanly possible to empathize with the feelings of others.

"Fourth, let's give everyone an equal chance to speak. To ensure this, I suggest that we go around the table and let each person speak for three minutes—no more. After everyone has spoken, if people have more to say, we can go around the table a second time or even a third time. But let's not allow a handful of people to dominate the conversation.

"Fifth, and finally, let's agree not to interrupt when another person is speaking.

"If you all can agree to these conditions, then I will chair the meeting."

The people in attendance exchanged glances. It was clear that they wanted me to be the chair—after all, I was one of the few people in the room who could reasonably be considered a neutral, fair-minded, unbiased leader that all the groups involved were willing to trust. One of the politicians from Jammu offered a comment: "I'm not sure I can accept your three-minute limit, Mr. Kathwari. My friends know it takes me ten minutes just to get warmed up!" Everyone laughed. But in the end, it was agreed that I would run the meeting according to the rules I'd proposed.

We spent about three hours giving each person at the table a chance to offer his or her thoughts about how to create a solution to the Kashmir issue that would be peaceful, honorable, and feasible. I made sure that the three-word formula, originally devised by the Kashmir Study Group, was repeated as often as possible—another effort to market our approach to the people with the power to make it a reality. And I was strict about enforcing the three-minute limit on speeches, so that everyone in the room would have an equal opportunity to be heard.

As the differing voices in the room offered their contributions, a number of themes began to emerge. We gradually realized that all of us shared a number of beliefs and commitments that we were able to summarize in a consensus statement. This was something that everyone had assumed would be impossible.

When the session ended, the doors of the room were opened, and the conference participants from India and Pakistan, who had been holding their own meeting, were able to join us. They were surprised to observe the amicable atmosphere of our meeting—they'd expected to find us engaged in an intense, angry fight. They were even more surprised when I announced that we had agreed upon a consensus statement.

I read the consensus statement aloud. It contained four basic concepts:

1. The dignity and welfare of the inhabitants of Jammu and Kashmir are of paramount importance.

2. The process of peace should be developed around the following features:
   ° Solutions to be sought in a peaceful manner
   ° Solutions to be perceived as honorable
   ° Solutions to be feasible

3. Confidence-building measures to be taken include ending violence, steps to improve the economy and social institutions, and steps to create the conditions for the rule of law.

4. The dialogue process started in Kathmandu should be continued and institutionalized.

Of course, this consensus statement did not spell out a complete solution to the Kashmir issue. But as a statement of general principles, it represented an important breakthrough in what had been an atmosphere of acrimony and mistrust.

In the months to come, the dialogue process did continue for a time. After the Nepal conference, I was invited to meet with some of the top leaders in India. As usual, I was met at the airport by an agent from the Indian intelligence bureau who was assigned to escort me everywhere. I was surprised when the officer greeted me with the words, "Hello, Captain!" The officer turned out to be Surinder Kaul, a Kashmiri Hindu who had been a member of my college cricket team. He would go on to serve as my escort on a couple of subsequent visits to India as well.

During this trip, I visited in Delhi with the Indian National Security Advisor, J. N. Dixit, who pronounced himself very pleased with the results of the meeting. (Sadly, he died just a few weeks later.) Then I went to Pakistan, where I met with President Musharraf and his advisors in Islamabad, and they, too, were pleased with the progress we'd made. In fact, Musharraf almost immediately offered to host a follow-up meeting, organized by Pugwash, to be held in Pakistan several months later. It took place in spring of 2005, just as he proposed.

This enthusiastic support from President Musharraf was particularly important because it signaled a subtle change in Pakistani policy in regard to Kashmir. Because India controlled the bulk of the Jammu-Kashmir region—including the most desirable portion, the Kashmir valley—India was viewed as basically satisfied with the status quo. By contrast, Pakistan claimed the right to control the entire region, and therefore was the source of most of the pressure toward change. Thus, when Musharraf showed an openness to the principles of the KSG proposal—especially the idea that any Kashmir solution should be "feasible"—he was softening the traditional stance of past Pakistani governments by indicating a willingness to compromise with India. This shift was potentially an important turning point in the quest for peace.

However, the promise of that shift has yet to be realized. There are a number of reasons for this.

As has often happened in the history of Kashmir, unfortunate events derailed the momentum toward progress. During the decade of the 2000s, President Musharraf became embroiled in a number of domestic political controversies unrelated to the Kashmir question, and his attention was diverted to these internal issues. At the same time, in the wake of the September 11, 2001, attack on the United States, the international war on terror came to Afghanistan, and Pakistan became caught up in that conflict, further distracting Musharraf.

As a result, the Indian government concluded that Musharraf would probably be unable to deliver on any promises he might make to India. In addition, conservative nationalist elements in India were putting pressure on their government to refuse to make any concessions on Kashmir and instead to rely on force to solve the problem. It was also unfortunate that the government of Atal Vajpayee lost its parliamentary majority in the national election in May 2004. Vajpayee had developed a personal commitment to addressing the Kashmir conflict, despite his reputation as a "hard-liner" on nationalist issues. As the example of Nixon going to China reminds us, political realities dictate that in many cases it requires a nationalist to take the conciliatory steps needed to lay the foundation for an international settlement.

For all these reasons, India lost interest in serious negotiations with Pakistan, regarding Kashmir or any other issue.

Making matters worse, in the summer of 2005, Musharraf himself committed a political faux pas. He made a public statement about Kashmir in which he described a series of steps that could lead to a resolution of the conflict—steps that were almost the same as those described in the KSG proposal. That was good—but then he made the mistake of referring to this as "my plan for Kashmir," as if he had authored it.

Soon thereafter, in October 2005, an earthquake devastated portions of Pakistan and the Pakistan-administered region of Kashmir. In a matter of minutes, this quake took the lives of some eighty thousand people, injured thousands, and left more than four million homeless.

At that time, I was chairman of Refugees International. I went to the site of the disaster with seven of our directors, including Ken Bacon, president of Refugees International, and Ambassador Frank G. Wisner. President Musharraf provided us with a military helicopter to assist in our visit. We interacted with our Ambassador, Ryan Crocker, and US Navy Vice Admiral Michael A. LeFever, who had been sent to the region with a fleet of heavy-lift helicopters. Their search-and-rescue efforts saved many lives. We also visited the M.A.S.H. unit and saw dozens of US doctors and nurses caring for patients alongside military medical teams from many other countries—from Cuba to Turkey. This was pure humanitarian aid, and the sentiment toward America was as positive as I had ever seen.

During this trip, a meeting with President Musharraf and his top leaders was arranged, and I seized the opportunity to raise the issue with him.

"President Musharraf," I said, "with all due respect, in my opinion, you should not have said that the plan for bringing peace to Kashmir was 'your plan.' Saying this will make it impossible for conservatives in India to support the plan. How can proud Indians accept a Pakistani plan for Kashmir?"

Musharraf was a bit flustered. "Maybe you are right. But look at what I have done in accepting the plan. Pakistan has agreed to concessions it never accepted before. What we've given up for peace is amazing."

"That is true," I said, "but the Indians will not see it that way. You should have called it the plan from the Kashmir Study Group—a plan developed with the people of Kashmir."

"The people of Kashmir?" Musharraf responded in a scornful tone. "Who speaks for the people of Kashmir? Their leaders never say a word!"

"Again, with due respect, Mr. President, most of those leaders are either controlled by your intelligence agencies or by the Indian intelligence agencies. This is why they say nothing." Again, Musharraf was taken aback. He was not accustomed to being spoken to this way.

Finally, he responded, "If the Kashmiri leaders won't speak out, then *you* ought to say something." And he turned to the foreign minister, Khurshid Mahmud Kasuri. The previous year, at Musharraf's suggestion, Kasuri had visited our home in New York to discuss the Kashmir situation. "Please arrange for Mr. Kathwari to be interviewed on our national television," Musharraf said.

I agreed to be interviewed, as long as I could be joined by Frank G.

Wisner, the former American ambassador to India and a board member of Refugees International.

The TV appearance took place a couple of days later. After Wisner and I answered a few questions about the earthquake and the international response to it, the interviewer turned to the Kashmir question. "Mr. Kathwari is chair of the Kashmir Study Group," he said, "and in fact President Musharraf's plan for Kashmir is really a plan that the Kashmir Study Group developed." I believe that this statement had been suggested to the interviewer by the Pakistani government.

He then invited Ambassador Wisner and me to discuss the KSG plan—which we did, emphasizing the need for a fair and realistic solution to the Kashmir problem, and focusing particularly on the decades of suffering that the people of the region had endured. This was a message that had rarely been heard in the Pakistani media, where discussions about Kashmir were normally dominated by Pakistani claims of sovereignty over the entire region and denunciations of the Indian role.

I'm happy I was able to present my perspective to the people of Pakistan. But I couldn't undo the hardened attitudes of many in India against the KSG proposal.

There was another moment during this trip that has stayed with me. As we toured the devastated earthquake zone by helicopter, the air force colonel who was piloting the craft asked me, "Would you like me to take us over to the Line of Control?" This is the dividing line that separates the Indian-administered and Pakistani-administered portions of Kashmir.

"Yes, please do," I replied.

The colonel shifted the helicopter controls and carried us in that direction. Within five minutes, we were at the Line of Control. I was stunned to recognize how short the distance was. My family, among others, had suffered years of painful separation while being just a few short miles from one another.

This realization underscored for me how unnecessary were the human tragedies caused by hardheadedness on both sides of the conflict.

. . .

AS YOU'VE SEEN, THERE were moments in the 1990s and 2000s when it appeared that the work of the Kashmir Study Group and my own modest efforts at diplomacy might help produce a major breakthrough in the ongoing Kashmir conflict. In each case, we were impacted by unfortunate events on the ground.

Over the last decade, geopolitical realities in the region continue to fluctuate. Pakistan's position as a country has been negatively impacted as a result of its involvement in the conflict in Afghanistan. By contrast, India has become more nationalistic and enjoys a much-improved relationship with the United States. Meanwhile, life in Kashmir is still difficult, with sporadic deadly battles between the Indian government forces and rebellious militants.

Beginning in June 2010, a huge uprising took place in Kashmir that resulted in many deaths. An associate of Indian Prime Minister Manmohan Singh approached me with a request for help. I suggested an effort to open communications with local Kashmiri leaders through one or more credible interlocutors. The next day, my Indian contact asked me to take part in an interview with a journalist from the *Times of India* as a way of publicizing my suggestions. I did this, and my ideas met with some favorable response.

About a week later, the Indian government appointed a team of interlocutors led by a leading journalist. In turn, this team contacted me and asked me to update the KSG proposal. I did so, with the help of a small team of other KSG members, although the changes we made were quite modest. We submitted this updated version in confidence to the governments of India and Pakistan, and the Indian leaders were interested enough to invite me to visit their country in January 2011.

I applied for a visa through the appropriate bureaucratic channels, but I received no response. Eventually it became clear that the Indian government had had a change of heart. Hard-liners who opposed any effort at conciliation over Kashmir had intervened to squelch this latest effort at mediation before it had truly begun. It was yet another disappointing setback in our decades-long effort to bring peace to the region.

Still, I consider our efforts to have been productive in shaping the Kashmir debate. The global attention that KSG focused on the problem put additional pressure on India and Pakistan to moderate their approach to the region. Border clashes continue, but there has been no major war between the two powers since 2003, which has undoubtedly saved countless lives.

Furthermore, I believe that our work to reframe the international debate about Kashmir has borne some fruit. Certain realities that were formerly little known have now become widely recognized—especially that the region of Jammu and Kashmir is made up of disparate peoples, cobbled together into one country by colonial interests. The Kashmiri-speaking region, with its unique history, language, and culture, has been the prime area of conflict. There is now a greater recognition that this region must have the ability to govern itself, and that the self-governing option could also be provided to other regions of the former state of Jammu and Kashmir.

As for me, I've learned that peace is a project that demands enormous patience and a lifelong commitment. The seeds of change that I've planted may not sprout until later—but no matter how long they may take to grow, they will have been worth the effort.

11

DEFENDING OUR INDEPENDENCE

IN CHAPTER EIGHT, I described how the management group I led purchased Ethan Allen, took it private, then took it public again through an initial public offering (IPO). This series of changes was common in the 1980s and 1990s, a period when the market for corporate ownership and control was quite volatile. It left Ethan Allen with the independence and strong leadership needed to transform itself for an increasingly challenging competitive landscape. It also left Ethan Allen with a heavy burden of debt, much of it carrying a high 18 percent interest rate that was a legacy of the inflation spiral of the 1980s. This debt put even more pressure on us to improve our operations, upgrade our efficiency, and modernize our product offerings. We spent the 1990s doing just that. And by the early years of the new century, we'd drastically reduced our debt and put ourselves in a much stronger financial position.

By the early 2000s, Ethan Allen was focusing on building the resources, talents, and strategies needed to thrive in a new era of business. We were continuing to purchase stores from the individuals and families that had previously owned them, gradually bringing more and more of the Ethan Allen retail network under corporate retail management. We were assembling a strong leadership team, including many drawn from our cadre of interior designers to whom we'd given much greater power and responsibility. Over time, we pulled together a group of some two hundred highly talented managers to run our retail division. About 70 percent of them were women, and practically all had risen through the ranks from our front-line operations, which meant they had a deep, intuitive understanding of the needs and preferences of our customers.

The strengthening of our leadership corps came at just the right moment. The twenty-first century brought with it a series of economic challenges that would test the agility and skill of companies in practically every industry. Ethan Allen was no exception. I describe the three trends that would have the biggest impact on us as *globalization, commoditization*, and *technology*.

Let's first consider globalization. Throughout the 1990s, some 70 percent of the furniture sold in the US was also manufactured in the US. As I've explained, Ethan Allen was a big part of that tradition. Our production facilities in New England, the South Atlantic states, and other locations had long been an important part of the local and regional economies. We took pride in the skills of our American craftspeople, and the high quality of the work was a central element of the Ethan Allen brand.

But as the decades passed, the furniture industry began to change. International markets became increasingly important. The economies of Europe and Asia that had been devastated by World War II came roaring to life during the 1960s, 1970s, and 1980s; after the fall of the Soviet empire in 1989, the nations once isolated behind the Iron Curtain gradually became integrated into the world economy. First tens of millions, then hundreds of millions of new middle-class customers emerged, hungry for the high-quality goods they had once been unable to buy—including furniture.

At the same time, high-quality manufacturing operations began to spring up around the globe, not just in the furniture business but also in electronics, automobiles, apparel, and many other industries. And as technological advances made international communications and transportation easier, faster, and cheaper than ever, global supply chains became practical and increasingly efficient. Soon those global supply chains began outcompeting domestic suppliers in one industry after another.

Today, the impact of globalization on the furniture business is impossible to ignore. Now the share of furniture sold in the US that is manufactured abroad is between 70 and 80 percent. Countries like China, Vietnam, Malaysia, Indonesia, and India have become major suppliers of furniture to American customers, along with more traditional foreign sources like Canada, Mexico, and Italy. These overseas suppliers are gradually catching up to the US when it comes to production quality, labor policies, and environmental standards; and increasing portions of the populations of these countries are gradually coming to enjoy a standard of living that is closer to ours.

But their wages are still substantially lower than those of American workers—which poses a significant competitive issue for US companies. Even today, typical costs for skilled workers like upholsterers in the developing countries of Asia and Latin America run an average of $2 to $4 per hour. By contrast, costs for similar workers in the US average $20 an hour. Add in the costs of medical insurance and other benefits, and the differences become even greater.

Thus, the rise of globalization put pressure on US companies either to start moving some or all of their manufacturing operations overseas or to become much more efficient here at home. Ethan Allen has largely chosen the latter route. We have chosen to outsource some portions of our manufacturing to countries like China, Italy, India, Indonesia, and the Philippines. But 75 percent of our manufacturing is still done in North America, where we feel we have better control over the quality of the work.

To make it possible to continue building furniture in the US while competing with other companies that use cheaper labor overseas, we've introduced an array of efficiency-enhancing methods. During the 1990s, we began using technology to greatly reduce labor costs and other expenses associated with producing high-quality furniture. For instance, at the start of the decade, Ethan Allen had approximately one million square feet of space dedicated to making wooden parts for sofas and chairs. By the end of that decade, the space was reduced to 50,000 square feet. Computer-aided machinery making the parts, along with other efficiency improvements, made this possible.

Manufacturing isn't the only area in which we've trimmed costs while improving our operations. Not that long ago, much of the bookkeeping, recordkeeping, and data management was done with a fair amount of manual labor. Today, most of it is computerized and centralized in our Danbury headquarters. The benefits include not just reduced costs and improved accuracy but also vastly enhanced systems for logistics, customer service, human resource management, and other vital functions.

These changes—driven by globalization, directly and indirectly—have dramatically altered the shape of our business. We determined that we needed to have fewer plants in the right locations, coupled with major investments in technology and in our people. We decided to concentrate our manufacturing in two regions—northeast Vermont and western North Carolina. Ethan Allen once owned and operated three sawmills to produce wood for our products; today we have one. We once had fourteen US plants in which we manufactured wooden furniture and parts; today we have three. We once had seven upholstery plants; today we have three. We've made major investments in technology in all areas of our vertically integrated enterprise.

The transition was costly. We had to manage it as humanely as possible, which was not an easy thing to do. We had to close a number of operations—one in Maine, four in upstate New York, and others in

North Carolina, Pennsylvania, California, and other states. We provided fair severance packages to the employees whose jobs were lost, along with help in finding new work, training programs, and other support.

A trend that's related to globalization is commoditization. This is the trend whereby products once available only through a few suppliers become available through a growing number of sources, making them easier to get, less unique, and less expensive. Like globalization, commoditization has created enormous competitive pressures for countless businesses, especially those, like Ethan Allen, that once enjoyed price premiums because of the uniqueness and high quality of their products.

Some of the results of commoditization can be observed simply by driving around communities in the United States. Traditional Main Streets lined with family-owned stores that have been in business for generations have largely vanished. In their place, you find malls and shopping centers built around generic chain stores or "big box" stores selling mostly interchangeable goods at rock-bottom prices—stores like Walmart, Home Depot, Lowe's, and the giant drug and grocery chains. Now these big box stores are themselves under pressure from e-commerce, lower traffic, and diminished sales.

Other effects of commoditization are subtler. For example, in many industries, significant price deflation is putting pressure on producers and retailers alike. You can see the impact by comparing how the costs of various items have changed over the decades. In the late 1960s, you could buy a new car for $2,000 or so. Today, a comparable vehicle starts at $25,000. By contrast, a basic sofa that cost $500 in the late 1960s costs about the same amount today. And the television set you buy today is not only cheaper than the one your parents bought in the 1960s, but it also offers an incredible array of features they never dreamed of. As prices fall and production costs continue to rise—especially medical costs for our employees—we've had to grow annually by about 6 percent just to stay even.

Companies like Ethan Allen that are competing in markets where commoditization has wreaked havoc have been pushed hard to respond to the economic pressures it creates. Not only has the price of a sofa remained basically flat, but the choices available to consumers of where and how to buy a sofa have multiplied. Traditional furniture firms now have to fend off competition from mass retail stores and from many specialized retailers.

These are some of the trends that Ethan Allen geared up to respond to in the 1990s and 2000s. Thanks to our improved financial condition, our updated business model, and the talented team of managers we nurtured, we held our own. We moved many stores from locations where traffic was shrinking to newer sites where younger shoppers could be found. We broadened and enhanced our product lines, offering new styles that customers found attractive. We encouraged and rewarded the creativity of our designers, who gave Ethan Allen a degree of individualized service that few competitors could match. In response, our sales and profits grew, along with the value of the business.

Starting in the early 2000s, we also focused on international growth. Our expansion in China was accelerated after a visit from Richard Feng, founder of Markor, a Chinese furniture manufacturer, who expressed an interest in opening a retail network in collaboration with us. I visited Markor's head offices in Ürümqi, the capital of Xinjiang province, where I met with Feng and six of his associates. When I realized that Markor did not have much retail experience, I asked them, "Who will develop the national network of stores?"

Richard Feng said, "We will do it, with your help."

During the next two days, Feng and I hammered out a working agreement. Today Markor operates more than ninety retail locations in China and is a very strong partner to Ethan Allen. To me, this is the story of modern China—a society filled with people who are eager to develop good ideas and then work hard to implement and improve them. Richard Feng and his wife Iris have become good friends to Farida and me. Their son Mark, who earned his BA and MBA degrees at Harvard, spent a summer as an intern at Ethan Allen. He is now president of Markor International, focused on markets outside China.

China is not the only country where Ethan Allen has a growing presence. We now have Ethan Allen design centers in Korea, Taiwan, Thailand, Cambodia, Saudi Arabia, Dubai, Qatar, Kuwait, Jordan, and Romania. In each country, I met with the families who wanted to open Ethan Allen stores, and over time we've developed strong business and personal associations.

This international presence has opened up other business opportunities for us. For example, in 2017, Ethan Allen was awarded a five-year contract by the US government to furnish the homes of American diplomats all over the world—a prestigious task that we're very proud to undertake on behalf of our native land.

As the 2000s rolled on, Ethan Allen's business was expanding strongly. Then the Great Recession of 2008–2009 hit. And Ethan Allen, like almost every other company, was staggered by its effects. As economic growth ground to a halt and even went into reverse, millions lost their jobs, banks stopped making loans, and consumer spending plummeted. Ethan Allen sales declined by 40 percent, and an annual operating profit of $147 million shrank to a razor-thin $1 million. Our stock price, which had risen as high as $40 a share, fell to as low as $10.

We'd already had to reinvent Ethan Allen once—in the years right after my elevation to president, when an outdated business model drastically needed rethinking. Now we had to reinvent it again, this time in response to a world hit by an economic tsunami.

Some of the changes we had to make were painful. Every possible expense was cut to the bone, and we had to let go of about two thousand employees. We also used our ingenuity to adapt to the new circumstances—for example, by converting our wood manufacturing operations from producing large inventories to making just a handful of pieces at a time, thereby saving on labor, raw materials, warehousing, and other expenses. And we redoubled our efforts to make sure that our product line was as modern and broadly appealing as possible. As I write these words, in 2019, the new products we've introduced in the last three years constitute fully 70 percent of our offerings.

What's more, because the aftermath of the recession coincided with yet another sweeping change in technology, we simultaneously had to figure out how to respond to the explosion of popularity in e-commerce. With companies like Amazon upending entire industries, it was clear that Ethan Allen had to retool itself to appeal to millions of customers who were falling in love with the speed and convenience of online shopping.

This is a challenge we are continuing to work on by combining personal service with technology. Today, for example, customers can enjoy live online chats with our more than fifteen hundred interior designers in North America. Our focus on combining personal service with technology isn't just a new way for us to attract customers. It's also emblematic of our long-term retailing strategy. In a world where commoditization threatens to drain value from the majority of products and brands, I believe that Ethan Allen's distinguishing features— its high quality, its fine designs, and above all its exceptional personal service—will make the difference for us. The key for us to survive and thrive is to combine these highly desired traits with the speed and convenience provided by technology. If we can do this through a range of initiatives, then our future will be bright.

A leader never stops learning. One of the most interesting things I've learned over my last few years at the helm of Ethan Allen is that reinvention is a periodic challenge. My experience suggests that, in today's turbulent business environment, a company will most likely be required to reinvent itself every five years. The period of upheaval we are living through today is just the latest. Becoming accustomed to such periods—and developing a shrewd sense of how to take full advantage of them—will be a vital leadership skill in the decades to come.

. . .

IN THE SPRING OF 2015, even as we continued to rebound from the Great Recession, we also faced a different kind of business challenge. This challenge came not from an economic downturn, changing market conditions, or technological upheaval, but rather from an activist investor who sought to take over control of our company.

Ethan Allen is certainly not the first business to be targeted by an activist investor. Experts who study this phenomenon estimate that 15 to 20 percent of American public companies are faced with a similar challenge every year now. For that reason, the story of how we dealt with it may be of interest to others businesspeople—especially given the fact that the strategy we used to defend our independence was both very unusual and highly successful.

Our adversary in this battle was a roughly $1 billion investment company called Sandell Asset Management. Founded in 1998 by Tom Sandell, a former trader at Bear Stearns, Sandell Asset Management had engaged in thirty-five activist campaigns and launched nine proxy fights by 2015. Two of its previous battles had involved Bob Evans Farms, a national restaurant chain, where Sandell managed to win four seats on the company board, and TransCanada Corp., a pipeline management company, which Sandell pressured into reorganizing by spinning off its power generation business and putting its US assets into a tax-advantaged partnership.

In 2015, Sandell decided it was time to put Ethan Allen in its crosshairs.

Sandell Asset Management had begun buying shares of Ethan Allen stock early in the year. By June 1, 2015, the fund had purchased some 924,000 shares, or about 3.5 percent of Ethan Allen's total shares outstanding, as recorded in filings required by federal regulators. Around the same time, Sandell's leadership—especially the company founder,

Tom Sandell himself—began launching vocal attacks on our company's management, its business strategy, and on me personally.

The criticisms offered were far ranging. According to Sandell, Ethan Allen was stodgy and old-fashioned, having failed to adjust quickly enough to the new world of online retail and e-commerce. Its revenues and profit growth in the aftermath of the Great Recession had been too slow to satisfy Sandell. And our company was sitting on big, valuable real estate holdings that ought to be spun off through a financial mechanism such as a series of sale leaseback transactions or the creation of a publicly traded real estate investment trust—two tactics then considered trendy on Wall Street. As a result, Sandell declared, Ethan Allen stock was trading below its "intrinsic value," which they estimated was about $41 per share. He blamed poor leadership for these results.

At Ethan Allen, we're always ready to consider the concerns of our investors. (I myself was the largest individual shareholder of Ethan Allen.) So when Tom Sandell visited our headquarters in May, our management team listened carefully to his complaints and his proposed remedies for our company's supposed underperformance. Some of the points he made had a certain amount of validity—and, in fact, our management team was already aware of them and was working on plans to address them. For example, we were deeply engaged in the latest effort to modernize our product lineup, something that a design-based company like Ethan Allen needs to do periodically. We were also working on improving our approach to e-commerce, as many other companies were doing at the time.

In other cases, Sandell's complaints were based on a misunderstanding of how Ethan Allen does business. We did our best to explain the nature of our corporate strategy, which includes the unconventional embrace of vertical integration as a way of maximizing our flexibility and responsiveness. Selling off real estate would limit our ability to expand or move locations as economic and market conditions changed. What's more, it would saddle Ethan Allen with significant debt. Having worked our way out from under the major debts we'd incurred back in the 1990s as well as the impact of the Great Recession, we'd come to appreciate the strategic benefits of being largely debt-free, and we weren't eager to give those up. Sandell was not mollified by our explanations.

As spring turned into summer, Sandell escalated its assault on Ethan Allen. The fund's management demanded that Ethan Allen announce that the company was available for purchase, saying that if it did so, there would be a "line out the door" of private equity firms eager to make a bid. However, if Ethan Allen refused to put itself up for sale, Sandell suggested that a proxy fight would ensue, with Sandell nominating its own slate of board members to oppose those nominated by company management.

It was clear that Sandell was gearing up for a fight. Unsatisfied with the performance of Ethan Allen's management team, Sandell was determined to seize control of the business. My colleagues and I believed that Tom Sandell didn't know what he was talking about and that his strategy would have a devastating impact on the future of Ethan Allen. We decided we needed to stop him.

The most common response by company managers to this kind of challenge is to hire an outside team of advisors with extensive experience in fighting off activist assaults. But my colleagues and I were surprised when we investigated this option. We learned that the companies that specialize in these services charge up-front fees of several million dollars to take on a case like ours, with additional charges of millions more in the event of ultimate victory. We wanted to win the battle against Sandell—but not at such a high cost.

I told my colleagues, "We'll take our case to the shareholders ourselves. We'll explain what we think is right for the future of Ethan Allen. We'll talk to the people one-on-one and let them decide."

To my knowledge, no major American company faced with such a challenge had responded in this way. But we were confident in the strength of our position and the quality of our arguments. And we believed in the power of democratic processes to produce the right outcome, both for Ethan Allen and for our shareholders. We were willing to lay our cards on the table and accept the verdict of the shareholders.

Sandell mounted an aggressive communications campaign in an effort to move shareholder opinion in its direction. The campaign culminated in a sixty-seven-page presentation called "Re-Design Ethan Allen: The Case, Candidates and Plan for Change," which was publicly released in early November 2017. This statement leveled a number of charges against me and against our board—some based loosely on facts, others largely fabricated. Sandell also helped orchestrate a letter-writing campaign, spreading criticism of Ethan Allen as widely as possible.

My Ethan Allen colleagues and I were determined to retain the high ground in the face of these attacks. But we knew we needed to address the months-long Sandell campaign. Our most important response was to engage in direct conversations with Ethan Allen's investors. Some were individual investors, while others were managers of investment funds run by endowments, pension plans, mutual funds, and the like. We crafted a PowerPoint presentation loaded with facts and information that explained our business strategy. Then we hit the road. We put together a team that included me, our chief financial officer Corey Whitely, and three board members—Jim Carlson, a well-respected attorney and a professor of law at NYU; James Schmotter, former president of Western Connecticut State University and associate dean at the Johnson Graduate School of Management at Cornell University; and John Dooner, Jr., former CEO of McCann Worldgroup, a leading marketing and advertising company. The group of us made in-person visits to many of Ethan Allen's largest investors; in other cases, we scheduled conference calls with them. All in all, we managed to speak with investors representing about 85 percent of the total ownership of Ethan Allen shares.

As we expected, we faced many challenging questions from our shareholders. Some had studied the Sandell accusations in detail, and many wanted to probe to determine whether we had reasonable responses. For example, one major institutional shareholder used Sandell's arguments as the basis for his own questions during our meeting. In response, our management team spent a lot of time discussing our evolving e-commerce strategy, explaining the advantages of our vertical integration, and showing why divesting ourselves of our real estate holdings would be a mistake in the long term.

Most of the shareholders we spoke with appreciated our willingness to grapple openly with issues like these and came away impressed by the quality of our thinking. For example, the institutional shareholder I just mentioned ended up publicly defending Ethan Allen's decision to keep most of our manufacturing in the US rather than outsourcing it entirely to overseas factories (another point on which Sandell had criticized us). We "understood the importance of retaining most of the manufacturing here, from a quality standpoint," he told an interviewer.

In the course of our meetings, one positive discovery that came as a surprise to some of us was finding that most of our institutional investors were focused on long-term strategy and our plans for value creation—not short-term gain.

Most important, we used our conversations with shareholders as an opportunity to listen and learn. A number of the institutional investors we spoke with offered useful insights and suggestions about industry trends and potential strategic adjustments that deserved our consideration. The value of these meetings reaffirmed the wisdom of our decision to tackle the proxy challenge ourselves rather than turning the future of our company over to a team of outsiders.

In September, Ethan Allen's management named its slate of candidates for the eight board positions—including a couple of new members with expertise in areas like real estate finance, thereby addressing some of the concerns we'd heard. Sandell also named its own competitive slate of six candidates. Two of the six soon came under a cloud, based on accusations of conflict of interest: one was an executive with an investment ratings agency involved in evaluating Ethan Allen's debt securities, while the other had once been turned down for a job at Ethan Allen. As one journalist put it, these missteps meant that "the credibility of the rival slate had been dented." That was a small but meaningful victory for us.

Another victory came about a week before the annual meeting, when the experts at Glass Lewis, a leading independent proxy advisory firm, issued its recommendation to holders of Ethan Allen stock. After discussing the arguments raised by the Sandell team, the Glass Lewis report stated:

> Overall, we ultimately see greater reason in this care for shareholders to continue to defer to the board and management team with respect to strategic and financial matters . . . As such, considering that the Company has continued to deliver generally positive financial results below the "top-line" in the meantime, including strong cash flow generation and improved margins, we're more apt to recommend that shareholders afford the current board and management team additional time to realize the envisioned benefits of the Company's current strategic and financial initiatives.

Of course, we were gratified to have an objective team of knowledgeable outsiders endorsing our case against that of the insurgent shareholders. But most important of all, in my judgment, was the work my colleagues in Ethan Allen did to educate our shareholders about the nature of our business and the long-term plans we'd evolved to make it even more successful in the future.

When the proxy ballots were tallied in November, the vote was not even close. Every board candidate nominated by Ethan Allen's management won at least 53 percent of the shareholder vote. By contrast, only one of the candidates nominated by Sandell earned more than 38 percent.

Our unorthodox strategy for dealing with the proxy challenge won praise from many observers. For example, one of our major shareholders is the well-known Gabelli Funds. After the November vote, an analyst from Gabelli commented, "I've never seen a company mount a better campaign against an activist investor than Ethan Allen did. . . . [P]eople might study this as an example of how management can push back against an activist investor."

Our unusual decision to rely on the good judgment of our shareholders and to combat Sandell's accusations through our own campaign of open, two-way dialogue with those shareholders reflected the style of leadership I've always tried to practice. I've sought to be a hands-on CEO who treats all his associates—especially the employees in our plants and our retail operations—with the respect and dignity they deserve.

The success of Ethan Allen's battle to remain independent drew attention from many who study the shifting landscape of American business. However, so far it has not inspired many company leaders to imitate our strategy. Meanwhile, the trend of shareholder activism continues. Activist shareholders with a variety of motives continue to launch campaigns aimed at forcing managements to alter their strategies, or even seizing complete control of companies. They're encouraged by the continuing record of success these campaigns enjoy. As one commentator observed in 2016, companies "are settling with activists at a faster pace than ever before, sometimes entering into agreements to appoint activists as directors in as little as days or weeks following the initial public disclosure of the activist's position in the company's stock. . . . The end result is that activists increasingly are transitioning from outside agitators to influential insiders."*

---

* Marc S. Gerber, "US Corporate Governance: Have We Crossed the Rubicon?" *Skadden 2016 Insights*, January 2016.

Of course, shareholder activism is not always a bad thing. Some corporations are indeed poorly managed. There are also boards that fail to provide appropriate oversight of management activities and companies that seem unable to generate value for shareholders. Sometimes companies need the kind of shakeup a challenge from outside the boardroom can provide. And some shareholder activists dedicate their efforts to pushing companies to become more socially responsible, thereby changing their behavior in ways that are beneficial to everyone—by protecting the environment, treating workers fairly, and recognizing the value of diversity.

However, there is a significant downside to the current flood of shareholder activism—a downside that I experienced firsthand while waging the battle against Sandell. During the seven months between the time we learned of Sandell's holdings of our stock to the November proxy vote, my colleagues and I were forced to devote a huge amount of time and energy to respond to the challenge—correcting misstatements, preparing and disseminating informational materials, organizing and attending meetings, and dealing with media inquiries. This work was important and necessary. But it swallowed up resources that could have been invested in activities more directly related to growing our business and building shareholder value—an ironic reality, given the supposed purpose of the challenge. And there were other downsides to the battle, as our board member Jim Carlson noted in an article published by Columbia Law School:

> The activist publicity campaign against Ethan Allen was intended to create business uncertainty and inevitably created questions from our key business relationships and associates in considering whether to continue making long-term commitments to our company. These typical activist tactics risk our Ethan Allen business and also our shareholder values. It's very

difficult to see how this disruption improves Ethan Allen now or in the long term for the benefit of our shareholders.[*]

One unfortunate lesson some managers might draw from our experience could be to conclude that operating as a public company is simply not worth the expense, effort, and distraction involved in fending off assaults from activist shareholders. In recent years, a significant portion of US companies have shifted from public to private ownership. I suspect that experiences like ours are one of the reasons.

It's not pleasant for a company's managers to face the kind of challenge Sandell mounted against us. But we've learned from the experience. We've responded by deepening and improving our relationships with our shareholders. For example, we've begun holding daylong meetings with our shareholders twice a year so we can continue to benefit from their strategic insights and ideas.

In the wake of our battle for independence, we also made some modernizing changes to our corporate charter. For example, we eliminated the provision, sometimes called the "dead hand" provision, that would have barred a newly elected set of board members from voting on certain proposals. This provision is often viewed as a kind of "poison pill" designed to make it hard for shareholders who challenge current management to make changes in corporate policy once they join the board. We agreed that it was time to remove this provision in the name of enhanced corporate democracy.

In short, Ethan Allen has used the experience of being forced to battle for our independence as a springboard for running the company even better in the future.

---

[*] Jim Carlson, "Ethan Allen, Hedge Fund Activism and Prevailing Over Conventional Advice and Practice," *CLS Blue Sky* blog, December 16, 2015.

12

LEADING IN A GLOBAL WORLD

TODAY'S LEADERS FACE ALL the problems leaders have always faced—demanding populations, fierce competition, and economic uncertainty. In addition, they're being called upon to lead in a world that is rapidly changing. And one of the biggest dimensions of that change has to do with diversity. As global markets grow in importance, and as the US itself becomes more diverse, leaders must master the challenge of guiding a multicultural world.

I've been grappling with this for decades, both inside and outside business. When I arrived in the United States, I faced the challenge of learning and adapting to a very different culture than the one I grew up with in my native Kashmir. I had to master the mores and challenges of the modern business world. And I had to gain the acceptance and trust of people who might never have met—let alone worked with—a person from my corner of the globe. This was a particular challenge when I was asked not just to lead but also to transform Ethan Allen—an iconic American company with deep roots in some of the country's most traditional communities, from the historic towns of New England and the rural communities of Appalachia to the valleys of California and the prairies of Texas.

At the same time I was grappling with these business challenges, my international background, combined with my personal commitment to peace and social justice, sparked my involvement in diplomatic and humanitarian causes. The tragic loss of my son in a war driven by religious and political extremism only deepened my determination to do everything I could to promote greater understanding and tolerance among all peoples. Here again I found myself challenged to lead positive change in a world filled with people of varying backgrounds, values, and aspirations—the same daunting challenge leaders in every domain face today.

As the stories in this book have illustrated, I've been blessed to experience some success in these efforts—as well as some inevitable setbacks. Much of the credit for the successes is due to the exceptional people I've been able to partner with. This includes the remarkable experts, diplomats, statespeople, and scholars who worked with me in the Kashmir Study Group as well as the inspiring leaders at groups like Refugees International, the International Rescue Committee, the Council on Foreign Relations, the US Institute of Peace, the Center for Strategic and International Studies, the Muslim-Jewish Advisory Council, and other organizations dedicated to global peace, freedom, and security.

The people I've been blessed to partner with also include my colleagues at Ethan Allen. They have worked with me for three decades to grow our business in a time of challenging economic, social, and technological upheavals. I believe that our continued success in a world where so many established companies have faltered is a tribute to the remarkable leadership skills found at every level in our organization, from the board of directors to our designers and craftspeople.

In the prologue to this book, I listed the ten key leadership principles that define the commitment to excellence by which the people of

Ethan Allen strive to live and work. I think these same principles are reflected in many of the stories I've told in this book. Let me remind you of those principles and suggest some ways they helped shape my actions, both in the world of business and in the larger arena of national and global activism.

1. **SELF-CONFIDENCE:** "Have the self-confidence to empower others to do their best." Over the years, I've learned that self-confidence is essential to the leader who expects to empower others. If you're unsure of yourself, it's easy to be intimidated by those around you, which can make you want to stifle dissent or try to micromanage the members of your team, lest they show you up, challenge your authority, or make choices you might not approve of. It's the insecure leader who tends to take refuge in bullying and authoritarianism.

   In my own life, a sense of self-confidence helped me earn the respect and trust of others, making it easier for them to help me— from my college professors in Kashmir and the government officers who facilitated my journey to America to the many people who encouraged and supported me in my new homeland. Self-confidence has also empowered me to stand up for what I believe is right—in a small way in encounters across boardroom tables; in a bigger way as a leader in industry organizations and nonprofit groups; and in the biggest way of all when I seek to influence government policies on issues like international conflict, immigration, and the global refugee crisis.

2. **HARD WORK:** "Establish a standard of hard work and practice it consistently." The person who accomplishes great things, I've learned, is usually someone that others view as obsessed, maybe even a little crazy—someone who regards long hours that others would deem "too much" as normal. He or she is also willing to work hard in the sense of making hard decisions—not agonizing or temporizing when confronted with painful options, but making the best possible

choice based on the information available and then refusing to look back with doubts or regrets.

Hard work and a passion for the jobs one undertakes are essential for anyone who wants to lead others. Over the years, I've found that working hard in all senses of the phrase is good for both body and soul. It also sets the tone. When the person at the top of an organization is truly dedicated to doing whatever it takes to carry out the mission, there's scarcely any limit to what can be accomplished.

3. **EXCELLENCE AND INNOVATION:** "Have a passion for being the best you can be." As almost everyone in business knows, driving innovation at a tradition-bound company is one of the biggest challenges. And in many cases, some of the biggest obstacles to innovation can be very difficult—and even painful.

I've described how, during my first years at the helm of Ethan Allen, it was necessary to make changes in the leadership ranks of the company to create opportunities for people who were open to the future vision we needed to embrace. Some of the departures were involuntary. We handled these as humanely as possible—but we didn't flinch from the necessity of making that call. The result was that Ethan Allen benefited from an infusion of new talent as younger people stepped up into positions of leadership.

Innovation is equally important in the worlds of nonprofit management, global diplomacy, and social advocacy. The Kashmir Study Group has not been able to bring about a complete resolution of the long-standing regional dispute over my birthplace. But we helped open lines of communication among the adversarial parties, helping to save thousands of lives. The key to this accomplishment was our willingness to embrace fresh thinking and innovative approaches to a problem that had long been bogged down in outworn, rigid ideas. Perhaps the fact that the Kashmir Study Group was led by an entrepreneur and made up largely of scholars and experts with no personal axe to grind explains the positive role we've been able to play. Experience shows that it often takes an outsider to provide the innovative thinking needed to move a stubborn problem toward a solution.

4. ACCESSIBILITY: "Be open and supportive, and recognize the contributions of others." The effective leader is someone who is accessible to others. But this trait is not as easy to practice as it might seem. It's not just about having an "open-door policy" or reading all the emails people send you—although these are useful. True accessibility—whether in business, international diplomacy, or any sphere of human engagement—goes two ways and is separated from judgment or criticism. It's about inviting continual feedback and seeking buy-in from team members about any important initiatives. It's about listening with open ears, minds, and hearts to the concerns of others, and seeking common ground where everyone's perspective is considered.

One way I do this is by making sure there is continual, intimate communication between me and the fifteen or so executives who report to me directly. I also have taken the unusual step of asking my direct reports to share with me the weekly reports they receive from their own team members. I receive some fifty of these reports every week, which focus on five important leadership areas: talent development, marketing, service, technology, and social responsibility.

Of course, accessibility is equally important to success outside the world of business. One of the reasons I was able to generate progress toward addressing the seemingly intractable Kashmir dilemma was my willingness to bring an open mind to my interactions with people from a wide range of perspectives—Hindus and Muslims, Indians and Pakistanis, and military, religious, and business leaders as well as politicians. Listening to the feelings, aspirations, and dreams of everyone with a stake in the region earned me a reputation as an honest broker who could be trusted to tackle the key issues without any pre-existing bias.

5. **CUSTOMER FOCUS:** "Encourage everyone around you to make customer service their highest priority." One of the ways I've tried to instill the principle of customer focus throughout Ethan Allen is by redefining the very term "customers." We now use it to include not just the end consumers of our products but also the whole internal and external network of Ethan Allen team members. Anyone who relies on you is your customer; and every day it's important to rededicate yourself to meeting his or her needs as fully as possible.

To reinforce this way of doing business, I recently established what I call "WOW moments" as touchstones of customer focus. I invite managers and executives at Ethan Allen to share with me any experiences they have or hear about that embody the best of customer focus. The stories I hear are often inspiring, and I like to spread them throughout the company.

6. **PRIORITIZATION:** "Clearly differentiate between the big issues and the small ones." One of the rules of prioritization is to be fiercely disciplined about taking on responsibilities. If you have too many priorities, you really have no priorities at all. I advise my direct reports to focus on just five key initiatives at a time—and I practice the same discipline myself, which enables me to actually accomplish most of the things I set out to do.

The success of Ethan Allen can be attributed partly to our success in applying the principle of prioritization at an organizational level. Ethan Allen is frequently presented with opportunities to buy other companies, some of them well run and otherwise attractive. If we took advantage of these opportunities, we could easily be ten times as big as we are today in terms of revenues—and we'd be active in a host of arenas where we currently are not players. But we would pay a big price for that sort of unfocused growth. We're better off doing a few things and being the best in the world at them. It's a model that has served us well for generations, and we take pride in the fact that Ethan Allen has been continuously profitable for eighty-six years—a level of consistent success that we attribute, in part, to wise prioritization.

As I know from my own experience, defining and balancing life priorities is equally challenging and important. Today I continue to juggle more than one role in my life. I am the CEO of a company dealing with continued, dramatic change; an international diplomat with a humanitarian mission; a spokesperson for social causes such as religious and racial tolerance; and an advocate for business practices that include environmental protection and fair treatment of workers. I am also proud of my children and grandchildren. It gives me great happiness that living on Long Island Sound (as we've now done for some forty-five years) and at our farm in the Hudson Valley (which we've enjoyed for thirty-seven years) provides us with a balanced life, letting us enjoy sports and nature while also working hard.

7. **LEADERSHIP**: "Lead by example." With the terror attacks of September 11, 2001, global conflict hit the US more directly and painfully than ever before. I thought it was my duty as a leader of the business community to help shape a humane American response, and my colleagues at Ethan Allen agreed. Among others things, we published a full-page ad in *The New York Times* and *The Washington Post* mourning the tragedy and urging national unity and a renewed commitment to the "American values of tolerance, courage, wisdom, and justice."

Soon thereafter, I had the opportunity to meet with President George W. Bush and his chief political advisor, Karl Rove. In the wake of the attack, I'm proud that President Bush and the overwhelming majority of other national leaders resisted any temptation to scapegoat Muslims, instead setting a tone of compassion.

I also spoke up about the international repercussions of the new War on Terror. In 2002, as a board member of the Georgetown Institute for the Study of Diplomacy, I attended a discussion led by John D. Podesta, a former Senate staffer, chief of staff in the Clinton White House, and later an advisor to President Obama, about defense issues in this new era.* The session took place against the backdrop of a raging debate about the possibility that the US might go to war against Iraq.

I asked about the "unintended consequences" that often arise from such military decisions, particularly those made in haste. "This is something that leaders at the highest levels of government don't study enough," Podesta admitted.

"Perhaps we should," I suggested. I recommend that the institute sponsor a study of possible unintended consequences of an expanded US military presence in the Middle East and South Asia. The idea was accepted, and the report, written by Institute staffer Paul G. Frost, was issued in the spring of 2003 on the very eve of the ill-fated US invasion of Iraq. It warned of many of the disruptions that could occur if the US were to invade a primarily Muslim country, making the dangers posed by unrest in the Middle East even worse. Sadly, a number of the predictions in the report proved to be prescient.

8. **CHANGE:** "Understand that change means opportunity—don't be afraid of it." Today, the furniture business—like most industries—faces dramatic challenges as commoditization and globalization sweep the world. My mission has been to try to define and lead our response, and these efforts have taught me some principles about managing change. One has been the need for continual rethinking

---

* Years later, when thousands of Podesta's emails were hacked and selectively leaked as part of the effort to disrupt the 2016 presidential election, I was surprised and flattered to learn that in 2008, he and the Obama-Biden transition team had considered recommending me for the post of secretary of commerce.

of familiar assumptions. To make this a part of Ethan Allen's DNA, I've instituted the practice of zero-based budgeting, which means that programs and initiatives are continually reviewed and updated as necessary.

Another crucial principle is the importance of *preparing* people for change. Fear, doubt, and resistance can be minimized when the leader lays a conceptual foundation before launching the change effort. Educate your team members in the ways the business environment is evolving; help them understand the new competitive challenges and the new demands that customers are presenting; and then show them, step by step, how the changes you propose will strengthen the organization for a better future. The best way to do this is face to face, person to person—which explains the town hall meetings we convened around the country and the program by which we brought more than five thousand factory associates, together with their management, to our headquarters in Danbury. Efforts like these help people understand "what's in it for them" and make it easier for them to embrace change rather than shunning it.

The leader who wants to encourage continual change, growth, and renewal must accept the necessity for experimentation—and the inevitability of mistakes. Resist the temptation to launch a witch-hunt or to point fingers after a failure and instead learn from your mistakes. The leader who behaves in a judgmental, condemnatory fashion when an initiative falters guarantees only that his team members will shy away from trying new things in the future . . . and that's a path that leads to stagnation.

9. **SPEED:** "Seize the advantage by reacting quickly to new opportunities." In the twenty-first century, technological changes are in the process of revolutionizing retailing, manufacturing, and customer service—all critical areas on which the success of Ethan Allen is dependent.

For example, as more consumers have turned to online shopping, traffic in the average retail store has declined over the past six years by as much as 60 percent (though at our design centers the falloff has been less). The internet is a prime source of customers—and digital skills are now a crucial talent for Ethan Allen designers and other personnel. We've already trained more than five hundred designers in conducting live-chat conferences with customers that let them discuss and share design ideas online; more will be mastering this skill in the months to come. This is no longer something that's "nice to know"—it is a "must-know" capability that may well be a matter of life and death for our industry.

I've found that the new business reality may require modifying our value system to acknowledge the reality that *speed itself* is now a crucial component of quality. A new product line, customer service system, or process that is absolutely perfect but that doesn't get rolled out until a year after our competitors have it is *not* an example of quality in the twenty-first century. When time is of the essence, we need to realize that 70 percent of perfect can be good enough—if that enables us to be first off the blocks with a groundbreaking innovation.

Again, this leadership principle is equally applicable to challenges beyond the world of business. Those who want to promote peace, freedom, democracy, equality, and other noble social goals must also be aggressive about seizing opportunities for change. Recognizing moments when a lever applied in just the right place may be able to force real change takes judgment and insight. It's a skill that every would-be leader must work to develop.

10. **JUSTICE**: "Make decisions fairly. Justice builds trust, motivation, and teamwork." Leading justly is perhaps the hardest thing an executive is called upon to do. It requires a willingness to lose when an underlying moral principle is more important than winning. It requires being open to disciplined, respectful conflict; the readiness

to change direction when you realize you are wrong, and the courage to stand firm when you are right; and the ability to say no even to a valued customer or colleague when you're asked to take a step that your conscience will not permit.

Justice also requires tackling business challenges through the same lens of social conscience you apply to daily problems. My work with the Kashmir Study Group, Refugees International, and similar groups reflects my commitment to peace, freedom, and fair treatment of all people.

The same commitment lay behind my participation as co-chair in a task force on Muslim American civic and political engagement sponsored by the Chicago Council on Global Affairs. Also led by my co-chair Lynn M. Martin, a former US secretary of labor, the task force included many distinguished leaders from business, academia, and the nonprofit sector. It was charged with examining ways to strengthen the integration of Muslim Americans into our national fabric. As detailed in our 2007 report and in the testimony we offered before the US Senate, we found that the United States is actually doing a better job than countries like France and the United Kingdom in making sure that Muslims feel like true citizens of our nation and behave accordingly. We also offered specific suggestions about how to ensure that this positive trend continues and grows in the future so that alienation and disaffection do not become major problems in the Muslim American community.

More recently, beginning in early 2017, I have been involved in two other major social initiatives. One is the Muslim-Jewish Advisory Council, which I co-chair with Stanley Bergman, CEO of the health-care company Henry Schein, Inc. Its purpose is to recognize the contributions of Jewish and Muslim Americans to our country and to focus on the problem of hate crimes against both communities. The other is a congressionally mandated Task Force on Extremism in Fragile States. Co-chaired by former governor

Thomas Kean and former congressman Lee Hamilton, the task force is developing expert recommendations for US policies to help fragile states in Africa and the Middle East avoid the dangers of political extremism. Interestingly, the task force is using a version of the five important leadership areas that I ask Ethan Allen managers to focus on—talent development, marketing, service, technology, and social responsibility—as discussion points in analyzing the challenges faced by governments of fragile states. This reinforces one of the big takeaways from my life and work—namely, that the same basic principles of leadership apply in every area of activity, including business, government, nonprofit management, and civic engagement.

■ ■ ■

THE LEADERSHIP OF ETHAN ALLEN is also committed to applying the principles of justice to our business decisions, particularly in regard to the big challenges facing business and society in the years to come: issues surrounding immigration, employment, technological change, outsourcing, income inequality, environmental protection, human rights, diversity, and tolerance. In 1999, Ethan Allen created its Environmental Health and Safety initiative. It represents our determination, from corporate offices to design centers to manufacturing facilities to supply chains—end to end and top to bottom—to build both environmental commitment and outstanding business performance through sustainable operations.

At first we were guided by voluntary efforts. In 2010, we stepped up our commitment in a big way. We partnered with the American Home Furnishings Alliance to start our journey toward becoming a Sustainable by Design company.

The Sustainable by Design process provides a sound procedural framework for our environmental efforts, but make no mistake—sustainability is in our DNA. Ethan Allen has always made the extra effort to minimize our effect on the environment, and we did it when no one asked us to.

We manufacture approximately 75 percent of our products in our US and other North American workshops. Yet to keep supply chain costs manageable, we've formed additional partnerships all over the globe. To give our clients the quality they always expect from Ethan Allen—and as a statement of our values—we're working to standardize processes in product development, manufacturing, and distribution.

We also meet or exceed a range of product safety regulatory standards. From the way we source wood to the way we craft custom upholstery, our efforts coalesce around three core concepts: delivering quality without compromise, forming transparent partnerships, and ensuring accountability throughout the supply chain.

At its core, Ethan Allen is about people. Every piece we create begins as an idea in a human mind. Everything we manufacture is touched by human hands. Every item we sell becomes a treasure in a human's home or workspace.

Our commitment to humanity defines the way we do business. It includes such values as managing employees fairly, caring for communities, and being consistent in our treatment of all stakeholders.

No matter where our products are made or sourced, we strive to build partnerships with vendors that respect people, the law, and the land. To make our expectations clear, we've developed a Supplier Code of Conduct. In addition, in our Mexico and Honduras plants, we maintain similar environmental, safety, and social responsibility standards to those in our US facilities. These are not things we do because they are legally required. We do them because they are the right thing to do.

On the related issue of outsourcing, I've continued to insist that Ethan Allen make the bulk of its products here in the US, maintaining the tradition of quality workmanship that helps define our brand. This comes at a cost: The company earns about half the profit margin on furniture made in its Vermont and North Carolina facilities as compared with what it could make in some cheaper labor markets overseas. Our shareholders have been supportive. Rather than demanding that we squeeze every penny out of our manufacturing strategy, they agree that treating US workers with respect and fairness is the right thing to do. Overall, our operating margins are among the highest in our industry thanks to the efficiencies we enjoy as a vertically integrated enterprise.

· · ·

THE TWENTY-FIRST CENTURY is a time of tumultuous change—social, economic, political, environmental, and technological. Progress in some areas is offset by troubling trends in others. Even as a younger generation arises that is more tolerant, better educated, and more creative than any cohort in history, we also witness in some quarters of society a disturbing resurgence of prejudice, xenophobia, and narrow-mindedness. Humankind is blessed with unprecedented technological tools that have the potential of bringing prosperity, progress, and global connections to more people than ever before. Yet while at the same time we struggle to solve looming problems such as climate change, income inequality, and the misuse of digital tools to spread misinformation and distrust.

Leading actively in a world of complexity and difference is hard—but like many hard things, it is also very rewarding.

I hope that the stories I've shared in these pages inspire you in your own leadership journey, wherever it may take you!

ACKNOWLEDGMENTS

WRITING THIS BOOK HAS served to remind me of so many people to whom I am grateful—people without whom my life and career would never have been possible.

I am thinking first of my father and mother—my father who cared for me and made plans for me, and even arranged for me to come to America, despite being separated from our family during years of exile; and my mother who, despite her own struggles with health and other challenges, helped me understand what it takes to be a good person and to care for those around me.

I am thinking of my wife Farida, whose courage and strength have been a lifelong inspiration to me. And of our children, Irfan, Farah, and Omar, whose love has helped make my life joyful and meaningful.

I am thinking, too, of the many people who made it possible for me to survive and flourish from the age of five until today. Many of them appear in the pages of this book—people like my teachers, professors, and friends in Kashmir; the members of my cricket team, who taught me lasting lessons about leadership; my friends, colleagues, and mentors in the business world, including Richard King, John Birkelund, Nat Ancell, Clint Walker, and thousands of wonderful associates from the worldwide family that is Ethan Allen; and my partners from the world of diplomacy, including Howard Schaffer, Frank Wisner, Joseph Schwartzberg, and many others who have dedicated years of hard work to the cause of peace.

Finally, I must thank the individuals who helped make this book a reality. They include the dedicated and skillful editorial, production, marketing, and management team at Greenleaf Book Group Press, and my talented writing partner Karl Weber, who helped me navigate the unfamiliar territory of authorship and publishing. I also want to thank Dr. James Schmotter and Dr. Marshall Bouton, who read the manuscript and provided valuable suggestions.

To these people, and to many others who are too numerous to name but who have touched my life in ways great and small, I will always be truly thankful.

Farooq Kathwari
February 2019

KASHMIR AND ITS REGION—A HISTORICAL OVERVIEW

THE RECORDED HISTORY OF Kashmir, though partially shrouded in myth, extends back nearly three thousand years. Throughout that time Kashmir has been recognized, to a degree matched by few, if any, other areas of South Asia, as a culturally and physically distinct entity. Though subject for brief periods in ancient times to various powers ruling over much of the Indian subcontinent—notably the Mauryas, Kushanas, Gupras, and Hunas, in that order—Kashmir generally remained, until its incorporation into the Mughal Empire in 1586, an independent state. Like scores of other South Asian states, it witnessed periods of imperial glory, initially under the Karkota dynasty in the mid-eighth century and intermittently under the Shah Mirs in the fourteenth and fifteenth centuries. But, such moments in the sun were short-lived, and the control that Kashmir was able to exert over distant territories was typically tenuous. Rather, the political norm for Kashmiri states was that of controlling the region's fertile Vale and relatively small adjoining territories, mainly in the Himalayas and their foothills.

Portions of the pre-independence state of Jammu and Kashmir, other than Kashmir proper, have, of course, had their own distinctive—although typically sketchily known—political trajectories. The Jammu region has been, for most of its history, the domain of small hill and mountain chiefdoms. Jammu proper, apart from its conquest of Kashmir (while under the suzerainty of the Sikhs), occasionally expanded its power southeastward into parts of present-day Himachal Pradesh. The Gilgit region too was generally characterized by the existence of petty, essentially tribal polities. The large, thinly populated region including Ladakh and Baltistan was independent for most of the period from the mid-tenth century until its submission to the Mughals in 1680, at times under a single Ladakhi state (which occasionally expanded into western Tibet) and more commonly in two or more states. There were also brief periods when it became subject to the control of neighboring powers centered mainly in Kashmir, Tibet, and Turkestan.

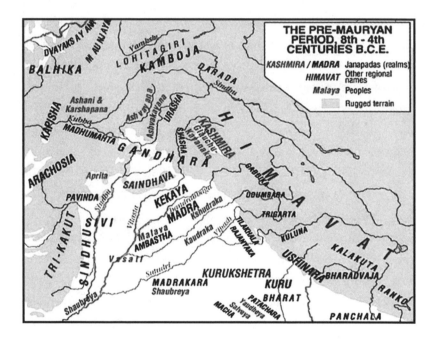

The Pre-Maurya Period, Eighth–Fourth Centuries BCE

The names on this map, including "Kashmira," are attested to in numerous ancient Hindu and Buddhist texts relating to the period from the eighth to the fourth century BCE. However, apart from Kashmir itself, barely a handful of the scores of realms and peoples noted here are recognizable, even in altered form, in the current political or cultural landscape, or for that matter, in the one depicted on the map that follows. The polities shown on this map, including Kashmir, were generally small in size, as were most South Asian states over the greater part of history.

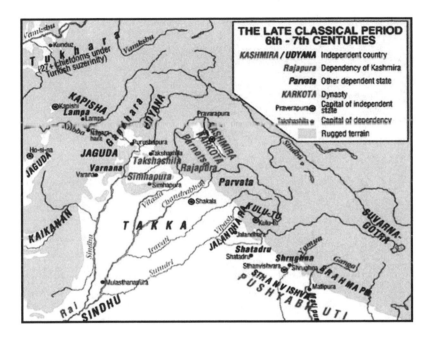

The Late Classical Period, Sixth–Seventh Centuries CE

This map depicts the area encompassing Kashmir as it existed in the sixth–seventh centuries CE during what might be considered the late Classical period. Over most of the roughly one and a half millennia that elapsed from the beginning of the period depicted on the preceding map until the end of the period to which this map refers, Kashmir was a small, independent state. Existing on the periphery of a politically fragmented India, it also maintained commercial and cultural ties with Central and Southwest Asia. The situation depicted here is what prevailed shortly before the mercurial imperial expansion of Kashmir in the reign of the Karkota monarch, Lalitaditya (724–761 CE). Following this reign the state lapsed back into its customary position of relative weakness.

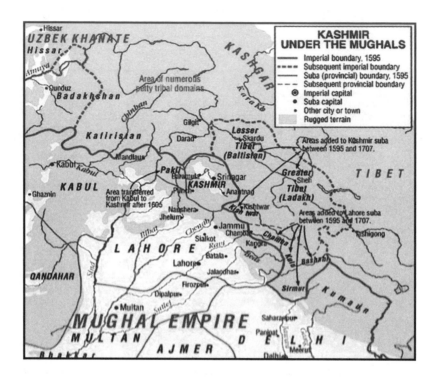

Kashmir Under the Mughals

The Mughal conquest and annexation of Kashmir in 1586 ended nearly a millennium of continuous Kashmiri independence and ushered in one of several periods during which an external power extended the territory of the political entity known to the outside world as Kashmir to well beyond the actual area of Kashmiri language and culture. Thus, by the death of the Emperor Aurangzeb in 1707, the Mughal suba (province) of Kashmir was extended to include the great part of what was later to be incorporated within the Dogra domains, as shown in the map that follows. It then included both Ladakh and Baltistan, but the core area of the Dogras, centered on Jammu, remained a part of Lahore suba.

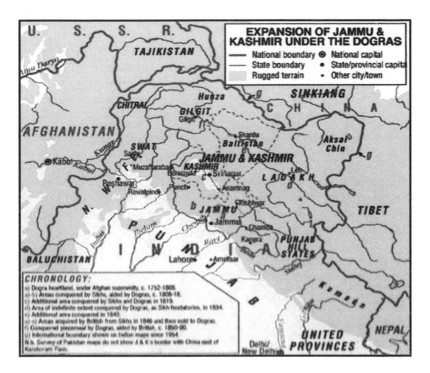

Expansion of Jammu and Kashmir Under the Dogras

The final period of Kashmiri expansion occurred under the Dogra dynasty of Jammu, which ruled the state from 1846 until the partition of India in 1947. This century witnessed a remarkable increase in the area and, consequently, in the cultural heterogeneity of the state. This accomplishment was due in large part to military and political assistance from the British Raj, without whose imperial protection the territorial coherence of the state might not have been maintained.

MEMBERS OF THE KASHMIR STUDY GROUP

M. Farooq Kathwari
Chairman, Ethan Allen Inc.

The Honorable Gary L. Ackerman
US House of Representatives

Dr. Nigel J. R. Allan
University of California, Davis

Dr. Walter Anderson
Johns Hopkins University

Ambassador Harry G. Barnes, Jr.
The Asia Society

Dr. Marshall M. Bouton
Chicago Council on Foreign Relations

Dr. Chester A. Crocker
Georgetown University

Dr. Ainslie T. Embree
Columbia University

Dr. Fen Osler Hampson
Carleton University, Ottawa

Dr. Robert L. Hardgrave, Jr.
University of Texas, Austin

Dr. Rodney W. Jones
Policy Architects International

Dr. Charles H. Kennedy
Wake Forest University

The Honorable James A. Leach
US House of Representatives

Dr. Peter Lyon
Institute of Commonwealth Studies, London

Dr. Barbara D. Metcalf
University of Michigan

Ambassador Robert B. Oakley
Institute for National Strategic Studies

Ambassador Nicholas Platt
The Asia Society

Ambassador (retired) Anthony C. E. Quainton

Dr. Leo Rose
Asian Survey

Ambassador Howard B. Schaffer
Georgetown University

Ambassador Teresita C. Schaffer
Center for Strategic & International Studies

Dr. Joseph E. Schwartzberg
University of Minnesota

Ambassador William Phillips Talbot
The Asia Society

Dr. David Taylor
Aga Khan University, Pakistan

Dr. Thomas P. Thornton
Johns Hopkins University

The Honorable Robert G. Torricelli
US House of Representatives

Dr. Robert G. Wirsing
Asia-Pacific Center for Security Studies

KASHMIR—A WAY FORWARD (2005)

The following proposal was developed in consultation with persons from the Jammu and Kashmir Region from both sides of the Line of Control and with Indians and Pakistanis.

We recommend that portions of the former princely State of Jammu and Kashmir be reconstituted into self-governing entities enjoying free access to one another and to and from both India and Pakistan.

1. Three entities—Kashmir, Jammu, and Ladakh—would be established in the portion of the pre-1947 state now administered by India. These three self-governing entities would each take part in a body that would coordinate issues of interest to all of them, such as internal trade and transportation.

2. Two entities—Azad Kashmir and the Northern Areas—would be established on the side now administered by Pakistan. Like the entities on the Indian side, they would each be represented in a

coordinating body that would consider issues in which they both had an interest.

3. An All-Kashmir body would be set up to coordinate areas of broader interest such as regional trade, tourism, environment, and water resources. This body would include representatives from each of the five entities as well as from India and Pakistan.

Each of the new entities would have its own democratic constitution, as well as its own citizenship, flag, and legislature, which would legislate on all matters other than defense and foreign affairs. India and Pakistan would be responsible for the defense of the entities, and the entities would maintain police forces to maintain internal law and order. India and Pakistan would be expected to work out financial arrangements for the entities.

Citizenship of the entities would also entitle individuals to acquire Indian or Pakistani passports (depending on which side of the Line of Control they live on). Alternatively, they could use entity passports subject to endorsements by India or Pakistan as appropriate.

The borders of the entities with India and Pakistan would remain open for the free transit of people, goods, and services in accordance with arrangements to be worked out between India, Pakistan and the entities.

While the present Line of Control would remain in place until such time as both India and Pakistan decided to alter it in their mutual interest, both India and Pakistan would demilitarize the area included in the entities. Neither India nor Pakistan could place troops on the other side of the Line of Control without the permission of the other state.

All displaced persons who left any portion of the entities would have the right to return to their home localities.

The proposal represents a practical framework that could satisfy the interests of the peoples of the Kashmir region, India, and Pakistan. It would end civil strife and the tragic destruction of life and property in the Kashmir region. By resolving the principal issue that could lead to armed conflict between India and Pakistan, it would go far toward relaxing political tensions in South Asia. It would offer enormous economic benefits not only to the Kashmir region but also to India, Pakistan, and all the South Asia region.

Larchmont, New York
February 1, 2005

INDEX

ABOUT THE AUTHOR

FAROOQ KATHWARI IS THE chairman, president, and CEO of Ethan Allen Interiors Inc. He has been president of the company since 1985 and chairman and CEO since 1988.

Mr. Kathwari serves in numerous capacities at several nonprofit organizations. He is a member of the Board of Overseers of the International Rescue Committee; a member of the advisory board of the Center for Strategic and International Studies; a member of the Council on Foreign Relations; chairman emeritus of Refugees International; an advisory member of the New York Stock Exchange; former chairman of the National Retail Federation; director emeritus and former chairman and president of the American Home Furnishings Alliance; a director of the Institute for the Study of Diplomacy at Georgetown University; co-chairman of the Muslim-Jewish Advisory Council; and a member of the International Advisory Council of the United States Institute of Peace. He also serves on the boards of the Western Connecticut State University Foundation, the Hebrew Home at Riverdale, and Arts Westchester.

He is the founder of the Kashmir Study Group, and he served as a member of the President's Advisory Commission on Asian Americans and Pacific Islanders from 2010 to 2014. Recently Mr. Kathwari was tapped to join the congressionally mandated United States Institute of Peace bipartisan Task Force on Extremism in Fragile States, co-chaired by former governor Thomas Kean and former congressman Lee Hamilton, who led the 9/11 Commission.

Among his recognitions, Mr. Kathwari is a recipient of the 2018 Ellis Island Medal of Honor and has been inducted into the American Furniture Hall of Fame. He has been recognized as an Outstanding American by Choice by the US government. He has received the Yale School of Management's Chief Executive Leadership Institute Lifetime of Leadership Award; the New American Dream Foundation's Lifetime Achievement Award; the Connecticut Institute for Refugees and Immigrants Legacy Award; the Eleanor Roosevelt Val-Kill Medal; the National Retail Federation Gold Medal; the International First Freedom Award from the Council for America's First Freedom; Ernst & Young's Entrepreneur of the Year Award; the Anti-Defamation League's Humanitarian Award; City of Hope's International Home Furnishings Industry Spirit of Life Award; and the Entrepreneurial Excellence Award from the National Association of Asian MBAs. He has also been recognized by *Worth* magazine as one of the 50 Best CEOs in the United States.

Mr. Kathwari holds BAs in English literature and political science from Kashmir University, Srinagar, and an MBA in international marketing from New York University, New York. He is also the recipient of three honorary doctorate degrees.